Know Your Enemy

The Christian's Critic

Nicholl A. McGuire

Pittsburgh Pennsylvania, USA

Pittsburgh, Pennsylvania

First edition

Spirituality. 2. Religion. 3. Prayer. 4. Inspirational.

Printed in the United States of America.

Published August 2012

ISBN 1451526547

EAN-13 9781451526547

www.createspace.com

I dedicate this book to my fellow brothers and sisters in Christ who have shown me what it means to stand up for one's beliefs and to not be ashamed or fearful of sharing God's truth in ALL its forms!

Table of Contents

Introduction 1

1. The Profile of a Christian's Critic 19
2. Wicked Critic's Boss 69
3. Critical Tongue 125
4. Study Your Enemy 151
5. Wicked Critic's Strategies 161
6. When the Critic Attacks 205
7. Put on the Whole Armor of God 217
8. In the Name of Jesus 221
9. Why Love an Enemy? 233
10. Know the Power of Faith 241
11. Casting Out the Enemy 249
12. The Worst Enemy of Them All 263
13. Creating Distance from the Critic 267
14. Satan is Under Your Feet 271

Introduction

Do you know who your enemies are?

Before you can confront an enemy, you have to know one. Did Jesus know Judas? Did David know Saul? Did you anticipate your relative, friend, neighbor, or even a stranger was going to say or do something so upsetting that now he or she is deemed an enemy? Know that when you speak truth, any truth, you potentially become an enemy to all who refuse that truth. It doesn't matter whether that truth is related to the Bible, something said in conversation, an event at work, a news report, or an entertainer's deceptive ways, the one who just "loves" my mom, my boss, my job, this singer, that dancer, artist, basketball star, football player, etc. isn't going to take truth well.

Our adversary, Satan, will use those you suspect as well as those you least expect to cause what appears to you as "unnecessary, petty, ridiculous, childish stuff" in your saved, sanctified and Holy Ghost filled life. However, you can't very well say that someone is an evildoer or a worker of the devil in your life, if you have no evidence and proof, right? Of course, but once you have information that shows a person or group is no good to you, use your evidence and proof wisely.

We are to remain steadfast in all that we do when walking with the Lord, let him show you who your offenders are—those some would call, "a backstabber, a liar, an angry man, evil woman, or the devil!"

Do you sincerely know who your enemies are? Sometimes we falsely assume that our adversary is someone who: doesn't look like us, fall in a similar income bracket, vote a certain way, attend a top notch school, or belong to a special group. We deceive ourselves. Many times, in my own life, my enemies were the ones that looked like me, acted like me, knew me better than I knew myself, and liked many of the same things I liked. So when we automatically assume that someone is an enemy because of some political, religious, cultural, or monetary differences, we are actually putting ourselves in a position to be an enemy to others. We might find ourselves attacking or being attacked for any number of reasons including: past events, lies or exaggerations told, anger outbursts, hidden envy, unresolved issues, and more.

When you decided to give your life to Christ, there was a war of good and evil that developed within your spirit. Not only were personal challenges magnified, but you found yourself warring with self and those around you. Most of the enemies that became more and more prevalent in our lives are those that we know! It may have took days, weeks or even years to find these people out, but God showed you and I some red flags about certain individuals, and for some of us, the truth hurt, but it also set us free from being bound to those people who were keeping up drama in our lives. Consider the following statistics. An estimated 1.3 million women are victims of physical assault by an intimate partner (someone they knew) each year, according to The Public Policy Office of the National Coalition Against Domestic Violence (NCADV). "Most women and children know the person who committed a crime against them. In 2008, 70% of women in the United States who were victims of violent crime were harmed by someone they knew" as reported on the Partnership for Safety and Justice (PSJ) Website located in Oregon. Not only women in bad relationships are assaulted by someone familiar, but "almost 10% of high school students are victims of dating violence each year" (Youth Risk Behavior Surveillance 2009). Also, "most children, adolescents, and adult women are raped by someone they know. Almost two-thirds of women raped as adults are raped by an intimate partner. Nearly 3 in 4 victims of stalking know the person stalking them," the PSJ webpage states.

Women and children aren't the only ones abused by someone they know, so are the elderly. "In 2003, state Long Term Care Ombudsman programs nationally investigated 20,673 complaints of abuse, gross neglect, and exploitation on behalf of nursing home and board and care residents. Among seven types of abuse categories, physical abuse was the most common type reported" (National Ombudsman Reporting System Data Tables. 2003. Washington, DC: U.S. Administration on Aging).

If that wasn't bad enough, the enemy has also used Christians to take advantage of one another. For example, "Pastoral counseling is one of the pastor's professional tasks that is likely to offer opportunities for sexual abuse. We know that about 10 percent of professional therapists admit to sexual contact with clients, and we can guess that the same figure applies to clergy" (see Marie Fortune, *Betrayal of the Pastoral Relationship*, unpublished article available from the Center for the Prevention of Sexual and Domestic Violence). "Typical of recent treatments of the topic is *The Sexual Hazards of Pastoral Care* (*Christianity Today,* November 8, 1985), by Dean Merrill, which describes the minister as an attractive target for 'the Enemy,' or a "sitting duck for the romantically starved."'" (Religion-Online.org).

In this book, *Know Your Enemy: The Christian's Critic*, you will learn many of your critics' timeless strategies designed to kill, steal and destroy your spiritual relationship with your Creator. You will also receive biblical references to assist you in your walk. Like a soldier, you must do the following while reading this book: train, put into practice the knowledge that you have received, study your enemies, and recognize their battlefields. These difficult people cause problems over the phone, on the Internet, in your home, workplace, at the local store, while you're on vacation, and anywhere else they feel they can catch you off guard. By the end of this book, you should be better prepared to confront your enemy in the next book, *Face Your Foe: 28 Critics of Your Faith You Can Overcome,* also by Nicholl McGuire.

There are rulers of darkness in this world as the Scriptures tell us. These rulers do not want you or me to have a faith in Jesus Christ. The devil knows that if we connect with Christ, he and his demons will be exposed. Truth will be revealed. Vampire and werewolf type of relationships will come to an end. The Christian will be let out of his or her cage, a free man or woman ready to perform God's will.

Demonic spirits are real and work hard to hurt others mentally, physically and spiritually, this is why the Bible warns us to, "Put on the full armor of God so that you can take your stand against the devil's schemes. "For our struggle is not against flesh and blood, but against the rulers, against the authorities, against the powers of this dark world and against the spiritual forces of evil in the heavenly realms" (Eph. 6:11-18, NIV) in Chapter 6 I discuss more about this topic. Although Ephesians 6 sounds mysterious, understand there are not only spirits who move in darkness, but human beings who are very much willing and able to carry their messages. We read of many examples in the Bible where men and women chose idols over a righteous God. The end result: people lost health, wealth, family, friends, and even their souls. Some turned back to God in their weaknesses while others died a certain eternal death.

The Holy Bible (KJV) instructs us to, "Be sober, be vigilant; because your adversary the devil, as a roaring lion, walketh about, seeking whom he may devour" (1 Pet. 5:8). But how can you be on the look-out for someone or something that doesn't make a sound unless it's threatened, hungry or harmed? Why wait until the lion roars to know that he or she is in your presence? Further, why go into situations without a covering when you know Satan is on the loose? We mustn't ignore the devil's schemes, give up our faith, compromise truth, or do other things that make us appear unstable and foolish especially when fighting in a spiritual war!

Satan wants us ignorant of his plans. He tells his people to lie, cheat and kill for him. He expects a blood sacrifice for every promise made, oath taken, money exchanged, and opportunity given. You need an example? Think of the events leading up to Jesus' death. Here he was walking amongst a group of men and all around him were critics, traitors, jealous individuals, and more who wanted him dead. Not only that, the Messiah was tempted by the devil himself! Satan doesn't want you to believe that evil exists. We see evidence of this in satanic inspired teachings displayed throughout media from statements like, "Satan is a friend…" to "There is no devil." The late founder of the Church of Satan, Anton Lavey, said "Satan is a symbol, nothing more." He added, "Satan signifies our love of the worldly and our rejection of the pallid, ineffectual image of Christ on the cross." So while the Christian cries about Jesus dying on the cross each Easter holiday, there are those who enjoy looking at the re-enactment of the Messiah's death and don't even believe Satan is real contrary to what we know the Bible says about him.

In an article entitled, The Foundations of Satanic Belief by Jashan A'al, Satanic followers "believe in no gods; some believe in abstract forces; some believe in an ancient, pre-Christian being; and some believe in the Biblical Satan. Not all Satanists are devil-worshippers, and not even all devil-worshippers are Satan-worshippers." This sounds like any average man or woman who isn't interested in the Creator or his Bible, doesn't it?

You may be a child of God who is being tempted by Satan and those who follow him whether they know it or not. You might have noticed those who have rebelled against God are now going through all sorts of personal trials. When you observe the lifestyles and conversations of these people, you can't help but see the truth, they got in over their heads when they decided to walk away from the one true God to be their own gods, worship ancient demonic gods and goddesses or directly serve Satan.

Your lost and confused family, friends, co-workers, and strangers may have at one time or another discouraged you from walking with Jesus with their negative comments and reactions. Some of those who we deem as "saved" were guilty of causing us to stumble because of their hypocritical lifestyles. They might have attended church in the past, hold a title in a prestigious group, and do other things that make them look good in the sight of men and women while carrying a spirit who wars with God and his people. This lying, critical (and oftentimes religious) spirit comes in the form of a selfish individual who gossips, lies and twists biblical truth to suit one's personal agenda.

In an article entitled, *Do You Have a Critical Spirit?* by Dr. Dale A. Robbins, he defines a critical spirit as "an obsessive attitude of criticism and fault-finding which seeks to tear others down—not the same thing as what is referred to as 'constructive criticism.' Robbins further explains that "the only criticism that is ever constructive is that which is expressed in love to 'build up,' not to tear down—it is always expressed face-to-face, never behind their back."

The "saved," just like the unsaved, will do the following at times: make ridiculous statements about their own brothers and sisters in Christ, covet others' blessings, participate in outlandish behaviors, rebel or ignore the Father, and spread bad attitudes all in the name of religion. Remember the Pharisees? In Luke 23:10-12, "The chief priests and the teachers of the law were standing there, vehemently accusing Jesus. Then Herod and his soldiers ridiculed and mocked him. Dressing him in an elegant robe, they sent him back to Pilate. That day Herod and Pilate became friends—before this they had been enemies." I'm sure you know a few people who have acted like this toward you and others. I talk about the Pharisees' reactions to our Savior and similar behaviors in modern day churches throughout this book. Most of which, we are all at fault.

These days the enemy will use church-goers, who aren't sold out for God, to turn those who are sincere Christians away from the church. These Pharisee-minded thinkers put God in their boxes and restrict members from going outside of the church to help others by saying what they believe God does or doesn't do with new believers. These pretenders of the faith (hypocrites) falsely assume that because someone doesn't come to Christ in the way they believe, then a new, mature, or re-dedicated believer's confession of Jesus is invalid along with their spiritual experiences.

The hypocrite accuses Christians of things that are untrue. He or she reinforces lies by sharing some of the following: false prophecies, exaggerated dreams, testimonies, and other things that sound or look like God is in the plan, when in fact he is not! Meanwhile, the hypocrite denounces any spiritual gifts a believer might have. Robbins writes, "The person with a critical spirit usually dwells on the negative, seeks for flaws rather than good. They're a complainer usually always upset, and generally have a problem or a complaint about something. They often have little control over their tongue, their temper, and have tendencies for gossip and slander which Paul said were sins 'worthy of death' (Rom. 1:29-32)."

Wicked religious zealots hinder a new Christian's worship of the Lord by telling him or her, "To sit down…put your hands down…that's not the way we do it here." We don't have to worry or debate with these in-the-box thinkers. The Lord says, "The wicked are denied their light, and their upraised arm is broken" (Job 38:17, NIV). A hypocritical believer will not allow the Holy Spirit to teach a new believer and will often doubt whether he or she is really hearing from the Lord when the new believer says, "I heard from the Lord and he said..." despite the message being one that uplifts and encourages the church to trust the Lord. Church members, who do more acting than praying, like some strong-willed pastors, act as middle men between God and the outsiders' innate desire to draw nearer to Him. There is nothing wrong with middle men (such as an intercessor, prophet, priest, etc.) that is until they start taking the people's eyes off God and putting them on things like: self, money, buildings and traditions. Once a believer has spiritually matured, he or she comes to the realization that one doesn't need to solely rely on a minister to pray to the Father for things like: special needs, forgiveness of one's sins and other things. Although the Scripture says, "For where two or three are gathered together in my name, there am I in the midst of them" (Matt. 18:20), but it doesn't say that the only way God will show up is if we connect with a man or woman of God on a daily basis in a confession booth, at a church service, in a religious person's home or elsewhere. For some Christians, they have become so focused on what man or woman can do for them; that they lose sight of what God can do. The mature believer who has asked to be in-dwelled with the Holy Spirit, has a direct connection to God's will in Jesus name without the need of putting men and women on pedestals in his or her life. The Holy Spirit will guide the believer to pray, fast and do other things to bring glory to God.

You will find that with every roadblock a family member, friend, co-worker, brother, sister in Christ or a stranger may put up to get you off track spiritually, your Lord is always there to whisper instructions about those who claim to love you, yet their evil ways contradict their speech. God warns us about people closest to us who have fallen away from their belief in Christ and who are unsaved. He also admonishes us from intimately socializing with backsliders, unbelievers and idol worshipers in order to keep us mentally strong, safe from harm, and most of all keep us close to Him. Its one thing to share the gospel of Christ with these people, but it is quite another thing to share one's heart. The Lord says we are to guard our hearts. He doesn't want us to make his middle men and women gods in our lives—doing and saying everything they want as if we are robots and puppets; rather we are to be "salt of the earth. But if the salt loses its saltiness, how can it be made salty again? It is no longer good for anything, except to be thrown out and trampled by men (Matt. 5:13)."

You may have dismissed the voice of God, also known to many as the: "Holy Spirit, a gut feeling, conscious, something said, a small voice" and other statements both godly and worldly men and women use to describe that small voice who keeps their mouths and feet out of trouble. There are times that we do the total opposite of what God has told us (while talking about others) only to find out later, we should have been obedient to God's wisdom and not our own—he knows what's best for us. When we are disobedient, we simply confess our sin, turn from it, and do as Our Father instructs. What sound advice have you ignored lately from God and his messengers? Is your disobedience responsible for your stress these days? The Holy Spirit provides the words we should speak if we ask him. However, not all believers have or know of the Holy Spirit which I share more details later in this book. This would explain why some who claim to be Christian often struggle with whether they are saved or not, they have yet to receive the Holy Spirit.

The Lord supplies Scripture for us to say to people who need peace, healing, words of knowledge, a relationship with Christ, and so many other things. When sharing the Scriptures with others as well as the contents in this book, you might not be well-received. You may even be criticized more-so. There will be those who will attempt to discredit me for a number of reasons including not being qualified enough to write such information being that I am a layperson. Truth is a hard pillow to swallow so it's been said by the wise. The Bible warns us to, "Give not that which is holy unto the dogs, neither cast ye your pearls before swine, lest they trample them under their feet, and turn again and rend you" (Matt. 7:6).

If you have received the Holy Spirit, that Jesus left behind before ascending up into heaven, (Acts 2:33), then you will experience a more in-depth walk with God. The Holy Spirit will move on you to talk to those you know as well as strangers while utilizing various spiritual gifts. He will sit with you and teach you more about God and his Son, Jesus. However, many so-called Christians grieve the Spirit. "And do not grieve the Holy Spirit of God, with whom you were sealed for the day of redemption" (Eph. 4:30).

I have learned, since walking with the Lord, that "many believers choose not to quiet their mouths long enough to hear and do what He says," the Holy Spirit told me. "Therefore, they never move beyond simple church attendance."

While God is moving you ahead, the critic will try to steer you backward. In *Know Your Enemy: The Christian's Critic*, you will be instructed to further your study and pray. When reading can't be done, encourage yourself by listening to positive music, uplifting television shows, and visiting Christian websites, and churches. However, we should be mindful that even these mediums can't always be trusted, therefore always look to biblical Scriptures whenever in doubt, and of course, pray.

When writing a book like this, one can't help but reflect on his or her life and why there are moments in one's walk with God that he or she struggles to keep the faith. I thought of several points related to my spiritual journey that might help some who may have allowed others' criticism to cast doubt about your serving God. First, one must admit personal failures before the Lord and make rights wrong when it's in your power—be accountable for your actions. I have contributed to my own downfall spiritually over the years, not only by associating with negative individuals, but also by allowing bad habits and things to enter my life. Ignorance played a part in my self-destruction. Next, when one hears truth, there is no sense in arguing with it. Observers would call me naïve and young as a new believer. Now and then the enemy would use my trust and love for others against me. I learned the hard way it's best to keep some things between you and God. Third, when all else fails, faith is always there to strengthen you. I have had what the world would call pinnacles of success and then other times fallen so low that it isn't any wonder that I didn't die in my youth. Fourth, be mindful of what you do that looks like and sounds like the world. Besides the backsliders and unbelievers contributing to my failures in life, there were also things that helped me fall away from the Lord during the 1990s and then again later in life that included: listening to ungodly music, reading depressing news, entertaining myself with celebrity gossip stories, drinking alcohol, and frequent club dancing.

When you know who you are in Christ and where you have been, the criticism from others doesn't hold the sting that it once did. Dr. Alfred J. Poirier, former chairman of the Board of Directors for Peacemaker ministries wrote an article titled, *The Cross and Criticism* where he shares some insightful information about criticism. "I see myself as God sees me—a sinner. There is no escaping the truth. "No one is righteous, not even one" (Rom. 3:9-18). He writes, "In response to my sin, the cross has criticized and judged me more intensely, deeply, pervasively, and truly than

anyone else ever could. This knowledge permits us to say to all other criticism of us: 'This is just a fraction of it.'"
Take moments out of your life to build your faith then when the critic comes with, "I remember when you..." You can comeback with, "But do you know who I now am? For I AM has changed me." Trust me, God will be very pleased because this will open up a conversation about his glory being manifested in your life.

There are many things that can contribute to any Christian's downfall on a spiritual level. Some people spend their lives never attaining the levels of spiritual success that God has called them to because of worldly influences. Godly critics will look on with disbelief, anger and even resentment in their eyes for our poor decision-making, but ungodly people will support us in committing sins.

At times, we can find ourselves feeling crazy trying to make sense of some believers who claim to be followers of Christ. There are many televangelists and Christian radio teachers' that provide weird analogies, foolish statements, confusing biblical teachings, and false stories that are more about people-pleasing then winning people to Christ. In addition, we allow our own emotions, when listening to some of these false prophets to get in the way of truth. We must KNOW whether there is an enemy or a Christ follower in our midst, before opening ourselves up to him or her emotionally and physically. The enemy loves *spiritually* deaf, dumb, and blind believers who are more concerned about what pleases the flesh than what pleases God.

While reading this book, you will envision people from all walks of your life who you may trust. These people may appear on television, live with you, work with you or even see you on the street. While reading, *Know Your Enemy: The Christian's Critic*, it won't be any coincidence that some people's faces will pop up in your mind. While writing this book, there were some people, in my past, who I thought of that had once claimed to be my friend, but after careful reflection, I realized they were not. God showed me that people, whether believers or not, can be immature, rude, jealous and more toward anyone who is striving to become a better person spiritually, mentally and physically. Through careful observation of your actions with others and how they respond to you, a consistent prayer life and obedience to God, you become more wise and discerning. You also learn to guard your heart. So when certain people come to mind, while reading this book, give God the praise, because he is revealing to you some things concerning your relationship with these individuals that might be negatively impacting your walk with him. Pray for further understanding when this happens. God wants you to pay attention to those who you rely on for advice, those who help pay your bills, watch your children, and others who do for you as well as those who don't. We might falsely assume because people do nice things for us, like buy us things, take us out shopping, or speak highly of us, they are our friends. Oh, how easily we can be deceived!

New believers can also act credulous in thinking that everyone who says, "I believe in God" is in fact worshipping the one true God of the Holy Bible. There are many people who are seeking a god or gods and they aren't necessarily in the Bible. Just like in centuries past, we have money gods, fertility gods, lying gods, nature gods, and more. False spirits tend to have similar godly traits and will use some Christians to fulfill any and every agenda. According to 2 Corinthians 4:4, in the NIV Bible, "The god of this age has blinded the minds of unbelievers, so that they cannot see the light of the gospel of the glory of Christ, who is the image of God."

Examine the people in your inner circle like you would if you were a boss interviewing a new-hire. Find out the following: who these people *really* are who fascinate you, offer you things, advise you, and do other things to win your favor. Do all of these things, before you: buy their products, open your home to them, invest with them, share their messages, marry, and so on. This book will help you discern that critical wicked spirit before you do business, go out on a date, or even hand over your credit card to him or her. Whether some believe it or not, not everyone likes or cares about Christians, this is why we must be wise when speaking with loved ones and making friends with strangers. We all can be so quick to tell our brothers and sisters in Christ not to judge others when they are only trying to be discerning. *It isn't acting judgmental when you are asking questions of others.* I thought I might emphasize this previous statement, because we have far too many people in sin crying out, "Don't judge me!" When one reports the truth, there is always someone saying, "Don't judge." Understand that telling someone that something is wrong or stating that his or her behavior is causing others to fall, is not being judgmental! "Blessed is the man who God corrects…" (Job 5:17, NIV).

It isn't being critical when you are concerned about one's background, education, relationship with God or lack thereof. Most of all, you aren't a judge when you are trying to get to the truth. If anything, you are acting like Jesus, you desire to know if this person is worthy to join you in your quest to help others. Not every person followed Jesus and not every person will follow you. So how do you know the difference between constructive or destructive criticism? According to an article by John Maxwell, *When You Get Kicked in the Rear, You Know You're Out in Front,* "Here are the questions I ask to get to determine what kind of criticism it is: Who criticized me?...How was it given?...Why was it given?..." He advises to: "stay open to change…, accept yourself…if you have endeavored to know yourself, and have worked hard to change yourself, then what more can you do? And forget yourself…secure people forget about themselves so they can focus on others. By doing this, they can face nearly any kind of criticism—and even serve the critic."

You will see some of the good, the bad, and the ugly in everyone the closer you walk with God, and read his word. As the Scripture says, "Thy word is a lamp unto my feet, and a light unto my path," (Ps. 119:105, KJV). As we all know any time you turn on a lamp everything that was hiding in darkness will be illuminated and that's when you just might see some critters take off and run—like your pessimistic critic being one of them.

Once you see one's "true colors," as some intuitive older folks like to say, refrain from being self-righteous. Further, don't be tempted to "throw the baby out with the bath water," so the old adage goes. In other words, keep what is good, but the rest ignore. Rather, use what Christ has given all his followers, the Holy Spirit, as mentioned previously. Listen to him! Let him be your guide! Be reminded of Jesus' actions in the gospels and do likewise.

You can't expect a spiritually lost person who doesn't read and study God's Holy Bible to be like you. You wouldn't think to tell a mentally disabled person "to start thinking straight" when you know they are incapable, so don't expect your lost partner, family members, friends, co-workers, and strangers to act any differently. Just because they heard God's messages a few times, attended a couple of church services, or said some biblically sounding statements, doesn't mean that they take the Father seriously. Critics of our faith help usher us into negative situations especially when they aren't sold out for God, and we mustn't let them! So don't argue with them. In Proverbs 12:16 (NIV), "A fool shows his annoyance at once, but a prudent man overlooks an insult."

As you grow in your faith, you will find the more you learn about God, the more you will want to share with others. With God's leading, you will impact many and will be amazed at the people you have touched using your own spiritual battles with the enemy as examples. You will also realize just how much of a winner in Christ you truly are! However, don't get use to the adoration from others like, "Wow! You are a child of God! I wish I was more like you!" because these same individuals that may have been admiring you yesterday, can easily turn around and challenge you on your faith today, leaving you thinking, "Is this the same person that encouraged me not that long ago? He acts like he doesn't like me now, why? Is he an enemy of mine?" Questioning one's faith is one thing, but when you find people are treating you disrespectfully, talking badly about you to others, or ignoring you after what you thought was a harmless argument about your beliefs, you have to wonder whether this person is still a friend. "The heart of the righteous weighs its answers, but the mouth of the wicked gushes evil" (Prov.15:28, NIV).

Don't be deceived! The devil shows up where you least expect him, when times are bad as well as when times are good. In the book of Job 1:6-8, notice what Satan does, "Now there was a day when the sons of God came to present themselves before the Lord, and Satan came also among them. And the Lord said unto Satan, Whence comest thou? Then Satan answered the Lord, and said, From going to and fro in the earth, and from walking up and down in it. And the Lord said unto Satan, Hast thou considered my servant Job, that there is none like him in the earth, a perfect and an upright man, one that feareth God, and escheweth evil?" A similar thing is going on today. The enemy shows up at places like: your social networking page, in your email, at a Christian fellowship, on your job, at your home, or anywhere else you feel comfortable. It is clear, from the previously mentioned Scripture that Job was going to be tested despite being a "perfect" man. So if God will allow a perfect man to be tested, what do you think he will do with you? Of course, some will want to defend their goodness, perfection, righteousness and the like, but God has clearly shown that what you think you believe about yourself is irrelevant, when he is ready, you will be faced with the kind of trials in your life that will leave you feeling like, "Where is God in all of this?"

Notice in the Gospels Judas showed up at meetings where Christ was present. The devil waits for the right time to do whatever evil he (or she) was sent to do. What we must do is remain steadfast through it all! (See Jas. 1:12 and Heb. 12:12-13). Even when you slip, grow faint, ill, or have to run from someone or something while walking with God, "know that if God be for you who can be against you?" (Rom. 8:31).

Christ's followers who spoke the truth, as it is written in the Bible, have been lied to and lied on, shunned out of groups, threatened, ridiculed, ostracized by family and friends, removed from jobs, tortured, and even murdered. Presently, Christians are still being persecuted in places like the Far East, India, Asia, Africa, and the United States. From torture to unfair policies and restrictions, persecuted Christians are forced to go along with worldly events, programs and other things that go against their beliefs. Despite the fact that as a society we have changed mentally and physically since the days Jesus walked this earth, God's messages haven't—he is still the same yesterday, today, and forever, while Satan continues to roam in the earth. As Christians, we know that our gifts, await us in heaven—Halleluiah!

You will read in *Know Your Enemy: The Christian's Critic* about your enemies different character traits in various situations. The deceptive critic poses his or herself as a good friend, favorite relative, trusted co-worker or that person "who knows you better than you know yourself" in some of the examples in this book. The offender in our personal lives will tell us how much they love us or how much they need us only to drop us when we can no longer be of service to his or her needs. From an adult son or daughter, to a best friend, a wicked critic doesn't care or realize just how much his or her words and actions have hurt us. Your enemy may tempt you to argue by saying some of the most disrespectful things known to man, so that you will eventually abandon your faith. Further, your foe will talk behind your back in order to discredit your walk with God.

So why are some people so critical and judgmental? According to Light's Blog, an Internet site that talks about toxic and non-toxic people (Lighthouse.org), *Why are Most Judgmental, Critical People So Critical and Judgmental?* The writer says, "People with low or no empathy also have a difficult time understanding or caring about the fact that insisting your thinking is wrong and valueless will hurt your feelings." We also have to keep in mind that some difficult people have mental disorders. The blog lists three: narcissistic, obsessive-compulsive and antisocial personality disorders. Learn more about these disorders so that you can recognize people who have these issues before confronting them about their criticisms.

Wicked critics don't know when they are being used by the devil. They have walked with him so long that they have grown accustomed to his negativity. Some of these self-righteous critics think they are a blessing to all who meet them, when in fact; this is the furthest thing from the truth!

Know Your Enemy: The Christian's Critic provides you with life observations, personal experience, and advice to help you face wicked critics in your life. At times you may be offended with the information provided in this book, because you may see yourself in some of these pages. Rather than get angry at the messenger, pray and ask the Lord to help you change! The heat that might rise from your belly to your chest and end up sitting on the top of your head, while reading some of the chapters in this book, will be nothing more than a clear indication we need to go back to studying our Bibles!

We might also need to pray about something in our personalities that we overlooked. While reading this book, you might consider fasting from food and certain people, places or things that could be keeping you from: healing, getting blessed, having a better relationship with the one true God, or even finishing this book! Whatever your spiritual battle, know you will need to trust in God, and in time, make some changes. Otherwise, you will find the critics' negativity will rub off on you! Before long, you might be used by the devil to get a believer off course; rather, than point him or her in the right direction toward Christ.

Believe it or not, there are good critics, the kind that are like-minded believers who catch us in errors and help us not only talk the talk, but walk the walk. However, for purposes of this book, the focus is being exclusively placed on bad critics – the kind that our adversary uses to sow seeds of doubt about our faith.

So I wrote this book with a burden to help those who have recently got saved, those who are starting to question their walks with God, and of course, dear to my heart, the backsliders. To my new Christian friends, I know what it feels like trying to befriend people who call themselves "Believers" in the one true God, who has a Son named Jesus, and a gift called the Holy Spirit. People will doubt, question and debate your beliefs. Some will act as if they are in agreement, but are really nothing more than pretenders. Check out the fruit on their trees. When you are a new believer or one who has rededicated his or her life to Christ, you periodically feel alone in this unbelieving world. There are those moments it seems there just isn't anyone who sincerely understands your highs and lows when walking this walk.

I also wrote *Know Your Enemy: The Christian's Critic* for those who have recently been exposed to some things in the church which have left you bewildered to the point that you are about ready to call it quits. I remember feeling that way too and I almost gave up on all things spiritual until I was reminded of the blessings I received since walking this walk, and the unexplainable inner peace I experienced. Daily I had to make up in my mind that I didn't want to go back to darkness after having received God's light in my life for the first time back in 1997.

Finally, I write to those individuals who have no clue how significant their lives will be impacted now that they have chosen to walk with Christ. If you thought your life was boring, depressing, meaningless, and so on because a critic said that it would be because you now walk with Christ, it doesn't have to be. Since drawing nearer to the Lord, I don't struggle with my critics' insults concerning my faith like I once did. There is always something to do in the kingdom—walking with the Lord is never boring! You just have to make the time to ask, "What Lord will you have me to do this day?" Then watch for his signs. I have learned when those negative feelings come upon me to just ask God for help—too much idleness will get one in trouble. If one believes the critic's offensive remarks such as, "serving the Lord is "not fun, meaningless, and difficult." The Christian might be tempted to do things like: pick up the phone and talk to people who don't have one's best interests in mind, visit an environment that might cost one his or her anointing, or accept invites from people who are nothing more than devil workers.

By the time you are finished reading this book, you should be able to do the following: define which critics are righteous and which ones aren't, determine whether you are your own worst enemy and learn more about Satan's attempts to get believers to fall away from their faith. Then after reading this book, you will be prepared to confront your critics in *Face Your Foe: 28 Critics of Your Faith You Can Overcome* by Nicholl McGuire.

I pray that all who read this book will be enlightened and will trod carefully when it comes to befriending people who say that they love the Lord like you do. Seek the Lord when it comes to visiting places that are religious, secular, or otherwise. As Christians, we tend to drop our guards and when we do that, we will suffer every now and then publically and other times privately.

May this book be a blessing to you.

1. The Profile of a Christian's Critic

Is your critic tall, short, black, white, skinny, fat, crazy, or weird looking? I know I am putting some people on the spot with this question. Your answer should be, "Appearance shouldn't matter." Now if it does, then there is still a lot of growing up one must do spiritually. God doesn't judge on one's appearance, he examines the spirit of men and women. "But the Lord said to Samuel, 'Do not consider his appearance or his height, for I have rejected him. The Lord does not look at the things man looks at. Man looks at the outward appearance, but the Lord looks at the heart' (1 Sam. 16:7). So if we expect the critic to look a certain way, then we will be defeated every time!

An enemy of Christians, who delivers an encouraging or discouraging message, doesn't have a typical look. It's what comes from the heart and out the mouth that defines who this person really is and what group or personal interest he or she is representing. The critic could be tall, short, handsome, ugly, intelligent, or dumb. Instead of focusing on what someone looks like, we should be asking ourselves, what is this critical person's purpose behind the purpose? For example, a friend tells you one thing, but behind the smile there is another thing she is really thinking and planning to do. We should ask ourselves, what are the individual's true intentions? Does he or she want something from me? Does this person secretly hate my God and me? Does this relative or friend sincerely have my best interests at heart or does this person harbor ill feelings?

A personal opinion means nothing if you don't care too much about the person who is giving it, but those closest to us, we care a whole lot about what they say, don't we? When I refer to the Christian's critic in this book, I am not referring to just anyone, I am speaking of those people whose opinions you value the most. You love and care for them. You believe that they add value to your personal and professional relationships. A spouse, parent, child, relative, church member, coworker, classmate, neighbor, friend, or someone else we respect and admire can also be a hindrance to our spiritual progress.

Your personal advisor may be a believer in the one true God or other gods, a backslider, an apostate (someone who no longer believes or supports his or her faith), or is unsaved. God doesn't want us receiving advice or being at the mercy of the wicked one who blurs lines of right and wrong. In Proverbs 25:26 (AKJ), "A righteous man falling down before the wicked is as a troubled fountain, and a corrupt spring." We have to avoid the temptation to consult with people who are not of the Lord and have no problem compromising biblical truth. For some Christians, it doesn't matter much what their loved ones personal relationship with God or many gods might be, just so long as these people love them. But we should be concerned, very concerned, about one's relationship with God especially if this person is very close to us such as: a mentor, parent, grandparent, sibling, or best friend. *Do you know that one incorrect piece of advice can destroy your life?* Consider this; the devil tries to do the following things to believers: tempt, seduce, deceive, lie, test, torment, trouble, afflict, accuse, persecute, oppress, steal, kill, and destroy. Who might he use to help achieve his goals? One or more of those weak-minded people we trust.

Most of us have all been told by teachers and leaders about the importance of accepting constructive criticism to better us mentally, physically and spiritually. Concerned associates will share personal experiences, statistics, stories, and more to get us to stop doing certain things that don't bring out the best in us. Over the years, I have personally been blessed by others' knowledge, but I have also been cursed as well. I found myself doing the following: accepting negative words that had no basis in my life, allowing others' opinions to disturb my confidence, listening to advice that gave me a false sense of peace, incorrectly assuming because people were older, therefore they must be wiser, and believing that everything loved ones advised were true because they had "been through some things." Many of you have done the same, and it hurts doesn't it when you find out just how wrong, fake, harsh, crazy, or manipulative a person truly is? You discover that what someone said is not all together true, lacks substance, can't be proven, or is nothing more than a lie straight from the devil. You start to experience feelings of distrust, anger and bitterness toward your once favorite person.

I knew that things were very wrong spiritually with some trusted confidants once I noticed Christ tapping me on the shoulder (so to speak), to come and follow him. Criticism ran wild about the following things I did when I began to walk with Christ: my church attendance, where I worshipped, what I was doing while there, what God told me to do (like participate in spiritual fasts) and what not to do, what to eat, how to dress, who to be friendly with and who not to, what message I should receive and what shouldn't I listen to, and overall my choice wanting to trade my old life for something new which included distancing myself away from certain people, places and things. Nothing I said or did during my early years of dedicating my life to Christ was good enough, smart enough, big enough, important enough, or beneficial enough according to my critics.

So how do you handle such criticism from those who supposedly are looking out for your best interest? John H. Armstrong shares some suggestions in an article titled, *Dealing with Criticism.* He writes, "If the criticism is false, and it involves a public matter, it may be right to correct the error..." He goes on, "It is always right and good to speak truth regardless of what has been said or done in the past or by others."

When we notice that some thing said is true we tend to become agitated and are quick to respond; rather than take the time to cool and think about whether the criticism is worth discussing. Armstrong advises, "Recognize that the natural tendency to defend yourself is very human but it is a deadly game to play once you get into a shooting/shouting war with people...Humble yourself under the mighty hand of God. In due time, he will lift you up and bless you."

In my experience, what a few called, "constructive criticism" or "advice" about my faith and personal choices sometimes ended up being information that made me doubt, question or wonder whether walking with the Lord was indeed the right thing to do. When someone's so-called wisdom is not bettering you spiritually, you have to ask yourself, "Should I be listening to this person?" Just imagine this, had Jesus permitted the words of men to infiltrate his mission, his work on the cross would have never occurred; therefore, we would all be headed to a certain eternal death. When religious leaders accused Jesus of having a demon, they misjudged him. Jesus said, "He who is not with me is against me" (Matt. 12:30, NIV). When someone speaks negatively about who you are in Christ, they are not in support of you and most likely aren't interested in Christ's mission. Further, if someone is rejecting the word of God, choosing to continue to do things that harm his or her self and others mentally and physically, let God deal with them—no sense in showering this person with Bible verses every chance you get and church invites.

I found the more I observed my critics' lives (those who have fallen away from the Lord and the unsaved), the more I found them disqualified to say anything to me about God, country, family, or job. John the Baptist called the religious leaders of his day a "brood of vipers" (Matt. 12:34) and then he questioned them, "How can you who are evil say anything good?" When we listen to critics, they reveal to us what is really in their hearts by the words that they speak. Jesus said, "For out of the overflow of the heart the mouth speaks." Then in verses 35-36, The Messiah provides insight as to what a righteous man will bring to others. "The good man brings good things out of the good stored up in him, and the evil man brings evil things out of the evil stored up in him. But I tell you that men will have to give account on the Day of Judgment for every careless word they have spoken. For by your words you will be acquitted, and by your words you will be condemned." It is a scary thought to think that everything we ever said to someone, God will judge us accordingly. Ask for God's mercy while there is still time.

Trusting God

How can one say that he or she trusts in God when their lives scream, "I trust in man…I love money…I don't know what I would do if it wasn't for this person and that one…?" What I began to notice with my critics was a pattern of "saying one thing and doing another." In time, I learned that this business of constructive advice, whether on or off the job, can be used to either build people up or tear them down. If it wasn't for God sending dysfunction away and replacing it with functional messengers and prayer warriors in my life, I don't know where I'd be today! God is a merciful, righteous judge who loves you and I more than any family member or friend ever will! This is why we must trust that he will lead us to the right people at the right time in our lives; rather than us relying on our bias selves to obtain knowledge from people just because they hold certain titles. Not only do we have worldly people who are often critical but there are plenty of men and women of God who are wayward in the faith too as a result of negative criticism and being critical of others! When their emotions are not put in check, some Christian's mouths are nothing more than clanging cymbals.

The wayward minister skips around the stage yelling, "You're going to hell…" because he knows he is doing some things behind the scenes he has no business. He may scare some straight, but others may simply walk out the church and away from the Lord forever. Using the pulpit to "tell you about your sinful self," sounds more like a reverend venting, instead of uplifting the church. Falling out every five minutes while acting emotional for the public when delivering God's word in between "you need to…you ought to…you better" messages, is not edifying anyone but the speaker. Jumping up and down, running around and yelling at people seated in pews for hours is not bringing the house down, but is nothing more than a mere distraction from the convicting truth that the Holy Spirit wants to deliver to someone or a group in the audience. When I point out these things, am I leading anyone away from the Lord by mentioning the truth? Would one consider me a wicked critic or just someone giving him or her some feedback? Will a church leader have read what I just said and think, "You know what, she has a point. Maybe I should tone it down sometimes. Maybe I am getting a little carried away with the mic in my hand." Now if what I said is considered constructive criticism, then so be it. But some would read the same text, and think, "Now who does she think she is? Talk about know your enemy, she's probably one!" This is why we have to really know the difference between our enemies and godly advisors because we can easily confuse God's anointed with Satan's appointed.

People, who love sin, don't want to be judged. People, who believe they are okay with the Lord, oftentimes will refuse correction. "Seek good, not evil, that you may live," The Bible tells us. "Then the Lord God Almighty will be with you, just as you say he is. Hate evil, love good; maintain justice in the courts..." (Amos 5:14-15). If you are one, who believes judging a fellow brother or sister, who claims to follow Christ, is wrong, consider the following Scriptures: Rom. 16:17; 2 Cor. 6:17; 2 Tim. 3:5 and 1 John 4. You will find in the biblical text, believers are either instructed to teach, test, separate, or keep away from certain individuals and to hate evil. How do you do such things if you aren't judging people?

Critical people can use truth to build you up or break you down. They can say things like, "I'm just being honest...You want the truth don't you?" But they can say it in such a way leaving you feeling like you are the worst person in the world! "So it's the delivery you have a problem with, but not the critic, right?" I can almost hear a reader questioning me on this. Not just the delivery, but the person too if he or she is not right with God. Think about this, did people trust you more or less since you gave your life to Christ? Some probably are neutral when it comes to trusting you because they know your past and are still critical of you because of it. So if at anytime we showed we were difficult with others, a trouble-maker, most likely they will be discerning about listening to us talk about our faith or anything else. Not everyone trusted the Messiah and believed that he was the Son of God, and not everyone will believe his followers either. (See Mark 13:13, Luke 21:17, and 1 Pet. 4:14).

As we listen to what others are saying, we should be paying close attention for signs that their advice is Holy Spirit-inspired and has proven to work for them. How do we do that? We pray of course and we watch for positive character attributes that show us that this person takes God's Word seriously. For example, think of those you know like tall fruit trees. What kind of fruit might be hanging on your advisors' tree? Does the fruit make people sick? Is it spoiled, useless, bitter, or something else that is keeping you from receiving their messages? You know when Eve ate of the fruit in the Garden of Eden, she offered it to her husband and he too ate. The story would have been written differently had her husband consulted with the Lord first. Notice how much trust he had in his wife. Do you put other people's opinions, offers and suggestions before your heavenly Father's?

Once I know something about one who might be a potential friend, then I am moved to listen to their knowledge about a subject, but not before the Lord uses me to test them. Sometimes I am in tuned to the Lord and notice signs, other times I am distracted by enemy schemes. The following Scripture is one that keeps us safe if we follow its instruction, "Dear friends, do not believe every spirit, but test the spirits to see whether they are from God, because many false prophets have gone out into the world." (1 John 4:1). I would even go so far as to observe and or blatantly ask my advice-givers, "Have your gods or God really worked for you in this situation? I would be interested in hearing some of your examples." If they exaggerate, lie, or point the finger back at you as if you did something so wrong for asking them a question about their faith, you will know something is wrong with your critics and most likely God didn't use them to give you guidance. Besides, if you ask God to reveal truth, he will. I would also wonder where this so-called constructive advice is really coming from. Critical individuals usually have motive. Did someone who may know more about me, move this person to ask me certain things so that they can put their own personal opinion in my ear? Is this so-called wisdom coming from a jealous, sneaky, deceptive or angry heart? Could my advisor really be nothing more than a confused person serving false gods while hoping to get me to go along with his or her false ideologies? Of course, one would have to treat each advisor and information received differently before we can reach the conclusion that one is altogether wicked.

Jesus had a small circle of people around him that he kept close. Many of his relatives and friends from childhood were not traveling with him on his missions. We know this to be true, because Jesus went looking for disciples. No one was invited in his circle just because they were "family" and "my best friend." I can only imagine had he included his entire family in on his ministry, it wouldn't have accomplished much. "Jesus, why do we have to stop at this person's house? Do you have to talk to him? Why would you heal him, he ain't right? What was wrong with healing that girl, she was so nice? When is God going to give us food and drink, we're hungry?" We saw how Moses' followers treated him in the book of Exodus.

Satan will find ways to negatively impact Christ followers as well as his own devotees' by attacking things like their: finances, relationships, businesses, and anything else he can influence. Satan is no friend to man, woman, child, or animal. In Robbins article, *Do You Have a Critical Spirit?* He speaks of the devil influencing obsessive behavior. "He may use...negativeness, insecurity, immaturity, and an unrenewed mind or other techniques, to influence a complaining or critical attitude to stir up turmoil and strife within the body of Christ" (See Eph 6:12).

When we do things that are inspired by demons, read things that are endorsed by demons, and sit at the round table with demons, you have to know that the information you are receiving is coming from demons! People, who don't draw near to the Lord, study his word and actually have some fruit to back it up, are not good advisors. If anything, you are more valuable to them (the lost, backsliders, and apostates) by opening up your Holy Bible and directing them to some Scriptures, but not the other way around. "The mouth of the righteous speaketh wisdom, and his tongue talketh of judgment" (Ps. 37:30).

True believers have no problem saying they are children of God. They will talk about Jesus, share the gospel, and will not be turned off by the Word of God. Every one of us who believe in God and work hard to be obedient to his will have a variety of spiritual gifts. The Holy Spirit provides these gifts and we act on them as God leads. "…the fruit of the Spirit is love, joy, peace, patience, kindness, goodness, faithfulness, gentleness and self-control. Against such things there is no law. Those who belong to Christ Jesus have crucified the sinful nature with its passions and desires" (Gal. 5:22, NIV). But those that serve other gods, "Ye are of your father the devil, and the lusts of your father ye will do. He was a murderer from the beginning, and abode not in the truth, because there is no truth in him. When he speaketh a lie, he speaketh of his own: for he is a liar, and the father of it (John 8:44). So when I decided to share what I learned about the Bible to others and talked about what God showed me or said to me, those who didn't want to hear truth shut me out. It wasn't until personal challenges came that they were more open to receiving God's Words.

If you question how involved Satan really is in the lives of human beings, think about this, there are countless records written centuries ago, besides the Holy Bible, that provide specific details about an enemy, an evil entity, or something terribly negative in this world that harms every living thing. There are far too many deceased people that have left behind their recorded experiences with dark forces while they lived not to believe that evil exists and has helpers. Take a moment and check the religious section of a bookstore on or offline and you will find many writings about evil and demonic activities human beings have gone through such as: physical torment, mental disturbances and bizarre images and visions.

What is a Wicked Critic?

Think about this, if one calls you or someone else a devil, evil or mean, apparently there is something they see, at least for the moment that you and others may not see. Maybe you have been guilty of saying or doing some unrighteous deeds lately. You could have been around some individuals that were into witchcraft and a spirit left the environment and followed you home. You might have an enemy who prayed for something evil to happen to you. The reasons why someone would call you or someone else "a devil" are endless. The best thing you can do is go to God and ask, "Why?" For some people, they aren't as sold out for God like they think and for others they simply are attracting wicked, jealous people that want nothing more than to break them down mentally with all their negative speaking.

So what might someone do to be labeled "wicked" by others? The late American psychiatrist and best-selling author, Morgan Scott Peck defined an evil person as the following according to Wikipedia (Wikipedia.org/wiki/M._Scott_Peck). "Consistently self-deceiving…, deceives others…, projects sins on others, commonly hates, abuses and controls others, lies incessantly, consistent in sins, unable to think from the viewpoint of victim (scapegoat), and has a covert intolerance to criticism and other forms of narcissistic injury."

Now let's look at the critical side of this evil or mean-spirited person. Merriam-Webster Dictionary defines the critic as, "One given to harsh or captious judgment," this is one of three definitions given in the reference book. The first two definitions describe the character of the critic positively such as, "one who expresses a reasoned opinion on any matter especially involving a judgment of its value, truth, righteousness, beauty, or technique." Put wicked and critic together and you got a lying, deceiving, controlling, hateful, cold, self-absorbed, abusive sinner who is difficult to be around. *No wonder we all need Jesus!*

A fellow brother or sister rebuking, correcting or admonishing you, in my opinion, is not what I would call a wicked or evil critic. Those who have the fruit of the Spirit will be patient, kind and good to you unlike a critical person with a chip on his or her shoulder. The pessimistic critic's sole objective is to make you look bad while using your weaknesses to esteem his or herself. For purposes of this book, I will not be focusing on someone offering simple constructive criticism to help you; rather, I will be sharing information about a critic that is bitter, angry with you, and has thoughts of stealing, lying or possibly destroying your character based on the following: an offense committed, upset about your following Christ, has unchecked jealous emotions, unresolved issues with you, and many other concerns that might or might not involve you but somehow you got thrown into the mix.

The wicked Christian critic, unsaved, or backslider is moved by his or her boss, Satan and his demons, whether he or she knows it or not to draw men and women away from God. These evil critics in your life have allowed demonic influences to permeate their minds, bodies and spirits through anti-Christ books, TV, music, radio, print, Internet, ungodly family, teachers, and friends.

The critic of Christ's teachings usually has a made-up mind about a believer's faith. He or she isn't really interested in listening to biblical truth; instead, this negative person hopes that a so-called messenger of God will tickle his or her ears with messages that will do things like: stimulate the economy, improve self so that he or she can obtain more in life, uplift one despite his or her ugly ways. Of course, this is just a few of the many examples of messages that are not about glorifying God, but rather uplifting the one who thinks he is his own god. Our Creator doesn't want those who are responsible for spreading the gospel to spend so much time tailoring a sermon or speech around self and making others feel great that one loses sight of Him. Man's personal opinions are flawed apart from God. "He will oppose and will exalt himself over everything that is called God or is worshiped, so that he sets himself up in God's temple, proclaiming himself to be God" (2 Thess 2:4, NIV).

Your critic may complain about your Bible reading. He or she might discourage you from asking questions or making comments about his or her bible teaching, preaching, programs, classes, etc. This person may cause you to avoid church or other similar Christian gatherings without good reason. This detractor may accuse you of acting self-righteous, being a hypocrite or even worse a fool! Self-absorbed critics, who don't want you to furthering your knowledge of the Bible a part from the group, will find fault with your witness, testimony, spiritual gifts, and other things directly connected with God. The critical individual might have: name-called, questioned your faith or politely asked you to step down from a position without a good explanation. For others, your foe might have broken up with you or walked out of your life because he or she was turned off by your faith in God. This person could have verbalized his or her concerns especially when you spoke truth whether about your faith or another topic. Consider this, you were only doing what a sincere child of God should be doing, "My mouth speaks what is true, for my lips detest wickedness" (Prov. 8:7, NIV). In Proverbs 10:13, "Wisdom is found on the lips of the discerning, but a rod is for the back of him who lacks judgment."

We have to realize that people around us will dislike our walking with God. They may go so far as to harm us or people we know especially if we are playing with fire; in other words saying we believe in the Lord with our mouths; yet partaking in sinful activities and conversations. Someone in your circle may have tried to justify his or her actions or inactions by falsely accusing you of acting "too spiritual" or "better than me" and some of you reading this book might have agreed with the critic. This is why you are not praying as much, going to church like you use to, making time with like-minded people, and doing other spiritual things. Now for those of you who are very active in church, if you don't appear to be cutting back on any of your spiritual activities, your jealous or insecure foe might reason in his or her mind that you need to be taught a lesson so he or she turns up the heat on getting you to "stop being so spiritual."

How does one keep someone in religious or physical bondage? One way is by bombarding them with negative statements like, "You never do anything right...you could never be...you are incapable of...you are stupid...don't know what I saw in you..." Who wants to be treated in this way by someone who claims to love you? So what does the victim do? Try to prove his or her accuser wrong even if this means sacrificing one's personal happiness.

I had been exposed to emotional and spiritual abuse after having been around dysfunctional people who never seemed to see any wrong in what they were doing or saying. From narcissists to bi-polar personalities, these people had their own share of demons that were spreading venom designed to affect not only me, but future generations! Throw in some significant, stressful life changes (like childbirth for instance) mixed in with an abusive past while fighting with negative individuals and you got yourself one big ole' basket case—that was once me. But God redirected me from a future of self-destruction to one of peace!

I had been misinformed by a few family members, friends, and money-loving pastors over the years about what it meant to serve God. Their own lives didn't reflect what they preached to me as a young girl. I often found myself wondering why people would tell me about God; yet they showed no signs they were indeed children of God. I didn't see the fruits that the Bible instructs Christians to look out for in some of these people. They often lied, showed distrust toward the people of God, but put much faith in wicked men and women's pills and thrills.

When I was a child and shared my spiritual experiences, I was told to "go play" or "you're making things up." God was my imaginary friend that some didn't want me talking or singing about. Little did I know at the time, that the hypocrites were recruiting self-righteous critics. In other words, when a man or woman, who believes he or she is right about his or her sin, they give others a pat on the back and even help some to participate in more sin because "I use to do the same things." People like this don't bother to see that their actions are actually conflicting with God's Words. When told about their behavior, friends turn into enemies.

When I became a teen, the Bible was nothing more than a tool for some to get what they wanted, while not doing what God wanted. Since I didn't attend church, because that wasn't considered important in my household, and my several years of private school wasn't enough to impact me much, I had no understanding on how to apply a biblical God and his percepts to one's daily living. In time, it would become easy for me to act like the world and not like Christians, because I felt they were trying to make me become something that I wasn't called to be. It wasn't until I finally surrendered to our Lord and Savior Jesus Christ in my early twenties that I would take God seriously. However, in time, I would gradually fall back into sin while drowning out feelings of conviction.

An apostate, backslider or someone who simply doesn't like the Christian belief system, may start off his or her conversation appearing to be reasonable and truthful, but by the time a Christian provides Scripture after Scripture on why the naysayer's opinion is invalid, a lie or simply doesn't make any sense, this critic of the faith will either walk away, argue (while hoping to make a scene so others will support him or her) or stop talking. You may have recalled a time when this happened to you.

A critical person usually turns into an accuser when he or she feels threatened. This self-righteous person may contrive a list of reasons as to why you are disqualified for talking about "righteous me." Notice the Merriam-Webster dictionary includes the word "righteousness" in the definition. Most critics of any religion will play the part of, "Your wrong and I'm right" so as to appear like he or she is standing up for righteousness, throw in a little yelling and some tears and this person will try to keep you from confronting him or her about the false criticism he or she is hoping you will receive. "I don't know why I bother telling you anything, you don't listen...you are so self-absorbed...stubborn! Are all people like you a #$@%^#)!" The critic shoots his or her daggers, but refuses to listen to you when you attempt to defend yourself. There will be those moments that we can't walk away and we will have to take a stand. There is nothing wrong saying that you refuse to act on someone's unreasonable demands, belittling statements and outright lies!" The truth will set you free, don't worry, the critical person won't be spending much more time dishing out his or her self-righteous statements before coming up with an excuse to leave your presence. Combat the devil's lies with godly truths and he will flee! However, sometimes we might have to be the one to walk away from a critical person's insults. Jack Zavada, writer for About.com, shares in his article, *Dealing with Difficult People God's Way*, writes, "While we should not respond to bullies by hitting them in the head with a rock, (like David did in the Bible), we should remember that our strength is not in ourselves, but in the God who loves us." He adds, "This can give us confidence to endure when our own resources are low."

Jesus' Critics

Jesus received criticism from the Pharisees when he taught, healed, served, witnessed, slept, ate, prayed, socialized, and more. Some witnesses were "offended" by him in Matthew 15:12. Not all believed that he was the Son of God; therefore, they set out to destroy him (Matt. 12:14). The Pharisees condemned him for eating with "publicans and sinners" (Matt. 9-11). They also looked for ways to "entangle him in his talk." (Matt. 22:15-17). So if the presence of evil followed Jesus around, what do you think your critics will do to you for preaching the Gospel of Christ? They will hate us. (Matt. 10:22). But the Bible also says, "Blessed are you when men hate you, when they exclude you and insult you and reject your name as evil, because of the Son of Man" (Luke 6:22, NIV). We are still blessed when men, women and children criticize us. Jesus wasn't fearful of the Pharisees and neither should you be of your critics, "For God hath not given us the spirit of fear; but of power, and of love, and of a sound mind," (2 Tim. 1:7). However, even knowing all of this, we still respond to people's criticism with feelings of sadness, upset and confusion. "I was only trying to help…why did she react that way? What is wrong with my Internet video that so many bad-mouthed it? Am I really that bad of a…" How do we get beyond these feelings? We keep working, praising the Lord anyway, and carrying our burdens to Him!

Had Jesus and his disciples preached happy messages all the time during their walks on this earth and never hurt anyone's feelings, where do you think you and I would be today? It is understandable why our government creates laws to protect one's free speech; however, is talking about whatever you want really free? Our society has what you call, "political correctness" nowadays. Therefore, one speaking too much about the Lord or any god on a grand-scale platform broadcasted on a major television network or elsewhere, will attract certain Pharisee-minded thinkers and quite possibly be censored if they delve deep into certain controversial biblical Scriptures. There are rules to follow, and if one deviates from political correctness, he or she may be committing career suicide. I personally believe that is why some televangelists water down biblical truth, especially when it comes to living a godly lifestyle, because they are instructed by their superiors (board members and investors) to say the kind of things that will bring in the most money to their churches, while avoiding the biblical percepts that convict sinners. Let us remember that political correctness is man-made and God is not interested in man's programs, for our Father is the same yesterday, today and forever! So don't worry over people's programs. Respect your leaders (Col. 3:22-24, I Pet. 2:13-20), but at the same time, don't grieve the Holy Spirit when called upon. (Deut. 11:26-28).

When They Criticize You

Every critic has his or her own way of critiquing you. Throughout this book you will notice there are a variety of ways that a wicked critic may voice his or her opinion on what you ought not or ought to do among other things. On EHow.com, Mary Beth Viveiros, eHow Contributor, writes, "Criticism comes in a number of forms: As children it comes from parents and teachers; as adults we must deal with it in the workplace; and friends or lovers might have something to say about what we do or how we are. Reflecting on the validity of the criticism either helps us grow, or just makes us feel badly about ourselves." Viveiros lists four types of criticism which include: professional, constructive, personal, self scrutiny, low self-esteem, and abusive. Professional criticism is when one receives feedback about one's job performance. Constructive criticism is when one is giving you feedback in order to help you grow, keep you safe, and provide other helpful tips. Then there is personal criticism which is usually more about one's opinion and less about fact. Self scrutiny is when an individual is critical of self. Low self-esteem criticism is when a person is trying to make his or herself appear superior by offering unwarranted advice. Lastly, abusive criticism is when one is deliberately trying to hurt you by stating offensive comments.

When you are stressed due to your critics, remember a certain man after God's own heart, David. He wrote about taking refuge in the Lord from his enemies, "My times are in your hand: deliver me from the hand of my enemies, and from them that persecute me. Make your face to shine on your servant: save me for your mercies' sake. Let me not be ashamed, O Lord; for I have called on you: let the wicked be ashamed, and let them be silent in the grave. Let the lying lips be put to silence; which speak grievous things proudly and contemptuously against the righteous. Oh how great is your goodness, which you have laid up for them that fear you; which you have worked for them that trust in you before the sons of men!" (Ps. 31:15-19). After reading what David spoke to the Lord about his own situation, what you and I go through when dealing with enemies is peanuts! I love the part that reads, "Let the lying lips be put to silence…" Critics lie, falsely accuse and do much more to hurt us; therefore we must share our burdens with the Lord, like David did, and trust that the Lord will deal with their negative criticism in his own time. So the Bible reads in Romans 12:19, "Dearly beloved, avenge not yourselves, but rather give place to wrath: for it is written, Vengeance is mine; I will repay," said the Lord.

I was disappointed that soon after giving my life to Christ, relatives and some friends found my periodic talk about God strange, uncomfortable and misleading. I thought that it was okay to share the gospel with those that I loved, but I learned quickly that there was a time and place for everything. I was criticized when I didn't benefit them or warned them about things I read in the Bible, but praised when I was back to my old self as one put it. "I was worried about you," one friend said and then proceeded to call me a few names. But the truth was, I wasn't back to my old self, wisdom, for a time, had went into hiding with some people.

The biblical passages referring to "Love your enemies" (Luke 6:35, Luke 6:27 and Matt. 5:44) have been twisted by selfish people, like so many other passages of Scripture, to confuse, manipulate and make well-meaning Christians feel guilty when they refuse to do what is asked of them. Over the years, I have noticed some believers love an enemy beyond human comprehension! I mean to the point where everyone witnessing this person's love have said things like, "It couldn't be me...I couldn't love him after all he did to me...Nope, I would never love her again...Love my enemy? I don't think so. You can keep on loving your enemies all you want, but not me!"

I heard one day the Holy Spirit say to me, "You can't love an enemy you don't know." Ponder on that for a moment. I get into this topic of loving one's enemy more in Chapter 9. Many of us think that because we are walking with God we will be alerted to our enemies every move. This is why it is a shock to us when we find out they are doing and saying insolent things about us behind our backs. God doesn't want us to be in the dark any longer concerning those in our inner circles who claim to offer constructive criticism, when in fact they are offering nothing more than destructive verbal abuse! If you have ever acted like a wicked critic, then you know your enemy more than anyone else since that enemy might be you! Therefore, it's best not to take an enemy's actions so personal, because we all know we are guilty of many of the things we don't like about others. You just might have compassion for the offender and eventually manifest God's love—I'm not speaking of, those temporal, emotional rollercoaster feelings we, classify as love either! About.com writer, Zavada, pens, "The most difficult person each of us has to deal with is our self. If we are honest enough to admit it, we cause ourselves more trouble than others do." Sometimes we will need to enlist "the help of a pastor or godly friend to help us see our situation clearly. In other cases, when we humbly ask God to show us the reason for our misery, he gently directs us to look in the mirror," advises Zavada.

Whether you are a new believer or a seasoned one, the following scenario you may be able to relate, because most likely you have experienced some, if not all, since dedicating or rededicating your life to Christ. It's difficult to show love toward people who have hurt you; therefore, you must have a genuine relationship with the Lord.

Let's say you are stressed out, grieved by circumstances, and angry over relatives and friends' statements and behaviors. Simply put, you are tired of being sick and tired! So you decide to visit a Bible believing, Holy Spirit moving church. Now, imagine you are an unsaved, lost individual and simply at your wits end while visiting this church. What might you do? Well in this example, you find yourself walking down an aisle with tears in your eyes desperate for prayer. Someone takes you by the hand, asks you, "What is your need?" Then you hear words coming from a stranger's mouth that sincerely believes in a God described in a holy book centuries old.

This Christ follower says the sinner's prayer with you, mentions to the minister that you are interested in participating in a water baptism, and encourages you to join others who also desire to be saved. Meanwhile, someone else leads you by the hand and takes you down some stairs of the church where there are many people just like you waiting to be baptized in the name of the Father, the Son, and the Holy Ghost.

Still imagining you are that new believer, you proceed to walk out of the church with the hope that things will get better for you mentally, physically and spiritually in the coming days. You begin to read the Bible, attend more worship services, and study with fellow believers throughout the week.

In time, you notice your outlook on life is beginning to look a little better. You start listening to praise music. You avoid people and places that bring you down. Your new way of talking and walking, since drawing nearer to the Lord, can't be ignored by those who knew you when. Now some of your relatives and old friends wonder why you don't call or come around like you use to. They observe you spending more time in the church than over their homes and other places you use to frequent. At first, everyone seems to be okay with the "new you" until you start sharing some things about what you have been reading in the Bible and listening to at church. "Oh don't start with that…I don't want to hear it…" a relative abruptly says while you are sharing a story. "You one of them Christians now, huh!? You think you better than me?" It's obvious this person has had a few too many bad experiences with believers.

You are beginning to observe relatives and friends' reactions to you and it isn't always positive, especially when you open your mouth up about Jesus. Like a vampire allergic to a cross, those people who you use to trust with your very life, are now allergic to you and your views! It doesn't matter if the person is a spouse, mother, father, sister, brother, cousin, a boss, or someone else you confide in, if these people are not willing to make a sacrifice to follow Jesus, just like you have, then it's only a matter of time that those you love will one day become your foes if you walk with God long enough. Gradually, they won't call or come around as much. You will hear less than flattering comments about you from others.

Now that you have hypothetically walked down the aisle as a new Christian again in the previous example, how do you sincerely feel these days about your walk with your heavenly Father? Are loved ones giving you a hard time or a pat on the back because, "You haven't changed!" according to them? Are friends acting more like enemies than supporters? What is really going on with you and those around you? Is God pleased with you and what you are doing to fulfill his calling in your life?

Everyday there is a battle in the spiritual realm, but don't get me wrong, our foes don't have to show up for battle everyday of the week to affect us spiritually. When reading the Bible, you will notice that the rebellious created discourse within their camps with satanic influences leading the way. To date, the enemy doesn't have to work real hard to get a Christian to fall away from the Lord particularly when he or she is frequently taking breaks from church worship, God's people, reading the Bible, spiritual music, and other things God-inspired. In between breaks, the enemy will use familiar as well as unfamiliar people to attempt to kick you every now and then while you are already down by getting them to say discouraging things to you! Instead of having a brother or sister in Christ, you have a critical enemy. It is through these trials that the Lord will speak to you, through the Holy Spirit, about the things that you are and aren't doing to exemplify Christ teachings. In the Bible, we can all relate to Job in many ways, he too experienced a lack of support from his relatives and friends, but he also came out victorious because he kept his eyes on the Father.

Any individual can be a foe depending on situations, environments, beliefs, and settings. A mean-spirited person will use things that are not of the Lord to bring others down spiritually. What this person does may affect your spiritual relationship if you are around him or her long enough. The Bible reads, "Thorns and snares are in the way of the fraudulent: he that does keep his soul shall be far from them" (Prov. 22:5). A critical enemy may attack you about things you said or did that offended him or her almost immediately. Then he or she will leave you alone for a time while this person attacks others. In Luke 4:13, after the devil had tempted Jesus, "he departed from him for a season." This indicates that he wasn't finished with him. He knew he couldn't break Jesus. However, the Son's resistance didn't keep him away forever. The devil would later come back using people to attempt to discourage Jesus from doing the Father's will.

Your devil-influenced critic may surprise you with a sudden phone call or a warm pat on the back before striking you with an offensive comment or a complaint about "you and your God!" or some other issue. When a person is not making an attempt to act in ways that align with godly teachings, you have to wonder if you can continue to classify this person as "my dear relative (or friend) who has my best interests at heart."

Some people walking with God can't stomach the fact that people who have done so much good for them over the years could become an enemy. "How could she? I thought that we were close. Why would she lie on me?" However, if you know your inner circle of relatives and friends well enough, then you will see that those who you love the most are just as lost and confused as you were on that day you decided to give your life to Christ. The difference between you and "they" is you stopped relying on your own strength to pull you through trials and tribulations, you decided to trust in the Lord, but they didn't. In Psalm 118:8 we read, "It is better to trust in the Lord than to put confidence in man."

God wants us to trust in him and at times he will move us to do things that we may not want to do while naysayers will act critical of our actions. Not only that, we can be guilty of becoming our own worst enemy by allowing feelings of resistance to keep us spiritually bound. We may tell ourselves, "That's too hard. I'm not good enough. What will people think?" The key to overcoming our inner critic is to do what God says despite internal or external opposition. Ask God to remove doubt and fear so that you can be better able to do his will. If you don't know what you are supposed to be doing in a situation, do the following: pray, fast and wait for God to give you instruction. God will use messengers, dreams, signs and many other things to make his words clear to the hearer. In the meantime, criticism may not stop.

Jill Briscoe, a pastor's wife and a writer of *When They Criticize Your Husband* (JustBetweenUs.org), shares some ways she has learned to cope with criticism. "As you listen, ask yourself why this person is so upset. Are they under pressure themselves from other quarters…?" She advises, "Let the first thing you say be a quiet and gentle word. 'A soft answer turns away wrath' (Prov. 15:1, NKJV). "Thank you for being so concerned" is one possibility. She also mentions when refuting any unfair or untrue criticism say, "I'm not sure you've been given the whole story," or "If you knew all the circumstances, I think you'd judge the matter differently." The key to handle any criticism is not to give them anything more to talk about. Many writers who have dealt with critical individuals also suggest whatever you do avoid arguing with critical people, even when you know you are right, which you will notice I reiterate in this book. When you have been formally trained in persuading, debating and managing people this can be difficult to do.

Most Christians enjoy attending church. But some wayward believers, apostates and backsliders, who are against attending a church service might say, "Well, I don't need any church to help me! I can do bad all by myself." If you are a church-goer you might think, "Well, do bad all by yourself, I'll be praying for you in Jesus name!" Those who have fallen away from the Lord or who aren't disciplined enough to read the Bible on their own, need to attend church, join a Bible study group or consistently sit under a teacher who can help guide them. Denouncing a church just because one doesn't like the people, the music, this thing or that thing is no excuse not to visit a church. If you have found yourself disgruntled with a particular church, ask God to lead you to a wise person who centers his or her teaching on how to apply passages of Scripture to your life or better yet get a study Bible and start meditating on God's Word for yourself.

Some church members might be called to start their own ministries maybe you are one of them. Therefore, it would make sense why you or others are becoming restless in the church. Pray to God about using you and other restless brothers and sisters in Christ to do something different in his kingdom if you feel like you and others are stagnant, lukewarm or slowly falling away from the Christian walk.

The Internet

Everywhere you look on the Internet you can't visit a website without a box available for someone to comment. Whenever you create something, upload, broadcast, or type on the Worldwide Web, there is usually a place on most sites that allow people to comment. These comments distract readers away from the points the author is trying to convey with his article, video, forum post, etc. Before long everyone is talking about who said what, name-calling, lying and saying other things in the comment boxes, rather than focusing on the topic at hand. I personally encountered my share of hateful and threatening criticism online for speaking truth about everything from relationships to spirituality and had to go to God often with angry feelings and even tears because I couldn't believe how rude people could be.

Many critics seated in front of the computer screen sharing their thoughts about an issue, a video, a forum post or something else are unfortunately immature and unwise. You see the immaturity show up by the negative and shallow opinions about one's appearance, voice, education, setting, and personal interests. Most of these cowardly critics would never verbalize what they think about someone to his or her face because they know there are those who would like nothing more than to fight. So these immature critics get to say what they want about anything and usually don't experience any repercussions for their insults.

With so many voices on the Internet, anyone who is publishing material on the Web might as well be prepared for the evil that lurks on one's website. Someone somewhere around the world is going to be rattled by Satan to insult the Christian. He or she is going to come with lies, anger and abusive phrases designed to attack your mind, spirit and body. If he or she is successful, this person will put you out of business and off the Internet.

At times website critics will become upset with something that had occurred to them offline; therefore, they are going to take their emotions out on that person who happened to upload his or her video preaching the gospel online or speaking truth about the following: politics, celebrities, business, relationships, and more. Then the backslider, unsaved or apostate might visit another site where someone is blogging about Jesus and leave his or her negative two cents worth. Before the night is over, this person will probably log on to the Internet again, stop by his or her social networking page and possibly notice a Christian friend is, at it again, leaving godly messages. Being in an irritable mood, the unbeliever most likely will leave an insulting comment about a Christian's friend's status updates as well.

The more you use the Internet, the more likely God will use you to visit a forum, a social networking page, a micro-blog site, create a blog, a phlog, video, or a webinar among many other things and when you do, there Satan will be in the midst. Knowing this, learn to control and filter the information that comes to and from your page. If God has not led you to make everything you post available for comment, disable comments whenever available. If God has not moved you to let the world see your posts, mark them private. If you have a social networking page and you often see offending status updates, unsubscribe from the person's page or delete them from your account. You can get further help on the site. Ask someone knowledgeable in your network or search online on how to block messages in your news feed, chat, cell phone or anywhere else you are being fed wicked material. Explore all the options available to you to protect your information. Be sure to block others who are offensive, and keep your public pages family-friendly.

It isn't spiritually healthy or necessary to argue with a critic so don't bother offline or online as mentioned earlier. In *6 Lessons on Dealing with Criticism*, an article by Mark Batterson, he advises, "Don't get into an argument!" He refers to Proverbs 26:4, "When arguing with fools don't answer foolish arguments, or you will become foolish as they are." He adds, "'The very next verse says, when arguing with fools, be sure to answer their foolish arguments, or they will become wise in their own estimation.' Those back-to-back verses seem to contradict each other but I think they reveal a deeper truth: If you're arguing with a fool you can't win."

Jesus didn't spend time ranting despite all the evil that was going on around him as well as the negative opinions that came along with his miracles, signs and wonders. When Noah was building the ark, he didn't stop to answer every critic that had an opinion on what he was doing. The prophet Ezekiel did many things for God that was strange and he didn't bother explaining himself to everyone who thought what he was doing was bizarre; rather he chose to focus on giving God's messages to the people. I received criticism over the years from mentors and employers for doing the things of God that were outside of typical church business such as: applying for God-inspired jobs, selecting certain friends, and even eating healthy things. I knew right away that when I stepped out and did something influenced by the Lord, the devil was going to move on men and women's spirits to talk negatively about my actions. Some went so far as to name-call, ridicule, and curse me because of my educational and career experiences. In the end, they looked foolish in my sight and others, because God actually bettered me mentally and physically unlike their unspiritual doomsday prophecies. "They spread a net for my feet—I was bowed down in distress. They dug a pit in my path—but they have fallen into it themselves (Psa. 57:6, NIV). I experienced an internal joy and freedom that my critics didn't have. Every step of the way, God was with me and gave me the strength to endure during my personal trials. He showed his faithfulness to me and gave me peace and confidence to stand whether I had one critic or many in my presence.

If you know that a person is really not interested in making a difference in society, helping you or offering his or her service to help others; don't give this person your attention. "Trust ye not in a friend, put ye not confidence in a guide: keep the doors of thy mouth from her that lieth in thy bosom" (Mic. 7:5). Those who are sincerely interested in what God has inspired you to do will either add to it, share it with others, direct you to more information to help you, or want to connect with you; these are the people worth our time.

The Has-Been Christian: Your Biggest Foe

The worst critic of them all is what I call, the "Has-Been" Christian. You will read plenty about his or her character in my book, *Face*

Your Foe: 28 Critics of Your Faith You Can Overcome. Now I define "The Has-Been" Christian as an apostate. To be clear, the apostate is someone who once was a believer, but not anymore. This person may say something like, "I use to be a Christian." However, he will still claim to know the Lord despite rejecting him. "They profess that they know God; but in works they deny him, being abominable, and disobedient, and to every good work reprobate" (Tit. 1:16, AKJ).

When I think of the Has-Been, I think of King Saul who at one time was appointed by God to reign over the people. But after repeated rebellion, God's Spirit left Saul which I talk more about later in this book. Now what captivated my interest about this story is that despite the king's evil ways, David and others still referred to Saul as "God's anointed" and choose not to kill him. Could it be that you might be doing the same things that David did when dealing with Saul? Do you find yourself often running from or running to your enemy in the hopes that he or she will change? Are you also running your mouth too? Attempting to start conversations with those who have reprobate minds? I talk more about this later.

You know that someone (who used to be a Christian) in your family or elsewhere dislikes you, but because of your loved one's history of serving the Lord, you find yourself wishing, hoping and waiting for this person to stop attacking you with his or her words, mannerisms or worse his or her fists. Keep in mind, in your personal life, "You don't have to reenact the story between Saul and David, it has already been written," the Holy Spirit told me while preparing this book. In some situations, you might feel led by the Spirit to discuss issues with a critical person. Make the time to bring up your concerns during a time when you can handle your emotions. Tell this person how you feel and why it isn't right for you to feel angry so often about what he or she has said. Explain to this person that being often criticized is not going to make you want to do anything different. Also, share with the individual that his or her frequent criticism is making you feel like you no longer want to talk or be around her or him. You will want to end the conversation positively by stating how much you love or care about her or him. If you can't talk to this person face-to-face, you might want to write this person an email, handwritten letter, text or create a video expressing your feelings.

Like the apostate, the backslider who once was also sold out for God, but now simply believes, has chosen to still indulge in sin. This person will observe a new Christian passionate about his or her belief in the Lord and motivated to do well in life, and will grow increasingly envious. However, this jealous backslider may encourage you on one hand to follow the Lord, but discourage with the other. He or she will share his or her complaints, concerns and suggestions as they relate to your spirituality particularly if you have pointed out how his or her negative actions or reactions are making you feel. "It sure looks like God is with you, but you might want to watch what you say to people…I don't like what you said…what about you?" The Has-Been goes on with, "You know you might offend people with all your Jesus talk, keep it to yourself…I mean what you are doing is so nice for the unsaved, I remember doing that same thing, but it wore me out! I just couldn't keep doing that anymore." At some point during a conversation like this, a believer may feel led to rebuke his former brother or sister in Christ in the hopes that feelings of conviction might take over the talkative backslider. At this point the Has-Been might say something like, "So you think you are above the clouds trying to tell me what I need to do…You are so heavenly-minded that you aren't any earthly good…You think you are better than me…? You think you so holy now that God is in your life!"

Has-Been believers act like Know-It-Alls especially now that they no longer feel obligated in their own minds to live righteously. In Proverbs 14:14, "The backslider in heart shall be filled with his own ways: and a good man shall be satisfied from himself." Paul, a disciple of Christ, warns believers in Galatians 5:19-21 about "the works of the flesh are manifest, which are these; adultery, fornication, uncleanness, lasciviousness, idolatry, witchcraft, hatred, variance, emulations, wrath, strife, seditions, heresies, envyings, murders, drunkenness, revellings, and such like: of which I tell you before, as I have also told you in time past, that they which do such things shall not inherit the kingdom of God."

The backsliding believer, as mentioned in earlier text, can be the worst of all enemies to the new Christian. With his or her negative criticisms of Christianity, the Has-Been may use Scripture to justify many sins from lusting to lying. "I know the Bible. The New Testament says I am free from the law," the former Christ follower says while trying to find some more reasons why it's okay to keep right on sinning. Some will go so far as to say, "Once saved always saved…" But the Bible says, "For the sinful nature desires what is contrary to the Spirit, and the Spirit what is contrary to the sinful nature. They are in conflict with each other, so that you do not do what you want (Gal. 5:17) Read the acts of the sinful nature (Gal. 5:19-20). "…Those who live like this will not inherit the kingdom of God" (Gal. 5:19-21).

Many unsaved people will look to the Has-Been believer for information without knowing that the backslider is no longer in fellowship with God, church, or anything spiritual. "I thought you said you were saved. Then why do you do those things? This is why I don't bother with you hypocrites!" the critic argues. When it comes to Christian-like behaviors, concepts, churches, music, and more, the skeptic may notice hypocritical behaviors from the Has-Been and become a harsh critic, so much in fact, he or she may take revenge on the Has-Been who thinks he or she is still capable of talking about the Lord despite still looking and acting sinful. This makes it hard for sincere believers to try to talk to unbelievers about Christ and his teachings. Non-believers and skeptics may unfairly assume that because their backsliding Christian relative or friend has "been there, done that," this person is still a credible point of contact. Therefore, if their beloved is doing something sinful and seems to be okay doing it, witnesses will reason, "Then maybe it isn't so bad after all since God understands."

Now when the backslider is exposed on his or her actions and deeds that are contrary to the Bible, this person will: make excuses, become angry, grow distant, and even go into a depression. Rather than choose not to continue in a lifestyle that disqualifies him or her from running the good race toward his or her high calling, the Has-Been keeps right on sinning while looking for someone or something to blame while justifying his or her unrighteous behaviors. "I know you saw me do that, but I was only trying to help…I promise I won't do that again, but you know God is a forgiving God and I ain't perfect! Besides, you helped me into this mess, you should be getting me out of it!" says the Has-Been who loves to place blame and always believes he or she is saved no matter how much this person sins and has led others away from God.

A rebellious person may have once held a position in the church too, but now he or she has fallen away from all things righteous and may even put up a fight when advised to go to church. "I don't need to study God's word or be around his people. I did that already and it didn't help me. I told you I'm not interested in Christianity. Sure, I use to have a church membership, sang in the choir, and taught bible study, but that's not what I do nowadays," the former church-goer says.

The Lord warns in Isaiah 65:2 about apostates, "I have spread out my hands all the day unto a rebellious people, which walketh in a way that was not good, after their own thoughts..." The apostate trusts in self rather than God. A character description of an apostate is found in Proverbs 6:12, "A naughty person, a wicked man, walketh with a froward mouth." So this individual may be someone in your circle that once was like you, sold out for God, but now, you can barely get this person to say one thing about his past relationship with Christ. He may be jealous of your relationship with God. Apostates see you as a constant reminder of those times when they once worshiped the Lord. Therefore, these former Christ followers are reminded of their falls from grace whenever they see others busily working for God. The critical apostate often has a discouraging comment about what a Christian does for the Lord and will secretly compare one's deeds to what he or she *use* to do for the Kingdom.

Why would anyone trust an apostate, a Has-Been believer, or a rebellious group, who obviously doesn't want anything to do with the gospel of Christ, for advice? Further, I would have to ask, would you trust a doctor to perform surgery on you who is out of practice? Well, this is just what many believers, as well as non-believers, do with back-in-the-day Christ followers, because these people are trusted family members, friends or acquaintances that have done a lot of ear-tickling over the years to keep others believing that mom, dad, auntie, sister and cousin is still alright with God. Some Christians keep these backsliders and unbelievers as advisors, because they say the kinds of things that make them feel okay when they sin whereas sincere brothers and sisters in Christ will most likely hold them accountable. God doesn't care what title these backsliders hold or what past impact they might have had on you. According to Luke 12.53, "The father shall be divided against the son, and the son against the father; the mother against the daughter, and the daughter against the mother; the mother in law against her daughter in law, and the daughter in law against her mother in law." To believe and follow Christ, just might create war in one's household when members of the family aren't being obedient to the Spirit of God.

You may or may not see the ongoing havoc in your own life, because some critics just know how to keep their mouths closed long enough to build up a smoke-screen before attacking a believer on his or her faith in Jesus. They may be deceiving you with a "has-been" kind of faith. Meanwhile, these former Christians hope that you can still see the good in them even in their sins.

Most *past* Christ followers believe they are okay with the Lord despite being bound in their sins. I talk more about this subject on my YouTube channel: nmenterprise7. Apostates will not repent, and will refuse any correction because they believe they already know it all as mentioned earlier. "I've been there, done that! Saw the church, been in the church, and studied the Bible. My mom and dad were members. I went on missions, you can't tell me anything!" says the Has-Been. Yet, secretly a backslider, who loves praising this past believer, may know this person has been living foul for a long time, but won't admit it to you or repent to God for following the sinful deeds of this person, because he or she is also comfortable in sin. Apostates/Has-Beens, back-sliders and the unsaved usually feed off what little belief they all have in Christ from one another until someone gets the bright idea to get serious with the Lord, turn away from rebellion and seek Him for wisdom.

Reprobate Mind

Gone are the days when you could speak to certain relatives or friends about the word of God without them getting offended. Why is this? Because chances are God may have handed them over to a "depraved mind."

According to the *Free Online Dictionary*, depraved is defined as deviating from what is considered moral, right, proper, or good. Similar words that would describe such a person include: corrupt, abandoned, perverted, evil, vicious, degraded, vile, degenerate, immoral, wicked, shameless, sinful, lewd, debased, profligate, debauched, lascivious, dissolute, and licentious. A person fits any one of these characteristics when he or she has decided to abandon what is right and go with what is wrong. Rather than think about what God thinks about an issue, he or she consults with self and uses his or her own personal judgment on an issue whether it comes from what some might consider a good or bad place. How does one determine what is morally right when he or she has no compass to follow? This person will use his or her personal experience or what other flawed human beings believe is righteous in order to validate wrong-doing. What if most of this person's life was spent being mistreated and he or she never really paid close attention to when someone treated him or her fairly? Would he or she know how to make wise decisions to help others? What if this person chose not to receive sound doctrine, wise counselors' advice, or anything else that would lead him or her to healthy decision-making? I can tell you that this individual will almost certainly corrupt others. He or she will use his or her own selfish principles to guide others away from Holy Spirit inspired people, places and things especially if this person feels like God has failed him or her in some way. The misguided will create a life void of Jesus by building it on a foundation of war, deceit, anger, abuse, and more. Then he or she will reign over others carrying a host of unresolved issues. Ultimately, the confused and abused will direct relatives, friends and followers down many paths based on one's godless and equally confused teachers; instead of the one true path that a Bible (thousands of years old—mind you), tells us that the only way to the one true God is through his Son Jesus. Further, it is the only path where our Savior will meet us where we are; rather than us having to jump through hoops to get to him like in some religions where one has to make a large income, be a member of this group, sign your name to this contract, attend a set amount of meetings, recruit a number of members during a specified time, attend this school, and support that organization, and so the requirements go on and on while Jesus is suffocated with man-made goals, buildings, programs, and the like.

Many of our most respected talk show hosts, writers, musicians, doctors, lawyers, even ministers have reprobate minds. They pretend as if they believe in the Most High, but in truth, they believe in self. They borrow Holy Scriptures as to appear as if they are important and privy to the Word of God meanwhile void of the Holy Spirit. If you observe these people long enough, you will hear in their voices that they really don't know what to believe. They are often confused when God's wisdom comes forth. They claim to know the Lord and understand his purpose and existence, but the reality is they don't know their own minds and bodies, so how can they attempt to know God?

There are many believers that have studied and prayed to God for decades and still have yet to scratch the surface of who God really is and what exactly is his plan for our lives. So how can a flawed man or woman filled with sin know a righteous God especially when he hasn't revealed himself? How can a wicked man or woman claim to know something that he or she isn't sure that he or she really knows? It's like a person saying, "I know how to build rockets," yet never built one. He or she sounds like a fool! This is what many of pop culture's teachers' pets look like, fools who are trying to explain 2+2 is everything but 4. One actor said on a talk show, "...it is whatever I say it is..." Try telling the cashier, the accountant, or even math students that. You will get a good laugh. One's personal way of looking at things, cannot dominate a society unless that society chooses to embrace the foolish person's views and run with them. So the next time you allow someone to talk to you about their selfish and immoral views, examine your own personal beliefs. Be sure that before you share what's in your hand with someone else, you look inside your own and separate your personal reality from someone else's fantasy. Then check the Bible and see how your view of self and the world compares to wisdom. From the looks of things, we all need something to determine good from evil, so why not stick to the one true God as a our counselor, teacher and friend?

Doubters

Follow the teachings of Jesus long enough and you will be approached by the doubters. They will come with their, "I don't believe...I haven't heard...I don't know what you are talking about...Would God really say that? Are you sure that God does that?" statements and questions. After a lengthy discussion about their issues with the Bible, you will feel exhausted, and quite possibly mentally drained talking to these people who insist on disbelieving everything you say no matter how wise!

These bitter and sometimes envious skeptics' arguments are usually based on their five senses. They are bitter because of past experiences with God, church and family and jealous because you know something they don't (I give further explanation on this later.) The doubters' five senses play a big part in their unbelief, allowing their carnal minds to suppress their spirit. In other words, their five senses are more important than God. If skeptics can't feel or see something then it's not fact. If they don't have a personal experience to talk about, then they don't believe anyone's testimony no matter how much proof is presented in front of them.

Many doubters are bitter toward God and his people because past prayers went unanswered, they have had bad experiences with supposed Christians and selfish beliefs have over-ridded spiritual ones. These skeptics can also be envious of believers, because they may have tried once to walk with God but failed miserably at it and never got enough faith to keep on going. The Bible would also describe these people as covetous when behaving in these ways. When a Christian is talking to a doubter he makes the mistake of deviating from his point by going down that dead end portion of the conversation that the doubter has set up with all his "I don't believe" talk. In Titus 1:9 (NIV), here is a wise piece of advice when speaking to a doubter, "He must hold firmly to the trustworthy message as it has been taught, so that he can encourage others by sound doctrine and refute those who oppose it." Basically, stick to the point. When you keep with the truth, the doubter doesn't have much argument and will oftentimes just remain quiet when he knows he or she can't upset you with his or her criticism of your faith. Also, keep in mind, no matter what Jesus said or did in those towns he visited, there were those who remained doubtful. Did Jesus waste precious time arguing with them? According to Jude 1:22 (NIV), "Be merciful to those who doubt."

Free-Thinking Debaters

You can't walk with the Lord without someone critiquing your lifestyle. There will be those who feel like they are "led" or authorized to tell you how they feel about you and your God. Family and friends believe that by default they are privy to say what they want without sparing your feelings. When they bring their arguments, what will you do? If you already know that the person approaching you has shown much rotten fruit in his or her lifetime such as: back-biting, gossiping, lying, and having an uncontrolled temper, then it would be best to refrain from debating with such a person no matter how right you believe you are. In 1 Timothy 6:4 (NIV) "...he is conceited and understands nothing. He has an unhealthy interest in controversies and quarrels about words that result in envy, strife, malicious talk, evil suspicions..." Now some readers would say, "I already know that. You aren't telling me something new. You said something similar in an earlier paragraph." Of course, I'm not giving you any breaking news. But the true test on whether you have mastered this area of your life is to check your emotions the next time someone brings you an erroneous argument. Notice how your body responds and what comes out your mouth. Maybe you look good at the time speaking with the fool, but by nightfall this person may have made your blood pressure boil, your head hurt, and you find yourself spending far too much time talking about this person to your spouse or relatives. The next time you feel this way about your critic, do this "...refuse foolish and ignorant questionings, knowing that they generate strife" (2 Tim. 2:23, NIV). Apply this Scripture both on and offline. Some of us have been guilty of taking an argument from outside the home and bringing it home to our families only for them to become angry with us and our enemies. The following Scripture comes to mind, "A foolish son is the destruction of his father; and the bitter arguments of a wife are like drops of rain falling without end" (Prov. 19:13, NIV).

Mockers

"Flog a mocker, and the simple will learn prudence; rebuke a discerning man, and he will gain knowledge" (Prov. 19:25, NIV). It is simply a waste of time to address mockers of God. These people appear both online and offline spouting off how they don't subscribe to this belief or that one. They don't like Christianity. They prefer to be their own god and they don't like people telling them what is good or evil since most mockers are prejudice. They go on and on about how God is this and that and why they would never serve him, help this person or join a group because of petty reasons like the way people look, how they talk or what they might ask of them. Should we care about a mocker's immature viewpoints? The truth is this person is just looking to upset the Christian so that he or she can tell his or her friends, "Hey, come over here; listen to what this crazy Christian said to me after I told him that I wasn't going to his church because I don't like Christians!"

To some people, to walk with God is a sign of weakness, "Only sheep need a shepherd," says the mocker. "I'm no sheep!" But the Bible says, "All we like sheep have gone astray; we have turned everyone to his own way; and the Lord has laid on him the iniquity of us all" (Isa. 53:6, AKJ). Mockers of God will run with the sheep analogy which is used in the Christian church to demonstrate God's relationship with his followers. In 1 Peter 2:25, "For ye were as sheep going astray; but are now returned unto the Shepherd and Bishop of your souls." If the sheep don't follow the shepherd then they will be eaten up by wolves; therefore those who stray from the faith will fall for an enemy's schemes. "As a shepherd seeketh out his flock in the day that he is among his sheep that are scattered; so will I seek out my sheep, and will deliver them out of all places where they have been scattered in the cloudy and dark day" (Ezek. 34:12). Those that mock God's people and his word "follow their own ungodly desires" (Jude 1:18). What comes to mind when I read this Scripture are those comedians and others who joke about all things spiritual or consecrated to our Heavenly Father; unfortunately many won't be laughing on that Day of Judgment. Instead, mockers will be crying.

No matter how entertaining mockers are with their criticism of God's people, these jesters can't be trusted to advise, teach or preach. "A scorner loves not one that reproves him: neither will he go to the wise" (Prov. 15:12, AKJ).

Judges

We have a lot of judges in this world. Turn on any television channel and someone is judging needy people desperate for money, fame and power, on his or her talent, wardrobe, body weight, hair, ideas, legal issues, preferences, you name it! Everyone has an opinion on what they think should be, could be, or wannabe. With all this judging going on, who really has time for God in secular entertainment? Even Christian churches, schools and media are judging people for the sake of being entertained. Many are seeking their next great American IDOL! Now we all know how God feels about idols. So why do we support shows and ideas that force us to choose one person out of hundreds, thousands, even millions to represent us? We do this, because the prince of this world tempts us to choose. It is time to pray Church, "Lord deliver us from the temptations to use godly wisdom to judge the world for selfish gain. Remind us daily to keep away from idol worship in Jesus name."

God tells us, "Thou shalt have no other gods before me" (Exod. 20:3). Satan knows that when we start glorifying individuals, places and things our minds become focused on the frivolous, unimportant things of this life rather than thinking about our Creator and what he wants for us. So instead of doing the things of God that please him, men and women place much attention on the architecture of the gods, the mystery writings of the dead (who once followed certain gods), the magic of the gods, the myths of the gods, the music of the gods, the visions of the gods, and so on.

Every so often we need to be reminded of how our righteous Judge views us, "He will not judge by what he sees with his eyes, or decide by what he hears with his ears; but with righteousness he will judge the needy, with justice he will give decisions for the poor of the earth. He will strike the earth with the rod of his mouth; with the breath of his lips he will slay the wicked. As a follower of Christ, we are expected to live righteously. Righteousness will be his belt and faithfulness the sash around his waist" (Isa. 11:3-5). Too often we are putting man and woman's traditions and opinions alongside things we supposedly have consecrated to God. Yet, it is okay to praise idols that look and act like centuries-old gods!?

Think of all of the things that people connect to God but seriously have nothing to do with God. Examples include: Christmas trees set up next to crosses. Secular celebrities sold out to Satan singing along with gospel singers. Churches hosting events with groups who delve in witchcraft, horoscope reading and idol worship. Church members supporting pagan traditions, mythical characters and cartoons that boldly as well as subliminally teach and encourage children to act immorally. Programs, music and services within the church that look and act like secular business models. These are just a handful of the many things that people of God try to justify as "being okay" and "God understands." They become angry when God's prophets warn them about their actions and what will result if they continue to glorify themselves and ancient gods. These self-righteous believers turn on the messengers of God and become increasingly critical of them and their families.

The Lord has said in his Word, "Do not make any gods to be alongside me; do not make for yourselves gods of silver or gods of gold" (Exod. 20:23, NIV). Have we not learned from those who have gone before us? "Do not worship any other god, for the Lord, whose name is Jealous, is a jealous God" (Exod. 20:3, NIV). No matter how much men and women rationalize their thoughts, programs, statutes, traditions, and more, while claiming to love our Creator, we should always come back to our Bibles and ask, "Now would God really consider what I am doing a part of his will? Is what I am saying and doing really glorifying God, myself or ancient gods?"

Critics in the Church

The critic who works hard in the church emulating the leadership is one I have come across in my journey with the Lord. This copycat critic is usually born again and sold out for the Lord; but there's just one major issue, he or she "feels led" to do everything that everyone else does including: preach, teach and walk like the pastor or his wife (whether called or not) while belittling others.

The copy cat volunteers for most activities in and out of the church because she enjoys the praise she gets more than actually serving others. Besides, her church requires that she do these things if she wants a leadership position one day.

Now when things don't go her way or become difficult in the church, God's daughter becomes a wicked critic always having something negative to say about someone else. "Why is everyone always late when I pick them up? I'm not going to pick these people up anymore! Why can't I get the good part in the choir? That girl can't sing! Why don't people give more money? I'm tired of people saying they are Christian, but they don't do all the things I do! When will people help out?" Her criticism always starts with a question directed at specific individuals who have offended her, followed by tears so that witnesses will come and comfort her with, "Oh sweetheart, it's okay. Daughter, you have the victory! God knows all about it!" In Matthew 18:15-17 (NIV) we are given wise advice when dealing with a person like this, "If your brother sins against you, go and show him his fault, just between the two of you. If he listens to you, you have won your brother over. But if he will not listen, take one or two others along, so that 'every matter may be established by the testimony of two or three witnesses.' If he refuses to listen to them, tell it to the church; and if he refuses to listen even to the church, treat him as you would a pagan or a tax collector." When we think of how much time Jesus spent talking to pagans and tax collectors, we are to listen, have mercy for the person, counsel he or she, but at the same time not condone his or her bad-mouthing.

Most likely, God didn't call this believer to join every church group or program available, but she wants to look important so she volunteers for many of them leaving little time to manage her home and care for her family. She hopes to take on a certain position in the church. She desires to be noticed by one or a few people. Oftentimes, these workers of the Lord desire a stipend especially when they see the pastor is living well on the members' contributions. We can easily fall into the temptation of wanting to be something more than what God has called us to be and that's when we get into trouble. God will then put us on the sidelines to watch the game rather than participate in it. It is then that feelings of emptiness will begin to surface.

A righteous God will not allow anyone to take advantage of his people, but people will allow people to take advantage of one another. Some of you see someone (or a group) capitalizing right now off your blessings and doing ungodly things with them. God says, "You don't have to worry any longer about being taken for granted. If you simply learn to say, 'No' things will change in your household, on the job at the church, and elsewhere." What use is it complaining about someone to others when we're guilty of permitting this person to take advantage of us in the first place? Why talk negatively about brothers and sisters in Christ when you know there have been times when you have been guilty of the same things you have accused them of doing? "How can you say to your brother, 'Brother, let me take the speck out of your eye,' when you yourself fail to see the plank in your own eye? You hypocrite, first take the plank out of your eye, and then you will see clearly to remove the speck from your brother's eye" (Luke 6:42, NIV).

As much as we would like to think that our brothers and sisters in Christ would not speak negatively about us or our faith in God, the truth is a few will, especially if they are from another denomination and don't believe in the Father, Son and Holy Ghost. They also won't get along with you if they consider one's personal opinion or man's traditions more important than the Bible. In Romans 12:10, we are told to, "Be kindly affectioned one to another with brotherly love; in honour preferring one another…" All is well until one asks questions or makes comments about one's personal beliefs, attitude, actions, church affiliation or associations, etc. Some believers react harshly when it comes to their religious background. They don't want to be questioned about church protocol and traditions that they still follow despite attending a different church. Other members may not believe in certain spiritual gifts in the Bible while church-goers, with Holy Bibles in hands, want to know why leadership is allowing controversial things to occur in the church. The issues between Christians can grow into all out wars, simply because some don't want to visit other churches that might be a better fit for them. Members may be stuck in routines and refuse to change, and others might falsely believe that anyone outside their church home is of the devil.

God made our mouths; therefore, he knew what we were going to do with them before we said one word. "And the Lord said unto him, Who hath made man's mouth? or who maketh the dumb, or deaf, or the seeing, or the blind have not I the Lord?"

(Exod. 4:11). We incorrectly think that because God has given us something such as our mouth that it's okay to do what we want with it, so we don't bother to inquire of the Lord on how to use it for various situations. The brother insults the sister in Christ because he is use to having his way. The sister yells at the pastor because she doesn't like things being omitted out the program that will take her away from the spotlight. Members argue amongst one another and say things like, "At my old church, we didn't do it this way…My pastor was good, I don't like this new one, because he doesn't get you off your feet…God doesn't operate this way, he does things this way…You guys are fools…are you sure God is with you?" The following passage of Scripture, from Paul, is something we should all think about when addressing issues between believers in the church. "I appeal to you, brothers, in the name of our Lord Jesus Christ, that all of you agree with one another so that there may be no divisions among you and that you may be perfectly united in mind and thought... Is Christ divided?" (1 Cor. 10, 13). What solutions might God be sharing with you to help yourself and others agree on an issue you might be presently facing?

A Critical Partner

An intimate relationship that may have been close and drama-free at one time between two individuals will change once one accepts Jesus while the other drags his or her feet on the things that God has led him or her to do such as: cut off certain people, relocate, budget money, visit churches or become a member, study the bible, attend spiritual conferences, pray, fast, listen to Christian music, and anything else God-related.

It is inevitable that friction will occur in the relationship, because two people can't agree on studying the precepts of the Bible, attend a church, or even pray together. Even worse, one or both may or may not hear from the Holy Spirit in order to take the next step in their spiritual walks. This may happen because the couple may be suppressing the voice of the Lord with all their negative thinking and malice toward one another. A marriage partner may become the offender while the other takes on a victim role. Then the roles reverse again and again until someone cries out, "Let's end this…I'm getting a divorce!"

"But if the unbelieving depart, let him depart. A brother or a sister is not under bondage in such cases: but God hath called us to peace" (I Cor. 7:15). Some people remain together through their storms and have wonderful relationships while others end old ones and start new partnerships exclusively with God or with someone who seems more compatible.

Now take a moment to think about what a desolate land looks like, it is abandoned, dry, cracked, and has no signs of life, right? Well, that is what some of our relationships look like and the critic sees our dry, deserted lands. What might cause that desolate land that was once a plush green and vibrant to become dead? If you answered something like, "The weather or man," then you are right. So is the case in the life of one who is attempting to follow Christ, he or she is frequently bumped off his or her journey by natural or man-made environmental changes which, if left unchecked, will make the believer's walk nothing more than a desolate land of tumble weeds, dirt and abandoned projects! Trust in the Lord during those times of desolation in your life and permit him to guide you to the people, places and things that are meant to bless you and not curse you!

A critical partner can be an enemy especially if he or she is not interested in serving the Lord. This is why we must be careful not to intimately connect with someone who doesn't pray, worship the Lord, listen to Christian speakers and music, read the Bible, or participate in activities that typically draw believers to a closer walk with the one true God. The Bible warns, "Do not be yoked together with unbelievers. For what do righteousness and wickedness have in common? Or what fellowship can light have with darkness?" (2 Cor. 6:14).

Critical Saved & Unsaved Parents

You can't read a book like this and not think about those who may have scrutinized your life more than anyone else, parents. Now there are those mothers and fathers who tried their best to mold and shape children into productive citizens; however, for some they didn't quite know the difference between encouraging a child and discouraging him or her spiritually and mentally. There are Christians who have unsaved parents; and they can be our foes.

Gossip, bitter words, and angry discussions about what the Holy One is doing in a son or daughter's life can leave parents feeling like all their efforts to raise their children to become a worldly success are null and void once God has come into their lives. Rather than, defend one's faith or try to reason why God would or wouldn't do something, a believer should simply ignore the parent's selfish aspirations and verbal attacks. Once I became an adult, I realized that I no longer had to do things to appease my parents. After private school, there was limited discussion about spiritual things. My parents left it up to me to make my own decisions including my faith choice.

The same God who permitted an unsaved parent to be a parent also knows his creation's selfish ambitions, disobedience, and rebelliousness. Be assured God knows your troubles concerning difficult parents. Pray, fast and seek counsel from those who are wise about your situation.

A critical parent should place his or her focus on one's own salvation, rather than be critical of his or her son or daughter's deliverance. A parent is supposed to pray the kind of prayers and act in ways that will cause his or her family to want to walk closer to the Lord not run from him. However, some relatives might talk about how outdated the Scriptures are, what they don't like about the church and overall criticize the people and things of God. Some will even go so far as to say, "I don't need to do all that (pray, fast, go to church, read the Bible) Jesus did it all for me." Not so fast! In Matthew 5:17-19 (NIV) Jesus says, "Do not think that I have come to abolish the Law or the Prophets; I have not come to abolish them but to fulfill them. I tell you the truth, until heaven and earth disappear, not the smallest letter, not the least stroke of a pen will by any means disappear from the Law until everything is accomplished. Anyone who breaks one of the least of these commandments and teaches others to do the same will be called least in the kingdom of heaven, but whoever practices and teaches these commands will be called great in the kingdom of heaven." Notice those who teach others to break God's commandments will be called "least in the kingdom of heaven." A parent is our first teacher, if he or she isn't walking with God, then he or she is teaching others to follow in his or her unspiritual footsteps.

Too often people claim to know and love Jesus, but in all actuality they are more concerned about meeting selfish desires while expecting to feel comfortable in their lifestyles void of sincere worship and praise of our Heavenly Father. A critical backsliding or unsaved parent is not concerned about the things of God and will tell you so by his or her dismal reaction to conversations about God, avoidance of church and Christians, and encouragement of worldly behaviors and conversations. However, despite a parent's godless life, a son or daughter, who is a believer, must avoid the temptation to want to verbally or physically assault a parent who might be provoking him or her to anger. A parent who is not interested in God's precepts will not pay attention to the biblical text that reads, "And, ye fathers, provoke not your children to wrath: but bring them up in the nurture and admonition of the Lord" (Eph. 6:4). But you, Believer, know the Scriptures, and when a loved one is saying or doing things that are not of the Lord, put them in God's hands and keep with the mission God has called you on despite critical words and back-biting from your family. Too often parents will call their children's attention to the Scripture that reads, "Honor thy mother and thy father..." yet don't bother to read the rest of the Scripture or live righteously. Don't worry God sees all.

In Exodus 21:15, "And he that smiteth his father, or his mother, shall be surely put to death." Despite this Scripture being in the Old Testament, it still has significant meaning today. There may be someone who is reading this book that feels much anger toward a parent or relative. If so, may God be with you, keeping your heart and mind intact in Jesus name.

When we watch the news and hear of someone harming or killing a parent, society doesn't react with a forgiving spirit; instead, people suggest the murderer should receive the death penalty. In Exodus 21:17, God took cursing one's parent seriously as well. "And he that curseth his father, or his mother, shall surely be put to death." Although nowadays this would be forbidden, society's reaction to a son or daughter cursing his or her parent is still furious and it wouldn't be hard to find a group somewhere in this world who would support corporal punishment for cursing one's mother and father whether saved or unsaved.

Keep in mind, God is not finished with godless parents, relatives and guardians even if sons and daughters might be done with them and all their attacks on their Christian faith. "Brother will betray brother to death, and a father his child; children will rebel against their parents and have them put to death. All men will hate you because of me, but he who stands firm to the end will be saved" (Matt. 10:21).

As much as you may love your parent, if he or she is unsaved or a backslider ridiculing God and his people, our Father will judge him or her accordingly and this person might end up losing a significant place in your life. Sure, we are to honor our parents, but we aren't to be fools for them. God hasn't changed and he is still adamant about his people being set aside for his purposes. In John 12:48, Jesus says, "He that rejecteth me, and receiveth not my words, hath one that judgeth him: the word that I have spoken, the same shall judge him in the last day." Further we are told in 1 Timothy 4:1, "Now the Spirit speaketh expressly, that in the latter times some shall depart from the faith, giving heed to seducing spirits, and doctrines of devils…" This Scripture doesn't exempt loved ones. We are warned, "…a man's enemies are the men of his own house" (Mic. 7:6). You don't want to be subjected to satanic influences that might move you away from the Lord.

As mentioned in other places in this book, regardless of whether one is a parent, guardian, best friend, etc., children of darkness do not have believers' best interests in mind. Instead, a wayward believer, hypocrite, apostate, or the unsaved is asking, "What's in it for me?" when dealing with sincere believers. "What might I get from my son who now declares he is born-again?" What word can I get from my daughter who says she hears from the Lord?" Remember God knows the hearts of men and women. Let God give you direction when dealing with those individuals who might be self-serving and critical.

Fault-finders

Fault-finders, whether in or out of the church, will speak disapprovingly of all types of Christians, because they see that believers all have one thing in common: a heart for righteousness despite their short-comings. Job knew more than anyone how friends can be when you serve the Lord, "My friends scorn me: but mine eye poureth out tears unto God." (Job 16:20). Have you ever looked to a brother and sister in Christ for comfort only to hear them tell you, "Stop all that crying...You know that if you hadn't done this you wouldn't have experienced that...You know God is punishing you because you did what you did—you know better than that!" Men and women might remember our faults but, "Blessed is the man whose sin the Lord will never count against him" (Romans 4:8).

The Slothful

Lazy believers are unwilling to put the work in to draw nearer to the Creator, yet they will criticize others. "You are always running for that church, why don't you sit down? Do you ever know how to take a break? I hope God doesn't ask me to do what you are doing," says the slothful believer. This person spirals backward in his or her walk with God because he or she simply doesn't want to participate in Kingdom Business. They will verbalize their discontent about church matters to anyone who will listen. When something is said or done that convicts slothful people, they will make excuses, lie or place blame. The Bible reminds us not to be "slothful in business;" but we are to be "fervent in spirit; serving the Lord..." (Rom. 12:11). The slothful welcome prayer, enjoy praise music, a comfortable seat in church, and a free meal, but when called upon, they aren't interested in helping anyone but themselves. When they notice that you are on to them, they will place distractions in front of your eyes to appear as if they are hard workers.

Bitter believers

Bitter believers, who feel like God has failed them in some way, aren't good friends to anyone especially new believers. They remember how it once felt falling in love with God (which I mentioned with the Has-Been Christian) and secretly they want that old feeling back. These insensitive, serious people, with often negative attitudes, are like the fault-finders, they will purposely look for issues in others to deflect from their own personal challenges. "We don't dress like that...your idea won't work. They don't listen to me around here. They never do anything right. I don't even know why I bother attending church." When we have someone like this in our circle, think of Ecclesiastes 7:16 (NIV), "Do not be overrighteous, neither be overwise--why destroy yourself?"

Backsliders In and Out of the Church

Critical backsliders who attend church and other spiritually related events, can become easily angered when one attempts to correct them. This could be because many once walked with the Lord and recognize right away when God is using his messengers to communicate his words. Backsliders rather talk about you and your issues, but when questioned about their lifestyle changes, they are usually digressing or quiet. The periodic church-goer or backslider says, "Oh yes, I hear what you are saying about the Lord but... Well yes, I know what God's Word says but...I pray but...I don't need you to tell me that because...Since we are on the subject about me, what about you?" The "once saved always saved type" doesn't think that anything they ever do is wrong. "When pride comes, then comes disgrace, but with humility comes wisdom" (Prov. 29:23, NIV).

The unsaved and backslidden will ignore you at times when you are attempting to spread the gospel. Their disinterest in God's word is due to past disappointments, failures and abuse. They also don't want to be reminded of where they have come from and why they ought to come up higher. To become a better person in God's sight requires work, the kind that many backsliders, lazy Christians and the unsaved don't want to do. "I'm not giving up my life... That's too much work. There are a lot of people in this world; God can get someone else to do that. I don't need to do anything for God, he knows how I am." The backslider will hide behind Scriptures that talk about not having to do anything to be saved, but ignore the Scriptures about being obedient to the Lord. When you are trying to explain why we all are expected to listen to God and do what he asks, you might be tempted to argue with the unrighteous or experience feelings of frustration with them. Walk away when you feel this way. Proverbs 19:11 says, "A man's wisdom gives him patience; it is to his glory to overlook an offense." Keep spending time with the Lord and reading the Bible and in time you will look beyond those issues you might have with others.

One who is willing to serve our awesome Savior is not worried about what he or she has to give up in his or her personal life since what we do at times is unrighteous anyway. Right away, you can tell when someone is sincere about his or her faith; because he or she ignores objections and fights resistance in ways that you can't help but want to listen and take notes. From using a gentle voice to correct a fellow brother or sister in Christ to inviting the unsaved or backslider to dinner, God's anointed is used to convict the sinner. We have to remind ourselves that we are representing Jesus when dealing with difficult people.

Some of you are having pity parties in church right now about your former backsliding relatives and friends—thinking the worst of them—when you should be praying for them. What might a pity party look like in church, you say? A group of believers talking about who, what, why, when, where and how concerning other believers that might appear like they are not faithfully following Christ or attending church like them. They are conversing about these people as if they are judges for a show called, "America's Best Christian." Here's what the pity party sounds like, I invented the following thought-provoking scenario.

"I haven't seen Johnny in church for awhile, how is he? It's such a shame. I hope he's not back on drugs. He was doing so well. Singing in the choir, attending bible study..."

The critical listener responds, "You know Johnny is probably up to no good; he's been such a disappointment to his folks over the years. I thought he was going somewhere!"

How do we know what Johnny is really up to just because he hasn't been seen by two or three people in church? In Psalm 52:3 (NIV), the Scripture is a wake-up call for all of us, the Psalmist David says, "You love evil rather than good, falsehood rather than speaking the truth..." Keeping with the scenario, I ask you to consider all possibilities before jumping to conclusions about those who might have a bad track record. Could it be that Johnny, my invented character, is attending an earlier service at the church, running a home bible study or left the church and is going elsewhere? But others are adding to the gossip, "Not only is Johnny backsliding, but so is Terri, Scott and Mary. Such a waste! Oh their poor mothers! I feel sorry for them." says one dedicated church member. How does this self-righteous believer know that the group's absence is due to them going back to their old ways? "Friend deceives friend, and no one speaks the truth. They have taught their tongues to lie; they weary themselves with sinning" (Jer. 9:5). What are the chances that Johnny, Terri, Scott, and Mary would be coming back to church service if they found out that people were talking about them like these Christians are doing? Now in my scenario, there is a happy ending. About a week later, after the pity party, Johnny shows up to church along with other members. The pastor announces that the group was out on the mission field. Don't our Pharisee minded characters look silly? "If you are wise, your wisdom will reward you; if you are a mocker, you alone will suffer" (Prov. 9:12, NIV).

Ask God, right now, for forgiveness if you have been guilty of participating in a pity party with other believers, talking negatively about your brother or sisters' spiritual journey without knowing the full details. Maybe someone is really backsliding around you and maybe you or others are guilty of causing this person more pain and suffering by shaming them while exalting yourself and others. If you said disrespectful words about those who you are supposed to be witnessing to, whether behind their backs or to their faces, ask God to forgive you for that too. If you believe that you are a "good person," then I challenge you to request that God search your heart right now and show you the truth about yourself. Then ask God to give you the strength and knowledge to act according to his will and not your own. "And Jesus said unto him, Why callest thou me good? there is none good but one, that is, God" (Mark 10:18). However, what if you are the one who heard a relative, friend or someone else talking about you and assuming the worse, in the Bible we are told, "Bear with each other and forgive whatever grievances you may have against one another. Forgive as the Lord forgave you" (Col. 3:13). I know it is easier said than done, but try it anyway. What has brought me peace in the past when it comes to "he say, she say" situations is a few things: distance, gifts and honesty. When I feel tempted to act like a fool about something someone has done to me, I create distance. When I truly want to bring peace to a situation I offer a gift, advice, service, etc. And when I just need to express how I really feel regardless of the consequences, I am honest and I do not sugarcoat how I feel about what has been said.

The Enemy's Fiery Darts

Have you experienced any of the following recently: a snide remark, pessimistic statements, lies, ungodly behaviors, sinful music, TV programs, or something similar? If you notice, most people who do these things on a consistent basis irritate and anger us, they are usually those we love and trust the most. Why do you think God would permit such things to happen to his followers who might be struggling to keep from sinning at least for a time? I would say, for two reasons. The first being, the Christian's faith is being tested. How can you fight an enemy appropriately without a faith? Do you sincerely trust that God will deal with attacks made by your critics? A commanding officer would never send a soldier out into the battlefield without preparing him or her first within the group. God chooses to use various situations to teach us how to spot a foe. Then we are to learn how to act according to his will.

How do you know if you have a foe in your camp or simply a friend who is just having a bad day? How would you know how to fight a rival, especially if you have never seen him or her throw the first blow? What might you do to deal with various situations that occur on the job, at home, the store, and elsewhere with unexpected enemies? You can't answer these questions without wisdom from the Lord. This is why it is essential to have a life of daily prayer, fasting and biblical study under the direction of the Holy Spirit.

When relating to others, the believer must not only be able to spread the gospel of Jesus Christ, as well as other messages in the Bible, but also apply biblical teachings to one's life. Every fiery dart thrown by the enemy can be used as an opportunity to grow in faith. The wicked critic hopes that his or her verbal assaults will resonate with believers. In this way, the detractor believes the Christian will falter in his faith. He or she hopes a believer will be so distracted by what the critic has said or done that there won't be enough reaction time to say anything that would make the wicked feel uncomfortable. If a believer should lose sleep over a situation, stop eating, or do something self-destructive because a detractor has insulted him or her then the individual is only leaving his or her self open to more attack which will also increase his chances of sinning! We must stay sober and alert when we have an enemy in our presence. "So then, let us not be like others, who are asleep, but let us be alert and self-controlled" (1 Thess. 5:6).

The Psalmist David shared the Word of the Lord in Psalm 101:5 (AKJ), "Whoever privately slanders his neighbor, him will I cut off: him that has a high look and a proud heart will not I suffer." We shouldn't sacrifice our health, time or money getting upset over prideful people who slander us, it would be better just to cut them off and live out our short existence tending to the things of God.

A critical person, especially one familiar with the Holy Bible's precepts, knows God's Words have power; therefore His wisdom will convict the unrighteous to want to change—something that unbelievers may not be ready to experience. It feels good to many freethinkers not to feel morally obligated to do anything in their daily lives, but go to work, eat, sleep, watch TV, surf the Internet, and spend money on self and occasionally others. No major inconveniencies, responsibilities, conflicts or anything else to upset one's carefree world. What a perfect life for the godless skeptic! No one ever has to do anything unless he or she feels like it. Of course, you and I both know that kind of life is not characteristic of the God we serve and besides its non-existent for many Average Joes, particularly if you aren't wealthy. However, far too many people aim for a life such as the one described, only to be disappointed over and over again until their dying days while absorbing the words of secular motivational speakers telling them, "Live life to the fullest...Do you... You can do anything you want if you just put your mind to it!" Then when you don't look like what man thinks you should look like, these same motivational speakers turn on you like snakes saying, "You didn't follow instructions. You didn't buy my CD on... You could have been somebody!" The Scripture asks us this question, "Do you see a man wise in his own eyes? There is more hope for a fool than for him" (Prov. 26:12, NIV).

A selfish, rich, ungodly critic is always ready to listen to depressed, confused, weak, poor Christians who don't know why their God has forsaken them. The ungodly respond like this, "I told you not to get involve with Christianity! See how easy my life is! I have no troubles!" Sure, that's what the rich man or woman says now, but if one was to ask his or her partner, relatives and friends about what really goes on behind the scenes with this critic, we would be shocked. We are advised in 1 Timothy 6:17 (NIV), when talking to the rich, "Command those who are rich in this present world not to be arrogant nor to put their hope in wealth, which is so uncertain, but to put their hope in God, who richly provides us with everything for our enjoyment."

2. Wicked Critic's Boss

You can't truly know an enemy unless you know the enemy behind the enemy. Have you ever heard someone ask, "Who put him/her up to saying that about me? I don't believe he/she acted alone." Sometimes a critical person is doing things to hurt others because they have been motivated by someone or a group to say or do something to rock the boat. If you have watched television reality shows, you may have noticed that for a time, early episodes seem relatively peaceful between characters until someone comes on the scene starting trouble. The "villain" is most likely motivated by the producers behind the reality show (like television talk shows) to say or do something shocking, crazy or hurtful to one's supposed loved one or best friend to increase ratings. The "victim" might very well be in on the madness pretending like he or she didn't know what was about to take place. Well, with Satan, he is like that antagonist in a movie, the archenemy in a TV series, or that backstabbing friend you might know. The evil one is going to move men and women to attack one another with words first, next evil deeds and, in some cases, ending with unfortunately violence.

In this chapter, we will take a look at the Christian's Critic's boss, the devil. The name "devil" is defined on Dictionary.com as, "a subordinate evil spirit at enmity with God, and having power to afflict humans both with bodily disease and with spiritual corruption."

The Christian's archenemy goes by many names including: Satan, Evil Spirit, Adversary, Beelzebub, Red Dragon, Belial, Lying Spirit, Old Serpent, Prince of Darkness, Prince of Demons, Prince of the Power of the Air, Prince of this World, God of this World, and the Tempter according to the Holy Bible. Satan is also known as an accuser (Rev. 12:10). He is that voice that confronts us about everything we ever did even if we have forgiven someone, repented, apologized, or did anything else that the Holy Spirit convicted us to do to bring peace to a situation. Our adversary is going to create a hostile environment so that hopefully we can mess up something with someone whether that is a relationship, project, opportunity, or something else. What's worse, he will even use our weaknesses to cause us to hurt ourselves. Sometimes that critical voice inside our head sabotages every effort we make to try to accomplish a worthwhile task such as: work on a relationship, find pleasure in a job, build a group, take part in a project, or do other positive things. The Lord says, "Override the critical voice within by studying his Word. Listen to his voice and he will direct your path. Be still long enough to obey and do what is asked of you." Sometimes we spend more time listening to people and music that we miss the encouragement and instruction that God is providing us. "This is why some problems never seem to go away," says the Lord.

There are many signs and symbols in our modern day society that represent Satan's evil ways of: tempting us to sin (Gen. 3:1), stealing from us mentally and physically (John 10:10) and killing us overall (John 8:44; 1Peter 5:8). This is why Christians must be cautious when buying certain clothing, shoes, toys, trinkets, and more that blatantly advertise for the devil and his devious ways. Some symbols include: devil horn and number six hand signs, the physical numbers 666 hidden or in plain view, triangle with a one eye covered or decorated, a mixture of red, white and black colors along with occult signs, a goat or beast head, pentagram, and many other satanic inspired designs. Periodically a chessboard is also pictured with some of these objects. Researchers as well as former Freemasons have said the chessboard floor is tied to Freemasonry. The group has been known to boldly show its affiliation with organizations, concepts, products, projects, programs, people, music, games, buildings, etc. An example of some of these occult symbols extensively displayed can be found on secular artists' album covers such as: Michael Jackson's, *Blood on the Dance Floor and Dangerous*, Prince *Lotus Flow3r*, Rihanna, *Russian Roulette*, Justin Bieber, *Complex*, Jordan Sparks, *Battlefield*, Lily Allen, *Alright Still.* Other symbols can be found in photographs and music videos with secular entertainers like: Clash, Lady Gaga, Bob Dylan, Jay-Z, Beyonce, Drake, Game, Chris Brown, J Cole, Lil Wayne, Willow, and Mindless Behavior. Christian entertainers and ministers have also displayed various symbols related to the occult which are cleverly hidden. I learned about many of the mainstream Christian musicians and ministers on video and blog sites by performing detailed keyword searches. Because they aren't blatant signs, I will leave it up to the reader to determine who or what is of light. Although they are far more discreet, upon closer inspection there are Christian artists' album covers and music videos that appear to have occult symbolism, display sexual preference, and secular affiliations. Notice hand and arm signs, seated or standing poses, clothing, jewelry, accessories, colors and patterns in clothing, and other things influenced by Satan. There are many imposters who may act or say that they are children of light, but their fruit says something totally different.

A number of critics of the one true God will argue that the devil doesn't exist and is just something, like Santa Claus, made up by man. Funny, Satan's name is even evident in the name of Santa. I talk more about Christmas lies in a book I wrote called, *Spiritual Poems by Nicholl* (Blurb.com). When reading the Holy Bible and other centuries' old work, we find that the existence of a powerful, entity is not a figment of one's imagination or just an image in a book or movie like Santa and other mythical creatures. In the Holy Bible, Satan is mentioned throughout the Old and New Testaments. As mentioned previously, his character is often described as being a liar, an accuser, destroyer, murderer, tempter, and even unclean (Luke 4:33, Luke 8:29, Luke 9:42, Matt. 15:22 and Matt. 17:18). In the Scriptures, The Prince of Demons has assistants who inhabit men and women, push prophets to lie, move others to do despicable things, and tempt even Jesus Christ!

At times, Satan chooses not to enter humans, but comes in the form of the following: a serpent, an unseen entity that has power over the air, shows up in visions as a dragon, and many other forms including a spirit of darkness and one of light. In Genesis 3:1, he is described as a serpent. When he approaches Eve, he appears harmless. We notice he talks, persuades, and gets her to doubt what God says. I have learned that Satan gives you insight into things that sound wise, appear to be righteous, but really puts you on a suicidal path. He doesn't force you to sin, but he uses others to work his evil plans to convince you to sin.

The Evil One's Counterfeits

The devil performs various false signs and wonders to move both believers and unbelievers to do his will. Based on Revelation 13, Christian researchers believe in the last days Satan will reveal the false messiah (v.3-4), create a false resurrection, unite the world under his leadership (v. 7-8) and control the world economy (v. 16-17). God has repeatedly warned believers not to follow false prophets, but do they listen? False prophets nowadays come as rappers, talk show hosts, politicians, motivational speakers, mainstream media ministers, and more. There are many who will claim that they know when Christ is coming. The Scriptures tell us that Jesus will reveal himself to all in time and no day or hour is given in the Scriptures (Matt. 24:23-28).

Satan's Assistants

Our enemy has workers which are referred to as demons in the Bible. They too, are fallen angels. His assistants speak to the living and to the dead. There are many (legions) and when they inhabit bodies, they don't want to leave (Mark 5:10). Satan entered the body of Judas for a time, left and then came back. (John 13:27, Luke 22:3). Jesus knew the evil one was present. Apparently, there is something in the atmosphere that alerts you to the presence of Satan, because if there weren't, you wouldn't be reading a book such as this to help you learn more about how to deal with an enemy. In addition, the prince of darkness does scheme (Eph. 6:11). He also has dark power and forces in the world that are evil (Eph. 6:12).

In Revelation 13:2, the evil one also uses beasts to help him. One comes from the sea and the other from the earth. There is also a false prophet at work as well (Rev. 16:13). The Bible says the two-headed beast blasphemies God (Rev. 13:5). The descriptions of these beasts doesn't seem far-fetched to me considering the ongoing work of scientists to make superhuman creatures nowadays. With a mix of both human and animal genes, they have already instilled things in animal species that God never intended for his creatures to have. You can learn more about man's progress by researching genetic modification and human-animal chimeras.

The prince of this world has his share of prophets, mediums, teachers, and more who perform counterfeit miracles, signs and wonders. We are warned in the Bible, "Do not turn to mediums or seek out spiritists, for you will be defiled by them. I am the Lord your God" (Lev. 19:31). But what do some believers and unbelievers do? They look to dark forces to talk to dead loved ones, predict the future, find lost objects, restore marriages, or worse hurt or kill enemies. Don't be surprised when a critic approaches you looking like a child of light pretending to help you during your time of weakness. "I am gifted in healing," says the pretender. "Let me see your palm. Do you need me to perform a spell? I can help you pay off some bills, but first can you do me this favor?" The wolf in sheep's clothing is on his job, but are you? Deceptive so-called believers in a "Creator" do nothing more than deceive naïve Christians. If you should partake in the devil's work, it's only a matter of time that he or she will expose you as a hypocrite as well as show you their true identity. "You Christians are all the same, you claim to trust in God, but you always look to men and women to help you when you are in a crisis!" says the witch, magician, warlock, Satanist, and others. Meanwhile, you are standing there taking verbal insults from a child of darkness who you once thought was a believer just like you.

Satan has no problem using our weak-minded relatives and friends, who are disobedient to the Lord to commit temporary kind acts which over time end up being replaced with disrespectful, manipulative, bizarre, and even wicked deeds (ie. Judas betraying Jesus).

Satan Tempts

Satan tempts us to do his dirty work. In I Chronicles 21:1, Satan tempted David to take a census of Israel. At first glance, there doesn't seem to be anything wrong with his request. However, we learn later that the motive behind the request is the problem. David spent valuable time conducting a census focused on the size of his army and not on God. We must realize that the tempter moves us to do things that seem right, but eventually take our minds and hearts away from the Lord. "There is a way that seems right to a man, but in the end it leads to death" (Prov. 14-12, NIV). Whenever we are tempted to sin, God gives us a way out. The Lord gave David an opportunity to stop the census by using Joab, the chief captain, to question David's reasoning, but David ignored him. Once the king realized his error, it was too late, in I Chronicles 21:7, God gave David options for his punishment; unfortunately, Israel was punished (I Chron. 21:9), because of one man's disobedience.

Satan will attempt to make us think that our heavenly Father doesn't care about our needs. He will tempt us into thinking we should be our own gods by rejecting the one true God and the things related to Him. One of the ways the tempter gets us to start pondering on our own needs and less on the Father's, is to direct us to things he thinks we would want especially if someone has wronged us. What tends to come to our minds first? A hope that the offender will reap what they have sown. In Proverbs 27:20 (NIV), "Death and Destruction are never satisfied, and neither are the eyes of man." Being tempted is not a sin, but giving into that temptation is. In Matthew 4, Jesus was tempted by the devil, but he resisted the temptation. Many will say, of course he stood up against the devil, he is the Son of God. But remember he was a man while walking this earth. When Satan approached him it was during a time when his flesh was weak, he was hungry and tired, he had been fasting in the desert for 40 days and in that desert were wild animals. Does that sound like he was a superhero of sorts? In addition, the biblical text doesn't say that the Messiah had any supplies to protect him from the desert temperatures. What kept Jesus strong was knowledge of his Father's Word, his strength in him and fulfilling his Father's will—that was it, nothing more, nothing less. Jesus stood up against the enemy's temptations and spoke these words, "Man shall not live by bread alone, but by every word that proceedeth out of the mouth of God" (Matt. 4:4). After Satan stopped tempting Jesus and went away, notice God's angels came. During the time of temptation, Jesus had no angelic protection. Don't miss this point, if you feel somewhat alone during your trials know that you have God's Word to stand on even if there is no one around to defend you from your enemy's daggers. If God's Spirit can send Jesus out into the desert to be tested, what do you think he will do to us if we claim to be followers of Christ? Satan was not only tempting Jesus, but he was also attacking his identity during his fasting experience. Do you recall the Israelites being tested in the wilderness? Many didn't survive those tests and didn't see the promise land because oftentimes they were distracted ie.) idol worship. Which idols are you watching, building, protecting, paying honor to and more on a daily basis? Nowadays many Christians are like the Israelites taking trips with God that should have only taken days to fulfill his will, but end up taking years.

Satan is in the World

Besides being referred to as a serpent in the Bible, he also comes in the form of a dragon and is repeatedly referred to as the devil who leads the world astray (Rev. 12:8). It is evident that he is very much the ruler of the darkness of this world by the sheer number of movies, media and more that display his signs, symbols, and colors.

When one speaks knowledge that challenges others to think about right and wrong or good or evil, he or she is cut off, black-balled, criticized, or ostracized from certain circles. You might have people tell you that something they are wearing, watching or listening to is not of the devil and then turn around and accuse you of having a demon—sound familiar?

Remember Satan doesn't like anything that looks or sounds like God. Biblical Scriptures prove that Satan is not symbolic or a legend, he is real! "Jesus said to him, 'Away from me, Satan! For it is written: 'Worship the Lord your God, and serve him only'" (Matt. 4:10, NIV).

The Accuser

The Bible at times refers to Satan as an accuser. He accuses brothers day and night (Rev. 12:10). In Zechariah 3, Satan accused Joshua, because of all his sins he committed, but God had mercy on him. The devil will falsely accuse you, by using wicked critics, in order to distract you from doing God's will. How many times have we been emotionally caught up in a situation so much that we failed to follow through with something that God called us to do for that day? The accuser will make a case against us in order to divert us from God's plans.

A Manipulator

Satan can use his power to manipulate us if we let him. Those who often lie to us are being used by the devil. In John 8:44 we read about people like this, "Ye are of your father the devil, and the lusts of your father ye will do. He was a murderer from the beginning, and abode not in the truth, because there is no truth in him. When he speaketh a lie, he speaketh of his own: for he is a liar, and the father of it." If you questioned whether someone, who often lies to you, is really about God's business, there is your answer.

Consider this, the wicked one was at one time an angel in heaven; therefore, he knows and is familiar with God and his Word. There are many who claim to be Christians, as mentioned in a previous chapter, who have fallen away from the Lord and will use biblical writings to validate an ungodly lifestyle. Without exercising our faith in Jesus, we too are susceptible to falling under Satan's pressure. In Mark 14:27, Peter claimed that he wouldn't deny Jesus, but we learn later in the same chapter that he denied Jesus three times. There are plenty more examples of people in the Bible who allowed the enemy to trick them into disobeying God and unfortunately many were killed because they listened to the father of lies and his children.

Angry

Our adversary is filled with fury, according to Revelation 12:12. We see evidence of Satan's rage when we watch entertainment that have characters with sinister expressions, drenched in blood, coming from fiery scenes, surrounded by eerie looking trees with shadows all around, flashy thunderbolts, fallen angels, and other dark imagery. It is obvious that the producers of these films and music videos are being motivated by individuals and entities filled with Satan.

In Revelation 12:7 it is revealed that the dragon makes war with those who follow God's commandments and believe in Jesus.

This would make sense, because every time Satan releases his grand schemes to the public, they often raise a red flag to concerned Christians everywhere. He hopes that believers will war with him, so that he can say or do things to cause them to act on false promises, insults, lies, and curses.

The Power to Possess

As mentioned earlier in this chapter, Satan's assistants (demons) inhabit people and animals (Matt. 8:28-33). The devil's demons can't be removed without being casted out by the power of Jesus (Mark 5:9) which we get into in Chapter 8. We know that Satan does drive people and animals who are inhabited with evil to self destruct (Mark 5:13). The Apostle Paul tells us we are in a spiritual battle—good versus evil (Eph. 6:10-12). Satan bounds people with illnesses. For instance, in Luke 16, a woman was bound with an illness for 18 years. However, Satan is limited in what he can do and has to take orders from God. We see limitations put on the devil by God when dealing with Job (1:12).

Keep in mind, the devil cannot inhabit one who is filled with the Holy Spirit. "You, however, are controlled not by the sinful nature but by the Spirit, if the Spirit of God lives in you. And if anyone does not have the Spirit of Christ, he does not belong to Christ" (Rom. 8:9, NIV). Therefore, Satan will use others to tempt us to blasphemy the Holy Spirit. Men accused Jesus of having a demon, this is considered blasphemy. "And the scribes which came down from Jerusalem said, He hath Beelzebub, and by the prince of the devils casteth he out devils" (Mark 3:22). Jesus dealt with his accusers. "…I tell you the truth; all the sins and blasphemies of men will be forgiven them (v. 24-28). However, those who did otherwise, Jesus said, "But he that shall blaspheme against the Holy Ghost hath never forgiveness, but is in danger of eternal damnation…" (v. 29). For the Christian, being critical of the Holy Spirit is absolutely forbidden. Confess your sin and repent, says the Lord.

Believers, who are not filled with the fruits of the Spirit, will permit Satan to fill their hearts with ugly things. For example, Ananias and Sapphira were questioned about their lying to the Holy Spirit; as a result both died (Acts 5:1-10). Once again, Satan can use friends or supposed brothers or sisters in Christ to hurt us. When you know you may be going in the presence of demonic activity, one must pray and ask the Lord to deliver those around you from evil. In addition, we ought to pray for protection. (Refer to Ps. 91, Ps. 23, 2 Thess. 3:1-3, and also see Matt. 6:13, the Lord's Prayer). God will shield his children when they don't give into sin. "We know that whoever is born of God sins not; but he that is begotten of God keeps himself, and that wicked one touches him not." (I John 5:18, AKJ).

The Devil's Organizational Chart

When God operates he is very detailed and organized, we see this with the many building projects, programs, books, music, and meetings he assigns his children to manage. I think of Moses, Noah, Ezekiel, Elijah and others who were given specific instructions to perform God's will. But the Lord also assigns tasks for Satan that exemplifies his order and power as well. We see that disobedient rulers and others in the Bible who God had given responsibilities were handed over to Satan; God's Spirit had left them. Even with the distractions of the evil one, the Lord's divine plans were still accomplished.

When one is a part of God's organizational chart everything flows according to his plan. God's servants will witness blessings manifest in his or her life as a result. However, when one is far from the Lord he is welcomed with the devil's organizational chart filled with lies, false promises and counterfeits (ie. people who often help you, flatter you with compliments and want what's best for you—be cautious.)

In Matthew 13:24, Christ goes forth to sow the "good seed," but in Matthew 13:25, we read of the enemy going forth to sow his "tares" — which is an imitation wheat. Therefore, we know from this Scripture that just like God has workers assisting him, the devil has his appearing as if they are doing good deeds as well. Now there are those who are "the children of God," and then "the children of the wicked one" (Matt. 13:38). So individuals who participate in wicked acts are considered the devil's children.

God works in his children "both to will and to do of his good pleasure, (Phil. 2.13)," but the devil is "the spirit that now worketh in the children of disobedience" (Eph. 2:2). In your own life, you may have noticed a replica of what appears to be those who will look as if they are performing like Jesus in good deeds and appear as if they are acting obediently. However, we know that certain people are nothing more than counterfeits! The Christian's critic acts very similar to a Christian, but remember that old serpent has his assistants too!

Now that you have been reminded of who employs the wicked critic, know that the godless one doesn't put his people to work without giving them details as to what they ought to do in order to "succeed, benefit, grow, change" and do other things that God instructs his people to do as well. The difference between God's organizational structure and the adversary's is that one is designed to uplift, rebuke, correct, and exhort while the other is created to ruin lives in either the short or long-term for selfish gain.

Have you ever worked for a company that no matter what you did, it just didn't seem like "the numbers, the progress report, or the review," ever looked positive? Have you ever felt feelings of being bound, stagnant or dog-tired on the job? This is because some organizational charts aren't what they seem (more on this later).

Think of the many people, who behind the scenes are drug dealers, across our land that have a front-job that looks honest or a thriving business that seems harmless, but upon closer inspection their entrepreneurial spirit or good employee image is nothing more than a front. Behind the scenes, they are workers for someone or a group who isn't interested in doing the higher good for humanity, but rather they work to make higher dividends for a small elite group.

If you aren't doing what's right for any individual or organization as the Father leads, understand, "He that committeth sin is of the devil; for the devil sinneth from the beginning..." (I John 3:8). So you may work for a company that commits sins daily, it doesn't make you a bad person, but what puts your relationship with God at risk is you don't take your burdens before the Lord and repent of your wicked ways, you knowingly support wrong-doing and you don't bother to help your brothers or sisters do right.

When you do such things, you will find that your relationship with the Lord will become increasingly distant. I know from a couple of unfortunate experiences in my youth. One organization I worked for supported homosexual agendas and other ungodly things. I didn't think twice about what they were doing, being that I was getting a decent paycheck, until a Christian radio program convicted me about them. Another company had a contest to try to get customers to buy more of their products. So supervisors encouraged us workers to discount items, that were not supposed to be on sale, so that we all could get bonuses if we increased sales. Needless to say in both situations, God was not pleased. Soon after I felt convicted about working for both companies, one announced they were laying people off and the other most of us just quit. When wrong is done anywhere, sooner or later, unrighteous acts will be exposed and consequences will be paid. "Watch out for those dogs, those men who do evil, those mutilators of the flesh" (Phil. 3:2, NIV). If you were to compromise your belief system in order to stay connected to a devilish network, then what would that make you?

You recognize that because of the devil's work in the earth, "the Son of God was manifested, that he might destroy the works of the devil" (1 John 3:8). So if Christ is in you, most likely you are at your place of work or elsewhere, because God's intent is to do some house-cleaning! It may be filled with evil and disorganized right now, but before long a child of light will have that place in tip, top shape or else God will be moving you to leave that company.

You most likely were given an organizational chart at your workplace when you were first hired that showed everyone's function. You reviewed the chart, but learned later there was more to it—you are expected to go above and beyond. Well, the same holds true with God's Word. You may study his precepts, but you find out more as you go along that your actions write the rest of the Bible! Are you in Christ or of the devil? Your fruit, as well as others you know, will show whose side you are really on. "That ye might walk worthy of the Lord unto all pleasing, being fruitful in every good work, and increasing in the knowledge of God..." (Col. 1:10).

Periodically a company shares organizational chart updates. When we review these charts, we usually look at what has changed since the last report. But what we don't do is stay up-to-date on that invisible structure. Do you know about the informal organizational chart at your workplace—the one created behind the scenes?

There are those workers that have the leadership's ear. They earned their positions because of past associations. They may be the boss' spouse, a friend from high-school, a person who belongs to the same fraternity, or a member of a favorite non-profit group. If you are unaware of the personal relationships behind the scenes, then you may be blind-sided—particularly if you said or did some things without knowing you offended someone's mother, cousin or in-law. If you have commented wrongly or told a person a convicting truth about his or her work performance, it isn't any wonder that you might have critical enemies on your job, home, church and elsewhere. Know that in most organizational structures that is an invisible chart.

When you work for a company, if they are considered one of the best in their industry, then they will try to entice you with many things to make you feel comfortable about being their employee. Some will spend exorbitant amounts of money on meals. Others will acknowledge your birthday and anniversaries with thoughtful gifts. You will feel good about going into work, because of how good they take care of you. When workers are distracted with the beautiful arrangement of desserts put in front of them almost daily, many won't ask too many questions about possible shady activities going on in their departments or around them. They also won't bother to share information about deceptive and unfair company practices. It won't be until someone's job is at risk that he or she will stop bragging about the steaks, crab legs and devil's food chocolate cake served in the cafeteria or the entertainment provided to the staff every Friday along with daily, weekly or annual bonuses. Now the jean-wearing employee starts examining what part does he or she really play on the organizational chart?

Before he slaughters you, the devil will fatten you up like a turkey stuffed on Thanksgiving Day. Those of you who are of Christ know that you have been deemed trouble-makers both on and off the job! Some of you suffer almost daily for past and present deeds where you exposed irrational infrastructures, rules and practices. Rather than fly under the radar, you got Satan's attention; therefore he has you on watch. You might have offended certain people on that invisible organizational chart and now they want your head! Maybe you refused to work one too many Sundays due to church obligations, so they make a note of that. You showed up late on a day that leadership really needed you to be at your desk, so they pen that in your file. You might have made a conscientious decision that you wouldn't spoil the boss by working over-time every day (like those in the office who have no life outside of work), so now they have labeled you "unreliable." Maybe you are an expectant parent that realizes there is more to life than your job, so you aren't always available to assist co-workers, they will surely be talking. So what might the big boss do with so many little things appearing to grow into bigger things? Surround you with people whose sole purpose is to set you up to fail so that you will be legally fired or put so much pressure on you that you start hating your job so that you will voluntarily step down, "You Christ follower! You lover of your family! You trouble-maker!" Despite all the opposition, remember, "…greater is he that is in you, than he that is in the world" (I John 4:4). Keep track of your activities, have witnesses and do your job well, because the enemy is seeking who he can destroy.

The Devil's Management Style

Those of you that have spent any time managing people know there are typically four types of management styles used in business. The most popular styles include: autocratic, democratic, consultative, and laissez fair. Satan uses any one of these management styles plus a few more if he believes they will get his job done! Don't believe me? Try proposing a change related to business ethics at your current workplace or request funding to better operations. Like clockwork, top leaders will consult with their assistants about managing you differently than the norm. One of their worst fears is that you might disrupt workflow or be a potential trouble-maker with all of your "good ideas."

In an autocratic environment, a manager will make decisions without any input from the staff. Business experts talk about how there is a high turnover when this particular style is used, but it doesn't matter to Satan and his demons. The more control that is in the hands of one person, the more likely workers will have to do what they are told no questions asked. It doesn't matter whether people like or don't like the controlling boss, who acts more like a dictator than a friend and runs the work environment like a sweat shop, there will always be those people that love money more than what is morally right. Some employees may even feel like there are no alternatives to work elsewhere; therefore they will endure all sorts of on-the-job stress. They have allowed harsh leaders to imprison them mentally, physically or both. These same workers are often critical of directors, managers and supervisors behind closed doors, but rarely direct their concerns to top officials for fear of losing their jobs and reputations with the company.

The democratic management style is widely used in most businesses, and permits staff to complete tasks in ways that are comfortable for them just so long as deadlines are met. When looking at this style of leadership from a spiritual standpoint, we can see that both Satan and God let humans make decisions on whether they will follow through with a task. Despite consequences on either side for not measuring up, neither God or Satan will force any one to do anything he or she doesn't want to do, but fellow human beings will! They will encourage one another to pick this side or that one, to do this thing or that one, and to say what the other wants them to say or to remain quiet. When the righteous don't go along with the wicked, they are manipulated into doing immoral things and treated worse than the rest of the staff. The Bible-Toting Believer is ignored during lunch hour. The wishy-washy Christians are often talked about behind their backs. The angry, confused or ignorant workers are frequently in trouble for negatively commenting about operations and fellow co-workers. Anything you say or do will be used against you when dealing with people who don't like you for your integrity and work ethic. When the democratic leadership style is used in a good way, workers concerns are heard and addressed and the work environment becomes more stable.

The consultative or participative management style incorporates either the autocratic or democratic styles, but what sets this one apart from the rest is that it allows views and opinions from staff. Based on my personal observation with this style of leadership, I have witnessed people being taken for granted. Feedback is usually encouraged from employees then used to make management look good without proper credit given to the one who helped the boss in the first place. No significant pay raises are typically given for stellar service at some organizations. No complimentary awards or letters are distributed to deserving individuals by those groups who are more concerned about money than cultivating a positive work environment. Instead, Satan and his demons stir up trouble amongst staff by taking hurt feelings and using them to falsely accuse others, place blame (or pass the buck) and speak lies. When the workers are fighting amongst themselves they are distracted from organizing protests, making phone calls or writing letters to bring about change. They also avoid meeting with leadership about concerns. When the consultative style is used in such a way that gives all involved in the project, proper recognition, it is most effective. Constructive criticism is encouraged under this leadership style, but people aren't always wise about their feedback which only further divides leadership and staff.

The last common management style is laissez fair which in French means, "let them do," according to Wikipedia, an online encyclopedia. This style gives staff complete control with little, if any, input from the leadership. Therefore, the people are permitted to govern projects, make decisions, and create improvements with diminutive assistance from business owners and top management. When this happens, sometimes projects get done on time and other times they don't, because the tasks are not specifically outlined. Employees become perplexed, misunderstand exactly what management wants, and miss deadlines. Meanwhile, those who are the top-performing employees are sometimes stretched way too thin while management is idle. When the employees make errors, this is when the criticism starts despite challenges, time restraints and leadership assistance. Jesus replied, "And you experts in the law, woe to you, because you load people down with burdens they can hardly carry, and you yourselves will not lift one finger to help them" (Luke 11:46, NIV).

From discussions around the water cooler to emails of a new mother's baby photos, a team loses focus and often forgets minute details of job requirements. When tasks aren't complete, everyone points the finger, but no one takes responsibility for all the additional activities that are ongoing in the office. Simply put, the more unnecessary distractions, the more problems.

You might have noticed any one of the management styles mentioned used in your church group, on the job, at home when parenting the children, or elsewhere and you wondered the following: "Why didn't things get done timely, why does it feel like no matter what we do nothing seems to work, and why should I even bother? Further, why didn't certain people have some enthusiasm, listen to wisdom and follow instructions?" We must be mindful, that besides people not doing what they are supposed to, Satan and his demons are at work too.

In an article *Testimonies of ex-Satanist in Africa* by Brother Chris (TestimoniesOfHeavenAndHell.com), organizers of demonic groups assign their workers various tasks. Brother Chris wrote, "...they also have departments or categories just like we Christians have different gifts...(a) girl said she used to work in the department of Fornication and she would sleep with different guys and take some of their semen to where the Satanists met at the sea." In the same article he talks about how "...some former Satanists would mention they were responsible (for causing) divorce, accidents etc. Some young girls testified and said at their school (primary) each year, there would be a death of a child, at least one, and they said they were responsible for that." While many Christians sleep on God-given plans, Satan is at work to drive the Christian out of his workplace, home, church, and elsewhere by appealing to ones fleshly desires. Think of your workplace like this, there is an invisible structure that not only has people you don't know reporting to owners and top management, but there are dark forces who have departments that are responsible for: lust, laziness, greed, lying, cheating, stealing, and killing people mentally, physically and spiritually. Which department do you work in? Are your responsible for spearheading or aiding destructive behavior at your workplace by your conversation and mannerisms without even knowing it? "Wow, look at all these pretty young ladies here, which one would I take home...oh that one is ugly! I need these office supplies for the church—the company won't miss them, they have too much anyway!" says the supervisor. "I'm not doing all that work—they don't pay me enough, besides it's Friday; let the other department figure it out. Some of these people around here are idiots! I hate this job!" says the workers. And God hears and sees it all.

An employee who comes to work with a less than positive disposition, often upset, and has no sense of direction, will be used to distract others emotionally, physically and spiritually by the devil, because he or she is more susceptible to enemy schemes than someone happy in the Lord. In addition, those who are weak-minded fall into dark magic spells, are provoked to curse their neighbors, and do other things that bring trouble to their spirits as well as those around them. The unsuspecting will even eat the devil's assistant's potluck meals without giving thought to his or her jealous, angry and bitter spirit. The ungodly bring their trinkets to work with them, surround their atmosphere with decor and the ignorant have no clue as to the power of the enemy in their presence. But discerning Christians know better and that is why they too will bring their consecrated items to the workplace whether in or out of view.

After all of the work drama, then a parent comes home to a rebellious child, being used by the enemy, to shake up the family home when authority figures are absent or refuse to work together. "I want to go to my friend's party! You never let me go anywhere! Why do I have to do my homework—its stupid? I'm not doing my chores, you're the lazy one!" the child yells. The frustrated parent will then show up for work the next day, carrying the weight of a child's temper tantrum. By the end of the work day, the parent/worker may have revealed his or her personal upset, by being critical of others and disruptive.

Wayward Christ-following workers do not do well when walking with the Lord, much less business, because their sins keep causing them to stumble. They can't manage family or home because of a rebellious, stubborn will. Some errant Christians are unreliable as a result of sin or spend far too much time helping others overcome their sins that being employed becomes no longer important. Then these same individuals will try to make themselves feel better about their lukewarm spirituality and irresponsible behaviors by talking to others about their faith in such a way that people start looking for reasons to get rid of them. The unsaved may feel like one is bragging about his or her spiritual lifestyle, forcing religion down his or her throat or doing other things that do not benefit him or her in any way. The unstable Christian worker looks like nothing more than a hypocrite to others and will receive much pessimistic criticism as a result of their erratic behaviors.

Righteous as well as unrighteous leadership usually can see both the weak and strong workers. Effective, honest and caring leaders will encourage their team to do better. Prideful, critical and hot-tempered leaders may pit workers against one another using evil talk. In time, both groups will separate from one another; therefore causing further division between the two as mentioned previously. In Matthew 12:25 (NIV), "Jesus knew their thoughts and said to them, 'Every kingdom divided against itself will be ruined, and every city or household divided against itself will not stand." This Scripture may also be applied to one's home front as well. There are those people who will bring their work drama home to their families, right along with Satan's minions. They listened to angry, depressing, obscenity filled music on the way home. They answered a phone call that left them emotionally disturbed. They noticed neighbors repeatedly doing some things that upset them. They observed children acting out. From work to home, the devil is going to tempt the believer as well as the unbeliever to join in on the havoc ultimately for the purposes of drawing him or her away from the Lord. Uh oh, someone better take the dog out, grab the children, and get out the way, because the evil boss of the boss has influenced his or her worker to explode on someone!

The Devil's Assistants

From aristocrats to democrats, we find good teachers as well as bad ones. The bad instructors are those that are often described in the Bible as the following: false prophets, wicked, wayward, disobedient, and sinful. Each have their own way they prefer to deal with the public. For instance, There are those teachers who love money. We are told in the Scriptures,"For the love of money is a root of all kinds of evil. Some people, eager for money, have wandered from the faith and pierced themselves with many griefs" (I Tim. 6:10). Do you know someone who fits that description?

Some teachers run spiritual organizations and small groups similar to secular businesses and because of this, there is a combination of godly and worldly precepts which aren't always in the best interests of those who are on the lowest part of the totem pole. Most of these educated professionals follow various management styles, like the ones described earlier, and follow secular business models coupled with their training from private studies and personal experiences. Successful, worldly business owners know you can't incorporate ideas and opinions from one's subculture without eventually breaking a rule or several; therefore, they normally stick with teachings that reflect mainstream society. However, those who are appointed by God to teach men and women will not only share his Word, but their constant improvements in their private lives will also reflect his awesome power which at times will stir the critics up to talk negatively about them.

Organize a protest putting down "the man" and what might happen? Offending an aristocrat, or some other dignitary can get you dismissed from certain establishments or worse killed—remember Jesus? But God hasn't given us a spirit of fear but of love and a sound mind, according to 2 Timothy 1:7, NIV. Then in verse nine it reads, "Who has saved us and called us to a holy life—not because of anything we have done but because of his own purpose and grace. This grace was given us in Christ Jesus before the beginning of time, but it has now been revealed through the appearing of our Savior, Christ Jesus, who has destroyed death and has brought life and immortality to light through the gospel."

The Messiah had no fear of hurting someone's feelings, because he knew he was speaking truth that was heaven sent. Jesus couldn't be concerned with offending man or woman with the gospel; he refused to allow people to keep him from speaking his Father's Words. A wicked man or woman's personal opinions, ideas or suggestions shouldn't keep your mouth shut either. If you know the Holy Spirit is burdening you to say and do the things of God at home, work or elsewhere just do it! But whatever you do, don't grieve the Holy Spirit. We are warned in God's Word, "And grieve not the Holy Spirit of God, whereby ye are sealed unto the day of redemption" (Eph. 4:30).

Many of us rather act like Jonah did in the Bible--run and hide from a God-ordained mission. When God spoke to Jonah, he said, "Go to the great city of Nineveh and preach against it, because its wickedness has come up before me. But Jonah ran away from the Lord and headed for Tarshish" (Jonah 1:1-2, NIV). You may have been like Jonah running all your life from the people and things of God. You may have also spent a great deal of your life running from people who didn't mean you well too! But there comes a time, when one has to take a break from all that running and just sit awhile. Tell yourself, "In the meantime, I will just sit and wait for the Lord until he tells me something different before I make another decision I might later regret." In Psalm 11, we see a good example of David knowing when it was time to stop running. He took his refuge in the Lord. At times you will have to just sit back and watch the Lord handle your enemies too.

Most Christian workers don't want to rock the boat with anyone. We rather not say this statement or that one even if it might mean that we could be helping someone with their relationship, business, money issues, and more. "I know I should say something, but I'm not..." the do-good Christian says. Instead of speaking truth, we say nothing being careful not to offend a loved one, friend, co-worker or stranger with one of our Holy Spirit inspired instructions. However, we can get into trouble with God when we are supposed to be talking, but choose to hold back. There will be those moments in our relationship with the Lord that we feel like being a bold Christian is too hard emotionally and physically (Ps. 138:3), but we have to keep pressing on anyway. Sure, we can lose opportunities, friendships and more as a result of telling the truth, but wouldn't you rather suffer now then discover later that due to your disobedience there is no room in heaven for you? Of course, there is a time and place for everything and God will use his people to fulfill his will. Yet, some of us make matters hard on ourselves because we jump ahead (without God's approval) in an attempt to make others "say what I do, and do what I say." When a worker chooses to do what he or she wants without following proper protocol, there will be problems (Rom. 13:5). When one disobeys God, he or she motivates Satan to turn up the heat. As you know, the evil one's intentions are to destroy one's character and ultimately his or her life. God uses bad situations to rebuke and punish rebellious believers and then he calls his children back to himself. The Word says, "Therefore say thou unto them, Thus saith the Lord of hosts; Turn ye unto me, saith the Lord of hosts, and I will turn unto you, saith the Lord of hosts" (Zech. 1:3). Also read, Amos Chapter 3.

Respect (even wicked authority)

A demeaning verbal reaction toward your boss, an older relative, or a young friend who has rules and standards that they follow can backfire! Take heed to this Scripture, "Submit yourselves to every ordinance of man for the Lord's sake: whether it be to the king, as supreme…" (Pet. 2:13). People create rules, warnings and other similar verbal commands for a variety of reasons whether we agree with them or not, the least we should do is respect them. If they go against the Word of the Lord, then we must seek him on what to do so that we are not compromising our beliefs. But if we act like the enemy, choosing to rebel, there will be trouble! An insult might cause a boss to fire someone, a spouse to draw up divorce papers, a child to run away from home, and so on. When we find ourselves acting more like the devil's assistants and less like children of God, we ought to take the time to do the following: apologize to the one in authority (and others we may have insulted), learn from past mistakes, and listen to what the Spirit has to say before reacting the next time (that is if there is a next time).

At some point, you may have to confront someone in authority about his or her words, deeds or lack thereof about a situation. In 2 Samuel 19, Joab, chief commander of King David's army, approached his superior about his weeping and mourning for his rebellious son, Absalom, who had caused many problems for the king. The soldiers came out victorious in battle something that the commander thought David would be proud of. Joab told King David that the commanders and men who fought for him evidently meant nothing to him by the way he behaved. He warned that if the king didn't make himself available to the men, "…not a man will be left with you by nightfall" (2 Sam. 19:7). Imagine telling your boss that his reaction to a business venture was irresponsible and rude and that if he didn't make wrongs right, everyone might walk out on him. How might your boss react? To deliver bad news, rebuke or correct any authority figure, one must be a man or woman of great faith, confident, and courageous as well as be intently listening to the voice of God.

Deception of Being Your Own god

As much as I love hearing God's word, I'm not impressed with money-making rebellious people. Many borrow from this religion and that one in an effort to create a super study on how we should all live with Jesus sitting at our feet while we're sitting on his throne. Isn't this what Satan's workers do? Tempt us to be our own gods. While some believe the hype and become self-appointed gods, they also take on positions that God hasn't given them. When they act in these ways, they become disrespectful, arrogant and foolish in their decision-making.

Everyone has a role in the kingdom, but what some will do is try to take on titles that God has not given them including the Creator's position in unsuspecting individuals' lives. "Pastor said this…deacon said that…mama told me this," the gullible says. "…Daddy said that…my husband knows this, he's so smart." The loyal, but gullible follower of pastor, husband, teacher, and parent begins to live his or her life void of one's own voice. Instead of trusting in the one true God, he or she is listening to many people who believe they are their own gods! Meanwhile, calculating people (wicked rulers) take advantage of people like this "who do as I say, but not how I do."

There are groups and people in mainstream media titling their events, programs, and themselves as "I AM." They are posing as self-appointed gods in order to move the masses to buy their books, music and more. Let us be reminded, "God introduced himself as I AM. God said to Moses, 'I AM WHO I AM. This is what you are to say to the Israelites: 'I AM has sent me to you'" (Exodus 3:14). Once again, prideful men and women are not only desecrating the things of God by disrespecting his commandments, but they are also trying to take on a role that doesn't belong to them too. There are plenty of Scriptures that tell us who we are in Christ without disrespecting the Lord with statements like, "I am God." Moses had enough sense to remove his sandals on holy ground and to listen to the Lord when he called out to him, but because wicked freethinkers can't experience the one true God in a similar way, they assume he is non-existent. There are plenty of examples in both the Old and New Testaments of people who claimed to follow the Lord but then chose to follow after other gods, when this happened they experienced God's wrath. To date, men and women are still worshiping other gods.

From the boardroom to the street, many leaders are not God-appointed, because if they were, they would know that God doesn't approve of their deceptive views, "in the closet" lifestyles, love of money, evil thinking, and cold-hearted tactics that draw God's people away from him. Some religious leaders or believers promote this "I am god" philosophy while taking weak-minded followers' monies to the bank. These ministers say things like, "I told God...I commanded God...I know the Lord will do this for me...You give your money to our ministry and watch what my God will do!" the braggart minister proclaims. If you were to get indignant with your boss by daily commanding and demanding he do something for you, how long do you think you would have a job?

For some of these self-appointed gods, it's okay to act tough with the Lord, yet they will not stand for any member, visitor or observer challenging them including telling them the truth about their misdeeds. Rather they want blind submission and obedience from followers. Watch for people in your inner circle who act like this, you don't want to pick up their mannerisms and act in controlling ways with people who you are supposed to be sharing God's word. Manipulators use Scriptures like Hebrews 13:17 and Romans 13:1-2 to control people. Some readers may feel like their pastors can't be challenged because they are "God's anointed," but they can be and they ought to be for the right reasons. However, be sure to seek the Lord first before approaching anyone, because you don't want to end up on the wrong side if someone is in fact performing the Lord's will.

On a website called *Wicked Shepherds*, a posting labeled, Chapter 9 *The Subtle Power of Spiritual Abuse* by David Johnson & Jeff VanVonderen, the writers talk about pastors acting like false authorities. "We tell ourselves, I believe the Bible. I want to be obedient. He's the pastor, the shepherd, God's servant, His mouthpiece. He really must know more than me. I really must be out of line. I must be seeing this wrong. Who am I to question? I guess I had just better go along. Why? Because he's the pastor, that's why." The writers add, "This type of thinking is a symptom of living under leadership that legislates and demands obedience to their authority. It rests upon a false basis of authority."

One day I approached a minister after Sunday service to share with him something that God laid on my heart. The Lord told me, "Go up to him and tell him he doesn't have to act." So I told him this and he was surprised, but admitted he heard a Christian teacher on the radio that morning talking about ministers "acting" when preaching. He didn't react to what I did and received the word without becoming visibly angry and defensive. However, those who saw me deliver the message were nervous and concerned about what I did. I ignored the voices and odd looks, because I knew that God used me for a moment to remind his son that He was in control, there was no need to put on airs. If a king, pastor, president or someone else deemed important is in charge of small groups or masses, this doesn't mean that God, skill, favor, common sense or anything else is with them. For some, if they are honest with themselves, they are undeserving of the positions that they have received. However, so that reputations look good before skeptical eyes, deceivers will present a, "I got it altogether" persona. The false leader will then feel obligated to keep up his or her act by getting people to believe in him or her by any means necessary. Declaring that one is his or her own god is not enough, one must act the part. If one believes he or she is deserving of a position, despite the facts are showing something totally different, then one's god complex (also known as ego) will take over and before long he or she doesn't have supporters but slaves such as: "Yes" men, victims, complainers, and lost sheep in his or her group. The whole system revolves around a single person who refuses to listen to God or his messengers.

Counterfeit Messengers

In 2007, Senator Charles Grassley, a Republican from Iowa, launched an investigation of televangelists, according to an article written by Tom Barlow titled, *Televangelist Builds $4 Milllion*

Home While Employees Lose Jobs (DailyFinance.com). The Senator was "challenging (TV ministries) to defend their expenditures and justify their tax exemptions." On the list were: the ministries of Paula White, Joyce Meyer, Creflo Dollar, Eddie Long, Kenneth Copeland and Benny Hinn. Several had cooperated fully, a couple partially. Creflo Dollar, at the time of the writing, had continued to hold out. Kenneth Copeland Ministries had "pulled a clever dodge," Barlow reports. What was interesting on numerous websites, these ministers have received much criticism whether justified or not for what they say and do. Much of it had to do with messages that had nothing to do with God ie.) money, but everything to do with them or other agendas. Take the time out to research some of these mainstream ministers yourself and allow God to show you the truth.

It's great to stand on the promises of God, I personally believe God for everything from healing to where I will live next. I also trust God, not man, to direct me on where I should and shouldn't plant my seeds too. Yet, there are those Christian TV personalities that take "name it and claim it" messages and use them to shake the money trees of fellow brothers and sisters in Christ. They do this, not so much to perform God's will, but to fulfill their own unmet desires. The Holy Spirit shared with me that these TV ministers have long been receiving messages from God's messengers that they would never share with their audiences, like this one he gave me to share with my readers, "God just wants to know, what have you done for me lately besides: work people up emotionally, ask week after week for tithes and offerings in my name, and make promises to backsliders and apostates that you know I am not going to fulfill?" In addition, he says, "I'm wondering, when are you going to be quiet long enough to really hear from me? When are you going to stop making up prophetic messages to impress? When will you come to me and know that I am Alpha and Omega?" Those of you reading this know who you are.

It's one thing winning souls for Christ through prayer, fasting, advising and the like, but it's quite another issue when one is putting people in further bondage by taking the words of the Bible and making them say what they want for the following reasons: justify wrongdoing, suppress, oppress, manipulate or redirect an outcome—this all sounds like the devil's work to me. In my mind,

I thought of many movie scenes where a minister is in need of money and a church might have to close as a result. The once sold out for God minister says, "Listen our church needs money. Our staff is long over-due to receive their checks. I know someone who can help us." Before long, a secular group working behind the scenes has the false minister up on puppet strings. "We can help, but you will have to do us a favor," the representative of the group says. So hands are shaken, contracts are signed and money is exchanged, but then the minister gets a guilty conscious and feels like God isn't pleased with him, so he tries to back out the deal. He starts doing things apart from the group's requirements. "We told you to say this...why did you say that? Make another mistake like that and we will cut you off! Be sure to include our work in your bookstore, mention our teachers, invite your group to our events, or else!" the angry devil worker warns. The godless group also reminds the minister not to forget to signal one's superiors during his or her next interview if he wants those checks to keep coming. Although this is just an imagined scenario, in reality, I have noticed many ministers wearing symbols on clothes, vehicles, and elsewhere that have nothing to do with God and show hand-signs that are tied to secular groups. The Lord says, "Don't pity them when their handlers hang them in front of watchful eyes. They should have never sold-out to begin with." I then saw a vision of a hung man with a rope tied around his neck representing the destruction of those who rebel against Satan's group.

Some organizations make good on their promises of punishing members who choose to share details about the group's secret practices.

If you check the backgrounds of many leading ministers, teachers, and authors today, you will find that they do have ties to demonic associations. At times, members talked too much and have been shamed in front of their adoring fans. If you would like to further your study about fraternal orders and secret societies, read *Codex Magica* by Texe Marrs, a well-known author of three #1 national Christian bestsellers. He provides visual evidence of the satanic hand symbols and signs that many entertainers, church and government leaders and others use to communicate with one another. Also visit online video sites that expose ministers using tactics and effects similar to demonic groups in order to gain large followings and financial contributions.

Think about the latest scandals in various Christian ministries in recent years, many more are to come. Some teachers have long left God's public ministry and now perform a false god's work behind the scenes for fame, fortune and power. Sometimes he comes in the form of a sun, one eye, pyramid, star, dark angel, half human and half beast, as well as many other things as mentioned elsewhere in this book. I have seen countless photographs showing power players in the Christian entertainment industry holding up devil horns, wearing clothing showing their allegiance and affiliation to homosexual, bisexual and lesbian groups, covering one eye illustrating their praise to a different god, displaying demonic artwork and ancient Greek gods, hand signaling their brotherhood connections, and more. Watch who you are supporting and what music you are playing around little ones. One cannot be a believer and support ungodly behaviors nor should one be showing individuals special favor just because he or she has been on TV or sold much music. "My brothers, as believers in our glorious Lord Jesus Christ, don't show favoritism," Paul warns. "Suppose a man comes into your meeting wearing a gold ring and fine clothes, and a poor man in shabby clothes also comes in. If you show special attention to the man wearing fine clothes and say, 'Here's a good seat for you,' but say to the poor man, 'You stand there' or 'Sit on the floor by my feet,' have you not discriminated among yourselves and become judges with evil thoughts?" (Jas. 2:1-4). I think of the many people both in and out of the church who are talented, but no one will ever really notice them, because those who have a platform only support those who have a much larger platform. "I'm not letting them in my church because they are from that small church, they aren't known!" What happened to letting the Holy Spirit have his way in the church?

Believers should make the time to research church and political figure heads' intent and affiliations before jumping on their bandwagons. Ignorant Christians are very quick to defend freethinking relatives and friends as well as unrighteous establishments without knowing the full truth behind why they say and do the things that they do. Further, believers shouldn't make excuses for wayward brothers and sisters in Christ preaching false doctrines.

Yet, we have either witnessed or been guilty of encouraging others to accept lifestyles and things that go against a righteous God especially when he has specifically warned us in his Bible about the characteristics of evil workers and their false teachings.

Christian Research Institute (CRI) and similar groups do a good job of exposing leaders in mainstream media who are often in error when it comes to absolute truths. CRI has many articles, books and audio recordings that talk about the lies, witchcraft and other things used to manipulate Christians everywhere. You can check out individual's names and organizations by visiting the ministry's website. Investigate and report supposed Christians who are scamming and misleading the public. Allow God to order your steps.

Now when recognizing these counterfeit messengers, we must understand, like Paul did, in Galatians 1:6-7 that there will be those who have fallen from grace that preach, "Another gospel, which is not another." The Bible also warns in 2 Corinthians 11:13, "For such are false apostles, deceitful workers, transforming themselves into the apostles of Christ."

In an article *Freemasonry and Judaism Worship the Same Egyptian Gods* (Texemarrs.com), written by Marrs, who also wrote *Conspiracy of the Six-Pointed Star*, he shares that, "...the so-called "Christian World" is also permeated with Egyptian and Satanic doctrines and symbology." He specifically names some of the denominations that are involved including: "Southern Baptist, Methodist, Episcopal and other churches are packed with members who are Freemasons. Their ranks include many pastors. Most of these churches, especially the Baptists, are also radically pro-Zionist," Marrs reports. Although this statement might spark controversy, it is evident that some church-goers are not attending service to simply worship Jesus. When you notice signals, signs and colors representing one's fraternal affiliations, listen to the Lord and do your research. Marrs writes, "In evangelical churches, rabbinical Judaism is revered and promoted, and entire congregations are led to believe that the Judaic religion is holy and good, and that it is based solely on the Old Testament. The people in the pews have no idea that both the Masonic Lodge and the Jewish synagogues are snake pits of Egyptian religion."

Whether on the job or at home, when you are speaking truth and exposing error, someone wants to quiet you. “You got it all wrong!” he says. “Not my group—we don’t support no devil! We don’t have people like that at our church,” says the wishful thinker. But has this person followed every member home and does he or she know what a member does in his or her free time besides what he sees or has heard? In the Old Testament, the great prophets of the Lord were under attack by their own people because they delivered unflattering truths to the kings. Remember John who was beheaded because the queen was offended by him speaking up about her lifestyle? “Now Herod had arrested John and bound him and put him in prison because of Herodias, his brother Philip’s wife, for John had been saying to him: “It is not lawful for you to have her.” Herod wanted to kill John, but he was afraid of the people, because they considered him a prophet” (Matt. 14:3-5, NIV). How many people want to chop off your head for speaking truth?

You are no different than those prophets of the Bible. Sooner or later someone will want to rid your name from an organizational chart (or family tree) whether created publicly or privately over something you said, because you simply don’t fit in with those who belong to the invisible chart. You aren’t the kind of family member, friend, or employee who “goes along just to get along,” so now you are at risk for getting thrown out the house, the workplace or somewhere else. But it wouldn’t benefit the household or the company much if the boss didn’t get all he or she could get from you before firing you, right? “Let’s get him to do some training…Why not place her in another department…? We could use his expertise in this area before we let him go…” Even a family member or friend might say, “I will wait until after my birthday to tell her she has to go…Maybe it would be a good time to sever all ties after he gets my car fixed for me…I was thinking about ending our partnership after the tax season, because I really need that refund money.” So now what one might have considered a great boss, nice teacher, loving relative or faithful friend is nothing more than false, a mere user and abuser! However, despite your upset, remember to “Trust in the Lord with all thine heart; and lean not unto thine own understanding, In all thy ways acknowledge him, and he shall direct thy paths. Be not wise in thine own eyes: fear the Lord, and depart from evil" (Prov. 3:5:6 7).

Counterfeit believers of our faith will also appear like they respect Christ teachings. Devoted to the worldly works of those writers, entertainers, artists, and others who seem intelligent, false teachers and prophets will pledge to organizations they consider of the "highest order"—some of which supposedly reveal great mysteries. These "mysteries" are not of the Lord. Paul reminds Christ followers in I Corinthians 2:5-8, "That your faith should not stand in the wisdom of men, but in the power of God." He goes on, "However, we speak wisdom among them that are perfect: yet not the wisdom of this world, nor of the princes of this world, that come to nothing: But we speak the wisdom of God in a mystery, even the hidden wisdom, which God ordained before the world to our glory: Which none of the princes of this world knew: for had they known it, they would not have crucified the Lord of glory." Therefore, we shouldn't be impressed with the critics supposed knowledge of certain spiritual things. If one must know something, ask God for revelation! God willing, he will answer.

Believers are advised in 1 Corinthians 2:10 that, "the Spirit searcheth all things, yea, the deep things of God." But what then does Satan do? He too provides his "deep things" (Rev. 2:24). We also learn that God has his angel who will "seal" his servants (Rev. 7:3). As for Satan, his angels will set a mark in the foreheads of his followers (Rev. 13:16). So you see devil workers will wear marks that signify who they serve.

With the abundance of people receiving tattoos nowadays, there is no question what is in many of their hearts and minds. "For what is in the heart, shows up somewhere on the body or in one's physical surroundings," says the Holy Spirit, after I had prayed one day about this subject. "It will be easy for many to receive the mark of the beast since they have already been programmed that tattoos and other similar markings aren't harmful." Attention believers: a wicked critic will reveal his or her true intentions sooner or later just by: what he or she wears, collects and boasts about. If you doubt whether a person is sincere about his or her relationship with Christ, look for fruits.

Hand-signs are popular amongst elitists. They signal who they are and what they do all within one handshake. Others speak coded language or wear certain colors to show their allegiance to a particular group as mentioned earlier. This kind of behavior is typical in fields like: entertainment, law, medical, publishing, business, and many more. There are those who can't simply attend a college or trade school to be a top performer in this world nowadays; they must eventually denounce God and sell their souls to the devil. If you disagree, conduct research about people who sold their soul to the devil, and look up occult signs and symbols. I told you about Marrs books but there are many other researchers who expose the devil's schemes. It is a disturbing and ugly reality of our American culture. "No man can serve two masters: for either he will hate the one, and love the other; or else he will hold to the one, and despise the other. Ye cannot serve God and mammon" (Matt. 6:24).

For someone looking on from the outside in when it comes to various "successful" companies, he or she might ask self, "What would I be willing to do to get ahead?" Without ever asking yourself this question or setting boundaries long before you are tempted by Satan, you are allowing yourself to be susceptible to almost anything, including a critic who can't wait to call you a, "Hypocrite!" Remember the following passage of Scripture, "...believe not every spirit, but try the spirits whether they are of God: And every spirit that confesseth not that Jesus Christ is come in the flesh is not of God: and this is that spirit of antichrist, whereof ye have heard that it should come; and even now already is it in the world" (I John 4:1-4). Notice the antichrist is already here! This isn't some idea from a science fiction thriller. So many believers focus on Jesus coming and saving them that they fail to realize they can potentially die tomorrow. They fail to comprehend the following truth as told to me by the one true God, "One cannot be saved on works, nor on merely making a statement of faith. Christians must work together, like body parts all serving various functions. Believers must utilize spiritual gifts, pray, fast, and do good deeds in their walks—none can function without the other."

Can you tell the difference between real believers and fake ones?

It's imperative that we know for certain which side we are working on, the devil's or the Lord's? Some will respond with, "Neither, because I am my own god!" So where does that kind of reasoning leave them? I would say, like a sheep in a pasture wandering in circles without a shepherd—easy prey for a wolf!

Once you review the chart titled, *The Opposite of God is Satan*, which appears on an upcoming page, you will notice that whatever God does or creates, Satan has a counterfeit for each. Think about this for a moment; let's say there is someone in your circle that is often giving something away. At first, you think that this person is kind-hearted for sharing his or her items. These material things the individual gives to others appear high in quality. That is, until you receive a few things personally from him or her. You start noticing a pattern with each gift, something seems to be wrong. "This item is a fire hazard. That one is missing a part. This gift is a recall. That one made someone in your family very sick," an observer comments. It appears like someone is trying to pawn his or her junk off on anyone willing to take it. The so-called generous giver says, "It works…" But what this person fails to tell you, "It also has a few things about it that concerns me—this is why I am giving it away." Now you realized it isn't that the individual really cares whether you will benefit from the goods, this person just wants to get rid of one's bad mistakes. His or her things may have looked good, but they were indeed worthless! The same is true when we obtain employment with "too good to be true" companies or enter into commitments with partners, relatives and friends who aren't sold out for God. There is something always wrong with their so-called wonderful pie in the sky opportunities, gifts, promises, and "Be your own god" philosophies! When approached about one's error in judgment or faulty good, he or she becomes defensive, "Well you didn't have to take it! I know I told you that, but you didn't have to do it! Why are you always bugging me about what I told you, I know what I said! That's why I don't like telling you anything. You always make an issue about things!"

Like those "too good to be true" deals or so-called "inspiring" thoughts of men and women, there are also satanic teachings, attributes, signs and wonders that may look like God but really aren't, and many Christians are easily deceived because of the similarities. Why? Because some believers don't read and study their Bibles and don't carefully listen to God's appointed messengers before they are acting emotional. The church-goer is doing things like: yelling, sobbing, dancing, shouting, or running around the church without hearing from the Lord. Meanwhile, the counterfeit praise worshipper doesn't understand that a sincere believers praise comes from a place of knowing God is real and how do you experience the realness of God if you aren't trusting or making time for Him?

Let God lead you in your praise not only in the church but also at home and elsewhere. Some might want to stop tongue speaking, singing and dancing long enough to listen to what the Lord has to say too! With so much worldly distraction both in and outside the church, a number of Christians just don't focus long enough on God and his teachings. Let's review the following chart on the next page. Character attributes and spiritual works previously mentioned appear on the chart as well.

The Opposite of God is Satan

Deeds, Signs & Similar Things	*God (Good)*	*Satan (Evil)*
Worshipers	John 4:23	Rev. 13:4
Angel of Light	Luke 2:9	2 Cor. 11:14
Lion of Judah	Rev. 5:5	1 Peter 5:8
Angels & Demons	Matt.25:31	Matt. 25:41
Miracles	Heb. 2:4	2 Thess. 2:9
Throne	Rev. 7:15, 20:11	Rev. 2:13
Church	Col. 1:18	Rev. 2.9
Bride & Whore	Rev. 17:22	Rev. 17: 5-6,16
Vine	Psalm 80:14	Rev. 14:19
City	Rev. 21:2	Rev. 17:5; 18:2
Son	1 John 4:15	2 Thess. 2:3
Trinity	Matt. 28:19	Rev. 20:10
Seeds	Matt. 13:24	Matt. 13:25
Children/followers	Phil. 2:13/ 1 John 3:10	Eph. 2:2
Apostles	Gal. 1:6-7	2 Cor. 11:13
Wisdom	I Cor. 2:5-8	Rev. 2:24
The Seal, Mark	Rev. 7:3	Rev. 13:16
Truth & Lie	Eph. 4:11	2 Peter 2:1-22
Talks to Humans	Heb. 12:25	Matt. 4:1
Enters the Living	Luke 1:35, 1 Cor. 6:19	Luke 22:3, 8:3
Dwelling Place	Rev. 11:19	Rev. 20:14
Human Sacrifice	1 John 2:2; 4:10	Job 2:4, Hos. 13:2

Despite Satan's power in this world, he cannot move unless our Lord approves of his actions. We mustn't forget that the boss over all is also the owner, our heavenly Father! Do you recall in the Bible where Satan wanted to be like God? Well, do you also remember when God cast him and other fallen angels down from heaven onto the earth? Consider this; the Lord gave Satan his own place to be his own god. Rather than demolish him right where he stood for even acting like he wanted to take our Lord's position in heaven, he gave him something! The devil couldn't be God in heaven, but he could be a prince to the world. Our Father gave the devil enough space to roam the earth. "And the Lord said unto Satan, Whence comest thou? Then Satan answered the Lord, and said, From going to and fro in the earth, and from walking up and down in it" (Job 1:7). Roaming the earth may not have been exactly what this evil spirit wanted, but God gave him something. Think about this, Satan's response to God demonstrates that although a master of lies, he does periodically tell the truth just like a boss, family member or friend who, like the devil, might want your spot in life. When I think of God's reaction to Satan's rebellion, I think of a parent and a young adult son having the following conversation.

"You may want to run this house, but I can't let you do that," says the parent.

"Well what can I do?" retorts the son.

"You can pack your things and move out. I will help you get your own place where you can do as you please," advises the father.

God gives Satan freedom to be his own god amongst those who have a choice to follow him or not, they can do the following: accept the evil one, rebel against God with false teachings, and act in unrighteous ways. They may look good, but when one looks closer, something is wrong. Now some readers might ask, "Why would God allow something so evil, so vile to be the prince of this world?" I won't even attempt that study in this chapter, but what I will say is that God didn't cast him down to earth without giving us a Savior! *Praise Jesus!*

The Owner Overall: God

Now for some readers, the idea that a righteous loving God would order or approve of an evil boss, like Satan, to put lying spirits in prophets, torture people, and even destroy nations is hard to digest, but is so true!

We saw what Satan could do as a serpent in Genesis, but as a Pharaoh? In Exodus, we got a close-up view of how God can harden a man's heart by using the evil one. When I think of both the hardship and freedom of the Israelites, I also think of how God can use evil and turn it around for our good.

Stubborn, angry, bitter, or confused people just won't corporate with even a little conversation and a meal. You know that to be true if you ever tried to advise certain family members or friends to just get along. They don't seem to understand basic common sense until pain is associated with it. "Oh, now I get it…I'm sorry, I should have listened…please forgive me." The stubborn relative cries. You might think, "It's a little too late." Think of how many blessings we missed out on because we simply dragged our feet, refused to pay attention to wise counselors while choosing to remain in a pessimistic state of mind about a situation. God doesn't hang around those who are consistently disobedient and unrepentant; rather he will step out of the way and let the devil and his demons deal with the rebellious.

If you ever thought God couldn't or wouldn't allow Satan to cause a disturbance in your atmosphere, like use a critic to humble you, think again! God allows Satan to attack you and me, especially when we are unwilling to follow sound advice. Remember Romans 8:28, "All things work together for good to them that love God…" the keywords in this Scripture is ALL—which includes the good, bad and ugly, and those that LOVE God—people who don't love the Lord this Scripture doesn't apply to them. It's hard to see the good in every situation when you don't have a close relationship with the one who owns the environment and all that is in it.

During Saul's reign as king in the Bible we learn that the Spirit of God left him. In I Samuel 16:14, "But the Spirit of the Lord departed from Saul, and an evil spirit from the Lord troubled him." No matter how much we might respect or still love a person, when God isn't with someone, things just aren't the same. Think about this, God permitted an evil spirit to trouble a person who once trusted in the Lord. This is yet another reminder that the same God who created us will also destroy us when we refuse to listen to his instruction.

In another book of the Bible, I Kings 22:22, God tells Satan to be a lying spirit in the mouths of the King of Israel's prophets. "And the Lord said to him, With which? And he said, I will go forth, and I will be a lying spirit in the mouth of all his prophets,

And he said, You shall persuade him, and prevail also: go forth, and do so."

God also permits Satan to test (Job 1:12), "And the Lord said to Satan, Behold, all that he has is in your power; only on himself put not forth your hand. So Satan went forth from the presence of the Lord." In addition, God used Satan to commit what some would call "unfair" or "bizarre" actions upon the innocent. In Genesis 22:2, God tells Abraham to sacrifice his only son, who he loved, but then just before he does it, God sends his angel to stop him (Genesis 22:12). God tested Abraham in such a way that no parent would ever want to be tested. In Matthew 4:1, our Lord lets his only Son be tempted by the devil and then later murdered. Sounds harsh, doesn't it? A believer in his right mind could never look at God's participation or lack thereof to stop Jesus' execution as sweet and kind. It was barbaric, sad, but at the same time a powerful, righteous act to save mankind from eternal death! "Whom God hath set forth to be a propitiation through faith in his blood, to declare his righteousness for the remission of sins that are past, through the forbearance of God" (Rom. 3:25). Jesus was a living sacrifice for us who were once lost, but now are found! Therefore, if we agree that the Messiah didn't die in vain, then we can also agree that God letting Satan "roam the earth" (Job 2:2) is for good reason too. We see further evidence of God in control when he tells Job (41:11), "Who has prevented me, that I should repay him? Whatever is under the whole heaven is mine." We know that even Satan is owned by God. Once again, God shows us who is boss.

Every now and then we choose only to focus on the spiritual teachings that make us feel good; rather than on the wisdom that convicts us. As mentioned in a previous chapter, ministers know that the "feel-good" messages bring in the most money to the church; therefore, they stay away from the things in the Bible that reveal God to be angry, jealous and controlling. Money-loving ministers do not want to bring attention to God's wrath on rebellious people, because that would be bad for business.

Wolf in Sheep's Clothing

When the evil critic is chosen by the Tempter to hurt a Christian, he knows what kind of attire he wants his worker to wear in an effort to deceive an unsuspecting believer. Typically, the critic comes into your life wearing sheep's clothing. In other words, he or she appears trustworthy—wouldn't hurt a soul. The pessimist rarely announces the time of arrival, nor does this person share his or her true intentions. The critic may have eyes as friendly as a child, a charming personality, and a beautiful physique. He dresses handsomely. She dresses seductively. Both devil workers would go undetected by someone who lacks spiritual discernment.

You see, our adversary knows what people to use for what situations, because usually our weaknesses have been broadcasted out of our mouths. Therefore, like a marketer, the devil hears the problem; then creates a plan to meet the need. "Do you need some help? I know someone... You could use a new and improved look, let me help you. Free yourself, go out with me tonight. You work so hard for your family, how about we have a little fun?" All it takes are statements like this and others to get a Christian's eyes off Christ and onto sinful things. Everyone wants to be that sweet, popular friend that everyone likes including you and me. But sometimes, we forget about the godless critic's boss behind the scenes, Satan. He and his demons are often depicted with pointy ears, red skin, and arrows for tails; however, most believers know that our adversary is not restricted to any man-made portrayal. "Caricatures are nothing more than mere distractions from truths that sit right before naive eyes," says the Holy Spirit, while I thought about why man would create such ugly looking cartoons of Satan. Our enemy is very real and can inhabit ungodly human beings so we have learned in the Scriptures.

Some believers and unbelievers might say, "The devil is made up, a figment of one's imagination." But, try telling someone that who has experienced great evil after having performed a spell, curse or other actions rooted in witchcraft. Attempt to explain away the devil when someone keeps telling you that when he or she goes to bed at night strange shadows creep along the walls with nothing in a room causing the odd shapes. Further, what might you say to someone who keeps being touched by some entity who murmurs and speaks vile things? There is a world beyond this one and some are more sensitive to it than others. Just because some of you reading this chapter haven't personally experienced some paranormal occurrences in your lives, doesn't mean they don't exist.

Evil in the Eyes of Men

I have never witnessed a "real" fleshly devil, but I have seen demons with my own eyes in supernatural visions such as: odd alien looking creatures, dark shadows, evil looking humans possessed by the devil, and mysterious looking animals. I also saw wickedness behind the eyes of sinful men a few times in my life that from the looks on their faces, and the things they said and did, they didn't care whether I or others lived or died. It was as if they had went from being mere men to becoming possessed with some "thing," so ugly, hateful and downright scary. I have witnessed bizarre things in my life like, awaking to an upside down cross that I didn't touch the night before. I have also heard a voice trying to get me to join the dark side with promises of fame and fortune. Further, I have heard my name called when no one was there.

In the Bible, an evil spirit came from God and disturbed Saul. In 1 Samuel 16:23, "And it came to pass, when the evil spirit from God was on Saul, that David took a harp, and played with his hand: so Saul was refreshed, and was well, and the evil spirit departed from him."

When positive music is played with vocalists singing about Jesus, the ambience feels uplifting, peaceful and carefree. Yet there are those times that some Christian music (Rock, Holy Hip Hop, Jazz, etc.) really has nothing to do with God, but is more about promoting an agenda, encouraging a worldly lifestyle, and bolstering the singer's career. No matter how many times a mainstream singer says Jesus or God it doesn't make what he or she is singing holy. Over the years when I have listened to many secular Hip Hop, Rap, Rock, R&B, and Techno musical sounds, much of it seemed to further aggravate already tensed situations while the music played in the background. I have learned that some music is arranged with subliminal messages playing in the background and once recorded it is prayed over by worshipers of Satan. You can learn more about this by researching "occult sounds in music,

Satanism, devil music" and other similar phrases via the Internet. During back-masking (recording music backward on a track) horrific human sounds are heard while instrumental sounds are manipulated.

In James 5:13, when we are in need of mental and physical peace we can use music. "Is any among you afflicted? Let him pray. Is any merry? Let him sing Psalms." Notice, it isn't just any music, the Scripture directs us to the book of Psalms. If you are a singer or musician you might want to use your talent to communicate the Psalms to the born again, lost and other listeners. We need more music filled with the lyrics of the Psalmist David that uplift, correct, and motivate people to want to keep walking with the Lord; instead of music that puts down individuals and glorifies others for living an ungodly lifestyle and making poor life decisions.

I have been entertained by both beautiful women and handsome men with smooth voices filled with flattery, then almost in an instant, see these same people act so ugly that I had to question whether God even existed. How could such a wonderful piece of artwork exude such mean spirits? Like the celebrities we watch on TV, these people would praise God out their mouths while they dressed up in satanic attire.

"How can something that looks and feels so good be wrong?" You might think. This is your first mistake, like it was mine. "People act as if the attractiveness of one's outer appearance proves the goodness of the inner man," the Holy Spirit told me one day. "You reason away righteous behaviors, ideologies, and the like to suit what you believe to be right while justifying the evil that you do," the Spirit further explained. To top it all off, we tell ourselves, "We shouldn't judge!" The issue of doing what is right and what is wrong doesn't need a judge unless one has problems with following the law," the Holy Ghost reminded me.

The devil has a long list of strategies to get you to step out of God's will and if he can lure you out of it with someone or something that looks or sounds appealing, he will. The serpent did it with Eve. Apparently, the apple she ate looked good enough to eat; otherwise, she wouldn't have eaten it.

Satan's Schemes

For centuries, Satan has used manipulative tactics to get ignorant people to stray away from the light and walk into darkness. He usually starts with a proposal or tempts us with something that appeals to our senses or innate desires. The devil will then get us to doubt our current actions or inactions on a matter then move us to compare it with his offer which usually captivates our emotions. However, his tempting proposition will disturb our spirit or "gut feeling" as some would like to call it and what might we do, ignore the signs. With a little prompting from those around us, we arrive at a final decision that we usually regret later.

Think about the following situation for a moment. Let's say, I told you that I had a lot of money to give you, but you needed to do a few immoral things in order to obtain the money. Now the things you would be required to do wouldn't be described as "real bad." You wouldn't go to jail and no one would know outside our circle that you did some questionable acts, unless you told them. You would be given so much money that you wouldn't worry over your finances for years. What would you say to a hypothetical proposal like this? Would you want to know more? Now you don't have that much time to think about this. Right away, some of you would think, "Depending on how much money is involved and what exactly I would have to do, I might go along with this offer." Just that fast, you would be willing to set aside your personal beliefs and permit yourself to get sucked into one of many enemy schemes. The promise of big money is enticing, isn't it? Some of you reading this might have considered praying about the proposal first. But what's there to pray about? I already told you that what you would be doing is immoral, don't remember? Go back and read.

Some of us fall for tricks, just like the previous example, because we have unmet personal needs. We might feel like the following: God isn't interested in our wants, doesn't care about our feelings, or doesn't want us partakers in what others' call blessings, so we choose not to bother him with our physical and spiritual requests; rather we take on tasks by ourselves. We basically write God out of our lives until we believe we need him, but for some disgruntled Christians, they walk away from God and never look back!

But what if we detected a problem with someone or something before we walked out the door? Would this keep us from falling for the devil's schemes? Sometimes. "But, why not all the time?" A few of you might question. In answer to that, I would have to say because there are life lessons that need to be taught by our Father in heaven to better us spiritually, mentally and physically (Jas. 1:2.) Besides if we knew everything that would happen to us in advance then we wouldn't need God, now would we? "With him (God) is wisdom and strength, he hath counsel and understanding" (Job 12:13). There is no way God would let us know all that might happen to us for the rest of our lives. We need the following to help us grow spiritually: the Holy Spirit, life experiences, the Word of God, faith, like-minded believers, and more. In my personal experience, many things God doesn't reveal to me, because he knows I would spend more time focusing on the problems and less time receiving his wisdom. Think about this, psychics also known as fortune tellers, are not good confidants for Christians, because they deflect from God with their oftentimes false predictions. God reminds us in his Word of his power and doesn't want us following after witches, wizards and occult things. But what do some believers do anyway, trust in relatives and friends who talk to the spirits of the deceased, research numerology and study stars, use dark magic and other demonic practices. Consider the following Scripture.

"Thus saith the Lord, thy redeemer, and he that formed thee from the womb, I am the Lord that maketh all things; that stretcheth forth the heavens alone; that spreadeth abroad the earth by myself; That frustrateth the tokens of the liars, and maketh diviners mad; that turneth wise men backward, and maketh their knowledge foolish" (Isa. 44:24-25). Those that listen to fortune tellers and the like, become more concerned about the outcome of the dilemmas then the events leading up to them. The person receiving false prophecies can actually make things happen based on a liars' predictions—God may have never intended for certain events to come to pass. According to Zechariah 10:2, "For the idols have spoken vanity, and the diviners have seen a lie, and have told false dreams; they comfort in vain: therefore they went their way as a flock, they were troubled, because there was no shepherd."

God didn't always prevent trouble from coming on righteous men and women (ie. Job, Jesus, Noah, Moses, Abraham, etc.)—we are no exception! There are always lessons to be learned amidst difficult circumstances. If we really love and obey God, like we say we do, then life's lessons will cause us to want to listen to the Father. We live in an imperfect world amongst imperfect people, who by God's design have their own free will. Therefore, we could never predict all that man or woman will or won't do in life without fully knowing the minds and hearts of every living being—now who can do that, but God? However, some who believe they have god-like powers will sure try! Even if some think that they are strong enough in the Lord or believe in multiple gods (also known as demons) to forecast future events, one can still be caught in an enemy's snare both now and in the future. The Bible doesn't say, to worship self, walk in the ways of self or trust in self or gods. We are to walk with Jesus Christ and worship Him and only Him! "Give unto the Lord the glory due unto his name; worship the Lord in the beauty of holiness" (Ps. 29:2).

Deceptive Spirits

When living amongst imperfect people, some of us have an inner circle comprised of: a partner, family, friends, co-workers, and others who we consider our best and most shining examples of what love is. However, those that we esteem, love the most, and shout to the world, "How good she is...how wonderful a man I know..." will let us down, and even worse, may get the boot out of our circles for repeated violations. You may recall 2 Timothy 3 which reveals the kind of people in this world and what they like to do, "...in the last days perilous times shall come. For men shall be lovers of their own selves, covetous, boasters, proud, blasphemers, disobedient to parents, unthankful, unholy." Right away you should recognize those that you know from reading this Scripture. These people who fit this description are causing you the most trouble and they might even be attending church with you! The Scripture goes on to read that these people are, "Without natural affection, trucebreakers, false accusers, incontinent, fierce, despisers of those that are good..." Notice, people like this hate the good!

It isn't any wonder that some will become irritated even vengeful when you try to reason with them. You may want this person to turn right, but he insists on turning left. The Scripture has a few more personalities you might recognize, "Traitors, heady, high-minded, lovers of pleasures more than lovers of God; Having a form of godliness, but denying the power thereof: from such turn away." Some if not all of these describes many of us.

We live in a time where so many believe that they are their own gods. The Bible gives us an idea of how the sinful operate, "For of this sort are they which creep into houses, and lead captive silly women laden with sins, led away with divers lusts, Ever learning, and never able to come to the knowledge of the truth." When I read this, I thought of those of us who once partied like a rock star and laughed the night away. Then the next morning we were cramming over college textbooks—always learning but void of wisdom. The Scripture reminds us that these people "resist the truth: men of corrupt minds reprobate concerning the faith." The consequence of all their rebellion is that these men and women "...shall proceed no further: for their folly shall be manifest unto all men, as theirs also was." So many critics love to talk about how out-dated the Bible is, but when you read Scriptures like these, you can't help but say, "How befitting! This is so true of our modern day."

So who are these critics we love anyway? Are they really our friends or are they being used by the enemy to one day become our foes? Are they sincerely walking in the light or are they dancing in darkness? Do they really care about us or are they really connected to us for selfish reasons? There is so much to consider when dealing with difficult people and little time to think about it all. Yet, I will provide some thoughts that will challenge you to ponder about those people and things (also known as idols) that God may be warning you about. According to Romans 2:22 (AKJV), "You that say a man should not commit adultery, do you commit adultery? You that abhor idols, do you commit sacrilege?" We have to often check ourselves, before we can check other people.

There is a deceptive spirit confusing many believers into thinking that it's okay to give certain people more love, attention, affection, and costly things just because they wear special titles, belong to favorite civic groups, or have done some great things in our lives. Read James 1:1-4 on favoritism. This misleading spirit is also keeping the Christian bound to all sorts of godless precepts, contracts, traditions, conditions, rules, principals, and step-by-step programs which distract him often from what God wants.

There may be a special someone in our lives that we have told others, "I owe this woman my life for saving me…If it wasn't for that man, I don't know where I would be." Seems like harmless statements. However, when you think deeply about phrases like this and others, they sound as if someone has put a man or woman on the throne of God while pushing His majesty off! You will know whether the one doing all the praising of others is idolizing people rather than simply loving them. If he or she spends more time celebrating people and less time meditating on God's will, this person will take offense to a believer who is not adoring people like he or she does. You may have noticed this if you ever commented on how much time one is spending event planning and doing other things for people, but not enough time praying, reading and acting on the principles of God. If you share your personal opinion, he or she may retort with a statement like, "I'm not like you, I love people. I don't like sitting at home reading the Bible, I like getting out with others." We have to keep in mind, God uses men and women to do things for us such as: pray, counsel, uplift and give generously; however, we should not be consumed with people so much that we don't give God his glory and his time! The nicest thing we can do for someone or a group that has done something for us is to say, "Thank you" while never taking our eyes off Christ. Even God's Son took his share of breaks from being amongst people.

Difficult individuals love to be praised for their worldly ideas and actions. Some utilize what they have learned from secular teachers in order to control masses and gain things like fame, but not so much to uplift others. When a few in the group start to awake to a controlling person's true intent, that's when what was once considered a nice friendship or great relationship begins to take an ugly turn. It is then that God provides us with an escape plan or a new way of doing things so that we can be better off without these difficult people around us. But what do we do every now and then? Reject the truth and bypass God's plan preferring to hold on to a history with a foe that is filled with, "Remember when memories..." and statements like, "I will never forget how much she has done for me." Meanwhile, ignoring the signs that God's Spirit has long left this individual.

Oh, how wicked we are for tempting a jealous God to unleash his wrath upon us for the stupid things we say and do after asking God for answers to our prayers. "Dear Lord, should I trust this person...should I marry him, do business with her, give them this money?" we ask the Lord. Meanwhile, we disrespect God when we get a clear answer from him. Rather, we go off asking someone else what he or she thinks about a situation. We do this sometimes because we don't trust something we can't see or physically touch, we are in doubt of God's involvement in our lives. How foolish we are for thinking at times that because we saw people's hands help us, hold us or give us something, that all honor should be given to people! Even worse, some prideful individuals will ignore everyone including God and praise themselves. "The pride of your heart has deceived you, you who live in the clefts of the rocks and make your home on the heights, you who say to yourself, 'Who can bring me down to the ground'" (Obad. 1:3, NIV)?

We allow ourselves to be deceived, almost daily, by critical relatives, friends, the media, government, bosses, co-workers even strangers on streets who claim to have personal relationships with Jesus Christ. We refuse to listen to God's warnings concerning our enemies, because from time to time we are too lazy, arrogant, busy, or something else to safeguard our ears and eyes from lies, schemes, double-talk, and mean-spirited attitudes. Sometimes we don't bother to incorporate our Lord's daily teachings in our lives and then we wonder why things don't go our way.

People take advantage of us when we lack a discerning spirit and are unable to determine truth from a lie. For instance, look at how many people believe everything they see when watching television news and reading print media, but believe nothing when an average Joe looks up factual information and proves that the media has been covering up or blatantly lying to the public about everything from historical events to the latest tragedies. Most naysayers never bother to perform their own personal research. Instead, they give praise to the news reporter, the celebrity or someone else while cursing God's true messengers and accusing them of being false. We live in a fast food, fast TV, fast service, fast women, fast men, fast teens and everything else kind of fast society. Many people want to have it their way without trusting in a God that doesn't give them their way, but shows them The Way!

Ask God, right now, to begin to reveal truth to you in *all* its forms from the news stories you hear to the company that you work for! Tell him you are sorry for not listening to him in the past when he sent his messengers to speak truth in your life and you rather argue and defend people and things you don't know much about. Tell him you need his help to stop believing lies and spreading gossip in Jesus name! After you pray a prayer like this, be prepared for God's messengers in many industries to come along your path with truth whether it comes via email, a social networking page or in-person. God will direct you to individuals, places and things that are like you, seeking truth. Receive facts, don't fight them! Don't be like the fool always ready to dismiss truth because it makes you feel uncomfortable. I said a personal prayer including the information I previously mentioned some years back, and the Lord definitely answered my prayers—this book is one of many answers.

A lot of God's children refuse a fresh anointing, because they believe they are already "good," the Holy Spirit told me. There are those, who still hold on to childhood baptisms believing that is all one needs to enter heaven. However, they ignore years of evil that has been said, done and thought about concerning our heavenly Father, loved ones, neighbors and friends over the years. The Holy Spirit shared with me, "There is no place in heaven for the self-righteous." In Titus 2:12, God's followers are instructed to deny "ungodliness and worldly lusts, we should live soberly, righteously, and godly, in this present world…"

At times, we fall weak and seek comfort in things, being that we are often bombarded with signs that tell us to, "Buy this on sale…Get this with zero money down…Ask for that…You need this!" We falsely assume that purchasing certain things will satisfy our innate desires, but we deceive ourselves! Soon after a transaction, we are back to complaining about yet another thing: we don't have, doesn't work or don't need while being critical of sales clerks, managers and company owners. Some believers spend much time on their knees praying often for things, that they have forgotten how to pray about anything else like: put in me a clean heart, bless me with a renewed mind, give me the courage to use my spiritual gifts, help me receive and share wisdom, put your messengers in government, cause local pastors to walk boldly for you and stand for truth, move on rich men and women to help the needy, widows, children, and more. It literally took me years to get out of the habit of praying for things so often.

Some wayward Christians believe kind actions towards others are all they need to save them from an angry God and a fiery hell. Honestly, the only thing our niceties will do is honor the one receiving them. God has repeatedly shown in his Bible that man's sacrifices whether for him or someone else will not earn him a place in heaven. "Who hath saved us, and called us with an holy calling, not according to our works, but according to his own purpose and grace, which was given us in Christ Jesus before the world began" (2 Tim. 1). Think about this for a moment, whenever a relative or friend gives you something, somehow some way this person won't let you forget it. When you give a tithe or offering to a church, a minister won't let you leave his or her presence without reminding you to give more. I am so glad our Father doesn't operate this way!

Most people desire the world to be simple, comprehensive and nothing more than a place they can engage their five senses. Anything outside of what humans feel, see, taste, touch, and hear, for many people, is null and void. This is one of many reasons why the enemy can come like a thief in the night seeking who he can steal, kill and ultimately destroy mentally, physically and spiritually. When a critical, selfish man or woman sincerely wants something from you, it doesn't matter: how nice you have been, how close you are to the Lord, what you look like, or how much money or power you have, he or she will create a blueprint that will answer the who, what, when, why, where, and how questions in order to get what he or she wants. This wicked person or group will not stop until goals are accomplished even if it means: losing a partner or friend, sacrificing material wealth, never seeing children again, becoming sick, being imprisoned, or killing others. The enemy may look harmless on the outside, but on the inside, he or she is a beast!

I know for some that what I am about to say will be a hard pill to swallow, however that one or two you might love the most, who isn't interested in your faith, the Holy Bible, church or anything related to the affairs of God, is an *enemy*! Let me repeat that again, the one who fights, disagrees or distracts you from spending time with God and sharing his Word, is your foe! Pray for that person, but don't abandon God or ignore what he tells you because of how they make you feel. Every so often we tend to sleep on those who may smile in our faces, because of relationship titles. God may have used us for a season in someone's life, but that doesn't make him or her a lifetime friend. If Jesus Christ, King David, John the Baptist, Apostle Paul, and others had their share of enemies, we too will have ours. Ponder on the following Scripture for a moment, "Dear friends, do not be surprised at the painful trial you are suffering, as though something strange were happening to you. But rejoice that you participate in the sufferings of Christ, so that you may be overjoyed when his glory is revealed. If you are insulted because of the name of Christ, you are blessed, for the Spirit of glory and of God rests on you" (1 Peter 4:12-14, NIV).

Knowing your enemy—that critic of your faith—is the first step you must accomplish before you can engage in verbal or non-verbal combat about your faith. Jesus knew when to tell a story, heal, cast out demons, advise his followers, answer critics, spend time with our Father, and die. All of which incited some degree of trouble from those onlookers who were either for or against him. But you might say to yourself, "I don't want to start any wars." The day you decided to become a genuine follower of Christ, *you became an enemy of the enemy.* "Consider it pure joy, my brothers, whenever you face trials of many kinds, because you know that the testing of your faith develops perseverance" (Jas. 1:2).

The critic is just the middle man, but your true enemy sits behind the critic. The enemy "knew you when..." He had a plan for your life too, just like God, but he wasn't interested in walking with you on a journey to help you; rather, he was more interested in arguing, hitting, tripping, kicking, choking, and fighting with you on your way to hell! One plan of the enemy is to get God's people distracted with money scams and scam artists so that they spend less time listening and obeying the Father and more time chasing money dreams. "People who want to get rich fall into temptation and a trap and into many foolish and harmful desires that plunge men into ruin and destruction" (I Timothy 6:9).

Working for God

When you are sincerely taking God at his Word (and I'm not talking about lip service either), I mean seriously walking with him, your rival will be doing the following: criticizing, ridiculing, lying, blaming, fighting, and ultimately trying to get you out of your marriage, home, job, social group, and other things. An enemy may look and act like righteous critics, but you have to look beyond the surface. It is very easy to confuse an enemy from one who simply doesn't need something we are offering, a person may say something like, "It's just not working out…we no longer need your services…we think that it would be best for you if you would step down…we won't be calling you anymore…we don't need you…I don't love you anymore." The difference between the enemy and one who is verbalizing a concern is that what they say and do usually doesn't stop right there with mere words. He or she perpetuates a war by continuing a fight long after truth has been spoken and hands have been shaken or bags packed. The critic is going to talk to someone else about you. He or she is getting you out the way, because you might be a threat, a disruption or a trouble-maker, but your absence isn't good enough, now he or she wants to assault you with words. "If I just get her to leave, maybe I won't have to put up with her nasty, ugly…If I could make him stop going to church and stop acting like a self-righteous, wan-nabe…maybe he will go back to being that fun guy I once knew. I never liked his no good, sorry, good-for-nothing…"

Trying to keep the peace with an enemy for all the wrong reasons will not bring any solutions; instead you will face more challenges. The Bible says, "Blessed are the peacemakers: for they shall be called the children of God." (Matt. 5:9). When some read this Scripture, they assume that being a peacemaker means not to partake in or create conflict with others. However, if you are one who hungers and thirsts for righteousness (Matt. 5:6) then you should know there will be conflicts when it comes to speaking and acting on truth. When Jesus walked this earth and performed the acts that he did according to the Father's will, oftentimes there was no peace. Occasionally our actions, if we follow Jesus, might cause us and others' around us discomfort, but remember our suffering is for the higher good. We are reminded in Matthew 5:10, "Blessed are they which are persecuted for righteousness' sake: for theirs is the kingdom of heaven."

Think about the New Testament stories of Jesus for a moment. Now ponder this, when sinful man had enough of the God Man, he had to do away with him, right? We saw this when Judas made the first move in orchestrating a plan to get rid of Jesus. But the Messiah sent Judas away knowing he would betray him. Notice, Jesus sent the sinful man away beforehand. He let Judas go. A simple act, but it speaks volumes. Jesus let one who was close to him go do what he knew he had to do. Some of you keep holding on to loved ones' opinions, systems, and other things because you fear what they might do. Your keeping your enemy close is actually keeping you from progressing in your spiritual walk with God. We can keep unrighteous people so close to us to the point that they cause us to sin. It's time to send pessimistic people, thoughts, and things away in Jesus name! Your time with them is up! Let them go do what they need to do, so you can go do what you need to do! Maybe God has called some of you to a Bible study, missionary group, new job, business, relationship, relocation, craft/hobby, or something else, but instead of listening to the Holy Spirit's reasons as to why you should be doing something else, you keep listening to an errant man or woman. It's because of this person's opinions you can't move on with your life in peace. Follow the lead of the one who truly loves you and who sincerely cares about your soul, Jesus, the Son of God!

The devil tickles both man and woman's ears with talk about "a kill or be killed" mentality from the boardroom to the bedroom. It doesn't matter that you may have been light-hearted when you haphazardly said something about "taking over the company in Jesus name" to your boss, "making that woman my wife someday" or "buying the family business if God blesses me." When you made statements like these, you stirred up the devil and now you are a walking target. Don't you know that the devil doesn't want a Christian running or buying a business? He also doesn't want men and women marrying! The last thing the prince of this world wants is for a Christian to be a success on his territory. Nothing good, positive, uplifting, or beneficial Satan wants for the Christ follower. So he twists what was meant for good into something evil. The devil plays mind games, "You know she doesn't really love you. He is going to get you fired one day. They will leave you out of the will, because you're an idiot!" So the "kill or be killed" triggers are engaged and before long, feelings of regret begin to set in after the smoke clears. "I wish I hadn't said that…I hope she forgives me," the big mouth sobs.

If you thought your statements of faith didn't matter that much, someone listening took you seriously, like that popular quote some of you like to recite, "I will be the head and not the tail!" So your brother or sister in Christ thought, "I hope he isn't talking about taking my position. She better not be planning to make some changes around here. We don't have any room in the inn; they better stay in the barn." There wasn't any room for baby Jesus, so his parents had to settle for the barn. Did you ever give any deep thought to that? Some of you believe God for a mansion on Satan's turf, but for now the only room he is offering you is a barn. "Let's see what you are going to do with that," says the Lord. Your so-called brother or sister in Christ heard your preaching, and for some, bragging. So he or she started planning like Joseph's jealous brothers did with him. "How am I going to keep this woman/man in her place until I am ready to get rid of her/him?"

You may think you are the head, but the enemy has got some of you hoodwinked. Take a moment to pray to the one true God for revelation and wisdom; because it won't be long before you realize the truth about yourself, the situation and those connected to it. Watch and pray. Don't ask God for revelation if you are unwilling to receive instruction. Most of all, stop sharing your personal dreams with jealous people and worriers or that hole in your face just might put you in a hole! From rabbit holes to financial holes, there are many Christians sitting in holes waiting for spiritual breakthroughs. Holes are dark, lonely places and scary at times. Remember Joseph's brothers put him in a hole, but God moved on the young men to get him out. I wonder what Joseph was thinking about while he was in his hole. Most likely the kind of things we think about when we are in trouble. "I should have never said that…I wish that things had been different…I hope that I can get some help…I pray they didn't forget about me…" Every now and then, God will use the enemy that hurt you to also help you.

When you step out in Jesus name, the devil shows out! Too much talking, walking and praying about God, with that Jesus glow on your face, and your critic does the following: looks the other way, doesn't have time to talk, makes a joke out of what you say or finds fault with you. Now if your naysayer can gain something materially from you, then this person has time to talk. "Sister, you have a word for me? Oh by the way, you have that check you promised? Hey brother, I have a little time on my hands, can you do me a favor? Oh I almost forgot, you still volunteering for that event, right?" Critics might have had a problem with you, but their hang-ups temporarily go away when you give them something they really want. After the excited feeling goes away and the newness of what you did wears off, it's back to business as usual with the critic leading the conversation about how they don't like this or that about you.

None of us wants to be ignored or treated differently because we say, "I am a child of God." We also don't want to be mistreated because we choose not to act like the world by jumping on the bandwagon just because someone cries, "Get onboard with us!" No matter how much my feelings may be hurt because of someone else's insulting comments or immoral behaviors, whether on or offline, I understand that there are reasons why God isn't going to permit me to get close to specific people, groups or visit certain places. I realize it's for my own mental and physical protection. Some things just aren't meant to be no matter how much we reason that they are. Instead of being content with what God has already blessed us with like: our health, a place to stay, clothes on our backs, and food in the fridge, we still want more. It is then that we construct this internal fight within ourselves where there is "my voice" and "Their voices". "I know that I should be grateful but pastor said…I know that God is with me but deacon said…I really like what I'm doing, but my spouse said…I think I should start cutting people off but what if they say…" Instead of letting those critics we love go as mentioned previously in this chapter, we bring them along for the ride on our spiritual journeys (even when we know these people really aren't reciprocating our love back). I thank God for the times that he has made me aware of enemy schemes and allowed distance to help me sort out who is friend and who is foe.

We must remember that what good deeds were done in the past by loved ones, doesn't dictate who these people are to us today. He or she may have once been a saint in our lives, but as we all know, people change. The loved one may have once been a beacon of light, able to tell us night from day, sweet with his or her words, and kind in deeds, but inside of this critical person may now live an enemy who is bitter, angry, stubborn, and still holding on to the sinful "good ole' days."

3. Critical Tongue

A critical tongue either built you up or tore you down at some point in your life. When you heard the evil tongue pour out insulting words, at first, you went into shock. "I can't believe she went there! He really said that to me!" you said. Then angry feelings caused you to retaliate. After feelings were hurt, emotions of regret began to set in followed by blame. "I should have seen that one coming. I should have never said what I did, but if she hadn't done that maybe I wouldn't have." For some believers, they become sad while stirring up fault-finding thoughts and heated emotions. Meanwhile, other victims of criticism begin plans for revenge. "I think I will talk to a few people in his group about his ugly ways, then I will recruit a few to bring him down and hopefully he will lose his job," the wicked one thinks.

In James 3:5-6, the tongue is described as "a small part of the body, but it makes great boasts...The tongue is also a fire a world of evil among the parts of the body. It corrupts the whole person, sets the whole course of his life on fire, and is itself set on fire by hell." The tongue may have caused you not to perform as well as you should have in school or college, it might have run you out of a marriage or put you out on the street. Pessimistic statements may have hurt or abused you emotionally in relationships or inadvertently caused you to stumble by the things you listened to or read that were not of God.

Some people may have strategically planned verbal assaults against you to get you to conform to their way of thinking. For those, who may have once cherished a relative or friend, this person may have turned you off with his or her share of insults and caused you never to look at him or her in a positive way again. I don't blame you, who can view a person the same way when he or she has hurt you so badly? This is why we must go to God with our burdens so that we can give others the benefit of the doubt. "Cast your burden on the Lord, and he shall sustain you: he shall never suffer the righteous to be moved" (Ps. 55:22, AKJV).

When you gave your life to Christ, there were those critics who launched personal attacks against you both online and offline. These critics may have hoped that if they could attack you with enough mean-spirited criticism then they would be able to cause you to give up your faith in God. These offenders may have found every Scripture in the Bible where God looks like a big, bad mean deity to get you to distance yourself from him. They said things like, "Why would such a God do this…Why would you want to serve a God who does that…?" All the while some of you were probably dying inside, because everything that you knew that gave you hope seemed to be no more after the critic got through with you. This kind of evil programming is the worst of its kind! It takes away something that you believe in and makes it look ugly, harmful and worthless. Wicked people participate in such negative programming not only when getting people away from religion and similar practices, but with education, government, culture, relationship, family, and more. The more one talks about how bad, how ugly, how wrong, how useless something is, the more people will go along with the critic's programming. They fail to realize what manipulative practices are being used behind the scenes to assault their minds. The disgruntled critics know when to strike, don't they? They usually launch their attack while you are experiencing the following: soon after a tragedy, when you are tired, hungry, confused, busy with children, working on a project, or in pain. Here comes the critic like the serpent approaching Eve, "Now do you really think God cares about you? Have you ever really thought about that dictator you serve in the Bible? Did you ever think who really benefits from your imaginary friend?" Instead of questioning the critic's motives for being "so against" Christianity, most gullible people go along with the popular view that will win them more friends and material gain. Most often, when someone or a group is talking negatively about religion, a law, a program, or even a person, they usually have ulterior motives whether right or wrong, notice the following created example in this short dialogue between a believer and an unsaved person.

"I am so not in support of his view. I don't like that close-minded candidate he is always talking about his faith. He was the one that helped create that law which keeps homosexuals from marrying."

"Wait a minute; didn't you support him several years ago?"

"Well yes."

"So what is your real reason for not supporting him this year? You know he needs our votes."

"I mean he's not that bad. But if I agree with him or that law he helped create, then our organization wouldn't receive any funding."

"Oh."

"So why don't you help us? Vote this way the next election."

"I don't think so."

"You Christians are all the same, always sticking to your own kind."

Despite the unsaved person's negative view of the conservative candidate, he or she at one time voted for this person, yet now this individual stands to gain something if there is a protest against the not-so popular candidate. In this situation, the critical tongue is being used as a powerful tool to get others to go against someone else with the hope of affecting one's career for personal gain.

Breaking a Child's Well-Being through Brainwashing

Children are vulnerable. Those money-hungry adults who have time on their hands, know exactly how to use children to get parents to: buy a product, sign up for a program, or go along with a certain agenda. They create catchy songs, tell children what to say to make adults feel guilty and use other sneaky tactics. Some children may innately feel like a certain person, setting or situation isn't right. Yet, they don't always know how to communicate their concerns or physically protect themselves especially if charmed by sneaky individuals who give them things like: toys, entertainment, favorite cookies, candies, and drinks in exchange for information.

Many children are told by brainwashed parents to go along with a relative's physical demands or help this person mentally cope with personal issues even if this adult doesn't appear like he or she is good with children much less want them around. This unsaved relative or backslider might share inappropriate stories with the child or permit him or her to do things that the parent would be against. To explain this sort of behavior further, I have provided the following example. For instance, a grandparent suffering with depression may use a child to comfort him or her by asking his son or daughter to drop the grandchild off "to keep dear ole' grandma company." There seems to be nothing wrong, at first glance, until the adult starts expecting the child to act like his or her servant. What appeared to be a simple relationship between adult and young person takes a turn for the worse when his or her basic needs are disrupted like: eating, sleeping and playing; therefore, this youngster has no choice but to start objecting. "I don't want to do that grandma. Stop bothering me grandpa. Leave me alone. Can I please eat now? Could I go to sleep? I would like to play with my toys," says the weary child. It is at this point when the adult begins to criticize the young person for not meeting his or her demands. The controlling, selfish grandparent will take her critical tongue like a weapon and start going to work on the child's confidence, "You ungrateful, little…You didn't finish helping me! What good are you? Stupid! Dumb! Ugly! Hey cry baby, get over here!"

Once drawn into a mean adult's deceptive scheme or program (specifically designed to control the child in the worst way), the sneaky relative, handler, guardian, or caretaker, will use the child like a puppet. The programmer sets the "programmed" on a task to make puppets out of others. The wicked teacher enlists the hard-hearted pupil to recruit. The idle trainer encourages his troubled students to teach his methods. The controlling minister manipulates the immature to market his grand plan. Observers wonder why there are so many bad trainers, teachers, Christ followers and more. Think about your upbringing for a moment. Were there any adults around you trying to use you to get to someone else, abuse or threaten to hurt you so that you would operate like a robot for them? How did you feel about those people? What did you observe about their behavior? The Bible says in Psalm 127: 3-5 (NIV) regarding children, "Sons are a heritage from the Lord, children a reward from him. Like arrows in the hands of a warrior are sons born in one's youth. Blessed is the man whose quiver is full of them. They will not be put to shame when they contend with their enemies in the gate." We are not to resent them or pass them off to others with a negative disposition, but rather we should feel blessed that God chose us to give them life.

Conduct your own research on mind control, brainwashing, and other related topics. You may have seen evidence of similar tactics used on naive adults by popular American cultists like: Jim Jones, Charles Manson, L. Ron Hubbard, Anton Lavey, David Karesh, and Sun Myung Moon. In addition, there is a long history of government dictators throughout our world who were able to get seemingly intelligent adults to hurt self and others. How did they do it? They used their tongues before any other strategy first. Consider this these masterminds used their mouths to destroy many lives. Most evil workers have left behind their writings, audio recordings, videos and more sharing details of their evil ideologies, so that they may be repeated. These sick former leaders are still manipulating young minds, with their satanic-influenced teachings, despite many of them being buried six-feet deep. Researchers have exposed these false teachers and have uncovered that some were part of government experiments gone wrong. This is why we must be careful who we are listening to. We don't know about the masters who are holding the puppets' strings and what are their true intentions. Let the Lord be your guide.

Teachers (parents, counselors and others) are supposed to help students grow emotionally and physically without killing their spirits. But what do we hear in the media? News stories about some educators abusing children in sadistic ways. Depending on the type of punishment inflicted on the child, will determine how deep the scars have penetrated a youngster's emotional and physical well-being as they journey toward adulthood. What some parents fail to remember is that their child will one day grow up and all the unresolved hurt will only be dispensed onto the following generation. Who knows whether a child will grow up to be a productive citizen willing to make society a better place or a troubled youth seeking to tear it down because of all his or her abuse?

Far too much criticism can destroy a mind. The emotional affects of mental harassment whether from a caretaker or a peer, are devastating. "Name calling is one type of psychological bullying that is particularly degrading and harmful. It happens in the schoolyard, classroom – and even at home," according to an article entitled: *The Emotional Effects of Psychological Bullying: Peer Victimization at School, at Work, and at Home* (Suite101.com). "The results of psychological bullying include insomnia, anxiety, depression, and even symptoms of posttraumatic stress disorder. Different types of bullying have different effects on different individuals; rarely are the effects positive." So if this happens with children overtime because someone or a group simply can't control their despicable tongue, then what might happen if you are an immature Christian repeatedly taking such abuse from members of your church home? You too will experience similar feelings.

Spiritual Abuse

So what are those upsetting emotions one keeps grappling with when in the presence of those who are supposed to be teaching God's word and helping Christ followers spiritually, mentally and physically? One may be experiencing religious abuse in the church. On SpiritualAbuse.com, this kind of mistreatment is "when someone in a position of spiritual authority, the purpose of which is to 'come underneath' and serve, build, equip and make God's people more free, misuses that authority placing themselves over God's people to control, coerce or manipulate them for seemingly Godly purposes which are really their own." Some of the signs of spiritual abuse include: personal slander, elitism, social isolation, emphasis on finance, the belief that the minister always knows best, misuse of Scriptures, fear of leaving, and more. Some of which I personally experienced while attending a church many years ago and witnessed all at other churches I visited.

At one church, a simple church invite evolved into a weekly group meeting between myself and others behind closed doors where I was the focal point; rather than God. Several individuals spent more time studying me than the Bible. Over a period of weeks, I found these meetings to be disturbing and emotionally upsetting, so I simply stopped going, avoided inviting people to my residence and ignored my phone ringing when members called.

According to an article entitled, *Trusting God Again: Recovering from Spiritual Abuse,* by Dan Hitz (Recmin.org,) "The effects of spiritual abuse are very similar to the effects of sexual abuse – distrust, fear, lost hope, and inhibited development. Many survivors of childhood sexual abuse find themselves susceptible to strong church systems that seem to provide an ark of safety and protection, but they lack the discernment to understand why they continue to feel the familiar sense of control and manipulation." The church members, who I encountered, all had one common background story they joined the group when they were in college and going through emotionally difficult times in their lives. For a few, they dedicated their lives to the organization's creed, members' needs and leadership goals—notice I didn't say to the will of God.

Some Christians reading this book may be victims of spiritual/religious abuse, but just haven't labeled what they are experiencing in the church that, at least not yet. We see Scripture passages that often refer to us as "children," and we are that to God, but we adults aren't supposed to be treated that way by human leaders. It is unfortunate, that some men or women "of God" view their congregation like they do their own children. They may even go so far as to call themselves, "Mother" or "Father" or allow members to refer to them as such. This may be considered a kind gesture, but what it does is put that man or woman in a position that God never intended. This person may be your God-appointed teacher for a season—nothing more, nothing less. You already have a mother, father and Holy Father; you need not give anyone else that kind of parental authority over your life. When we look at church leaders, like we would our own parents, we are taking our focus off of Jesus and placing it squarely on men and women's shoulders while giving them emotional power over us. All the while we leave our hearts unguarded. The slightest infraction made by a leader can emotionally hurt an unstable follower for a lifetime while impacting his or her personal and professional relationships. If the follower has not guarded his or her emotions and has given the person (or group) access to the deepest part of one's Spirit, he or she has made man or woman top priority over his or her life and not God.

Divinely appointed leaders are indeed God's chosen, but as I mentioned earlier, they are in our lives for a season. Notice I said for a season. Eventually, God calls us to do things a part from these people. If you recall the disciples didn't always stay together, all were called to spread God's word and set up various ministries around the world over time. We have to keep in mind, no matter how sweet and nice some spiritual leaders can be, some are nothing more than money-loving ministers who abuse their power for selfish-gain. They sit behind closed doors discussing ways to make more money to fulfill personal needs like: buy this car, invest in that property, go on this trip, pay off personal debts, get children into college, help relatives, and more. None of these leadership's needs have anything to do with spreading the gospel. This is why many suffer much criticism from staff and church attendees. What's worse, some leaders strategize on how to effectively sell their personal needs and brand to the public with a God label on them. Now if one reading this isn't participating in such actions, mixing personal business with God's business, then there should be no ill feelings about what I have said. Take notice of the following example of how many pastors abuse their power. I think of a few who had big dreams and wanted the church to help them make their personal desires happen. One pastor created several "money" lines promising members they would receive their blessings if they gave a set amount of money. Those who gave the most received a special prophetic word from the pastor, and those who gave the least in the money line, received nothing. Members of a couple of denominational churches I visited passed plates around for birthdays, a honeymoon, building needs, and more at least several times in a single service. One church held regular services that lasted as long as three hours. When money is a focal point in a church, criticism should be expected.

Readers, watch for signs of spiritual abuse in your church. Notice how you behave around your church family. Ask yourself the following:

- Are you isolating yourself from likeable family and friends?

- Do you have a judgmental or critical attitude toward people you are supposed to be ministering to?

- Is your church family dominating all your time?

- Does your church leadership often put down people in the congregation as well as other churches?

- Does the leadership expect you to meet unrealistic goals and act in ways that have left you feeling uncomfortable?

- Do you feel pressure, anxiety, worry, or fear about disappointing the leadership?

If you answered "yes" to most of these questions, you really have to think long and hard whether or not God is still keeping you under a certain ministry or calling you elsewhere. Go to our Father and ask him for revelation concerning what he is doing in your life and how might your current church play a part in your future.

There is a great evil amongst us which involves children and immature adults being pushed by aggressive adults behind closed doors to be the best at everything. When the feeble, mentally unstable or handicapped don't meet abusive church expectations they are talked about badly and sometimes ostracized. The weak-minded and physically bound are programmed like computers to participate in acts that go against the Word of God. They are either deceived into performing despicable tasks or forced. Their handlers are not only proud of their creations, but especially excited about all the money they make from them.

Consider the long list of emotionally wounded and physically abused child stars who have grown up to become troubled celebrities still being pushed to bring in the harvest to their slave drivers. This sort of thing isn't just happening in the secular entertainment industry. Look at the lives of those who run mega-churches. Families have spent years of being manipulated and abused by leaders who they thought they could trust only to repeat the same behavior with those who trust them.

The critical tongue has name-called, cursed, chanted, lied, threatened, and more too graphic to explain here to get many of us to conform to someone else's twisted doctrine, fleshly desires or selfish demands; rather, than direct people to Jesus who gives us the Holy Spirit who reveals God's plans. Now the abused child, turned lost adult with possibly a past that also includes spiritual abuse, is repeating the same behavior with his or her children or someone else's. In time, some sons and daughters are visiting psychologists, psychiatrists, and others in the hopes of healing from past abuses.

Unfortunately, there are those children, specifically celebrity entertainers, who are given recommendations for help within their elitist circles that actually create more harm than good. You can read about many of their lives on-line and elsewhere. You will find that some of the so-called "help" or treatments they received from members closest to them involved drug use, alcohol consumption, mind control devices, and witchcraft practices. If these individuals were to go outside of their networks, some professionals may not know how to properly treat these severely brainwashed victims. Just think a person's whole life could be wrecked, by design, due to evil tongues that pay honor to Lucifer. I mention celebrities, because these are the people we see most often and who have the most influence on society at large. Someone who has been abused by evil speaking is being paraded in front of the masses spreading his or her dysfunctional lifestyle through music, dance, clothing and more. We have to exercise caution in what we choose to entertain our five senses. In addition, we have to correct our children when we see them mimicking entertainers, whether Christian or secular, simply because we can't afford to let the mentally ill sicken us and those we love. Remember if we are sincerely Christ followers, God will hold us accountable in this life and the next one for deviating from our faith to participate and encourage immorality.

Deceived by the Wicked Tongue

We can easily be deceived by someone's lips speaking flattery, giving us false encouragement, and sharing lustful thoughts. We consider such a person divine, wonderful, unique, funny, and more if we are not using spiritual discernment or are backsliding. But sooner or later, we realize the wicked critic is nothing more than a gossip, a liar, an aggravator, and even worse a murderer! Why is it that we are so ready to trust a godless person just because they look attractive and speak nicely to us? Is there something that we lack on the inside? Are we that desperate to want someone to love and appreciate us that we believe almost anything that they say?

When I pondered on these questions, I heard the Lord say, "My child, understand that a man or woman that comes in your life is after one thing, and that is whatever you can offer them to make them feel better about his or her self." He explained further, "If you can give he or she that one thing, this person most likely will be your friend for life whether he or she is good for you or not." So all these years, I wondered why I attracted certain individuals, and it all boiled down to that one thing I promised them in conversation and then later made good on it. Once their wish was granted, these difficult people would then feel that they had an "in" with me to say or do what they wanted in my life.

When you establish boundaries and stop doing for the critics in your life, it is then that they will start speaking negatively about you to others. I have experienced criticism from people for my personal and professional actions and reactions particularly if I didn't make a profit for a service. There were those who called me, "Weak, stupid, fool…" for being nice to people who couldn't help themselves much less me. Those who were wise advisers thought enough of me to give me guidance. But wicked critics, who misunderstood the teachings of Christ, were more concerned about their own interests. If we allow ourselves to be susceptible to enemy schemes, then the devil will stake claim to our minds, spirits, bank accounts, and whatever else he (or she) can get his hands on. Remember, most mayhem begins with an ungodly tongue!

Many Christians are guilty of following people both in religious and secular communities who talk deceptively. These smooth talkers have the "we are better than they" mentality. They are the self-righteous of our world as mentioned in a previous chapter. They keep people away from the church. They love their cliques and will say and do things to keep from their group being infiltrated by "the undesirables" or "sheeple"—a word that is used amongst some conspiracy seeking groups and elitist circles to describe people who act like sheep following a shepherd's (or church leaders) every move. Those who are supposed to be disciples of Christ do not take into consideration their own flaws and refuse to step outside the boxes of their own self-proclaimed righteousness.

Rather than help the confused, ignorant, lost, and poor, these Pharisee types will use their tongues to cut those who don't meet certain criteria. "She doesn't pay her tithes and can't speak very well, how did she get that position? That evangelist better start bringing in more visitors or else," you might hear one say. "Why do I get the feeling that God doesn't want him in our group," a critical Christian might say to encourage conversation from others. "I mean he doesn't read his Bible enough and he still lives with his child's mother?" A judge of a critical group might say, "Those people from that church don't have much money, we don't need to do much for them…I don't like that one member, she asks too many questions...I don't like her mother, so I know I won't like her!" Although these are not direct quotes, I have heard similar ones especially from critical tithe-paying church members.

Is it any wonder that some people end up having mental breakdowns trying to live up to unreachable standards put upon them by some churches? Some people bend over backwards trying to keep naysayers off their backs. With enough criticism, a new believer may end up abandoning his or her faith and checking into a mental institution.

In 1997 and in 1998, I was warned about two churches that I visited. I found out that they were known for running people away because of their very high standards. They didn't consider that people who have sinned for years needed to gradually distance themselves from sin. The unsaved, lost and backsliders who came to know Christ or re-dedicated their lives to Him, couldn't just walk away from sin overnight although some have. Instead, as soon as recently saved visitors walked down the aisle, they were expected to bring people to the next service, attend bible studies at least two times a week, and face the scrutiny of church members who outlined everything they had to do to maintain their position as a disciple of Christ. Members would report back to leaders about followers' "religious" progress. As I grew closer to certain people (I thought were friends), the more they demanded from me. Thank God, I stopped visiting a couple of these churches before I needed therapy. An evangelist friend told me that a member she once knew at one of the small churches I had attended, ended up being driven mad by all the pressure that was put upon her each day to study her Bible and recruit others.

Church Leadership

I think of leaders over churches who have been easily deceived by the promises of more money and bigger properties by the worldly elitists (who are very much interested in getting a cut of their donations from members and visitors). Some of these churches that were once failing, end up getting what they think is a blessing from God, but in time find themselves being pushed by board members to sell their souls to the devil for more fortune, fame and power. Some so-called Christians are no more than modern day Judas' still selling out Jesus for silver (and who knows some may be envious of Jesus' ministry as Judas was—Matt. 27:18). What's worse, various church leaders' confidants encourage them to keep up with their wickedness in the name of Jesus. And if leaders don't, they are criticized, set up, and banished from their church and local communities. Of course, God makes a way for the righteous and those who repent, I have heard some former leaders obtain employment out-of-state in other professions, participate in missions full-time, start up new churches, and do other things that continue to help others and glorify the Lord.

The church board, members and even visitors really want to believe that the attractive woman or man of God, who slithers his or her tongue like a snake, is really about God's business. But what they usually find out later, long after money and time have been spent is, that God had no involvement in appointing the leader in the first place! Instead, he or she was manufactured, created by a small elite (like some televangelists that we see when we turn on the television early in the morning or stay up late at night). Some church members become so disheartened with lies that they turn their back on God, church and family.

There are plenty of books that expose the misleading sermons of televangelists. For instance, one book written by the host of "The Bible Answer Man" radio program, Hank Hanegraff, provides insightful information about many popular TV ministers distorting doctrine while misleading the public with exaggerated story-telling and lies. His book is entitled, *Christianity in Crisis*. Before you listen to a televangelist, may I suggest you ask the Lord to lead you to truth? When I talked to God about what I saw on the TV screen and heard on the radio, he led me to books that helped me weed out some of these false prophets who base their ministries on prosperity teachings, twist Scripture in such a way that leaves the Trinity out and exaggerate God's messages to mean what they want them to mean.

Now when I mention these leaders over mega churches, I'm not just talking about televangelists, there are plenty of large churches in the United States and elsewhere who receive no television or radio air time, but are connected to worldly activities. Check out your own denominations online to find out the secular groups they support and other affiliations. According to Providence Baptist Ministries, a web-based ministry (Pbministries.org), there is "an estimated 400,000 - 500,000 Southern Baptist men (who) are Masons. Among this number are many well-known Southern Baptist leaders…" Now what might be wrong with this? Well, take the time to learn more about the history of Freemasonry and also think about what was discussed in Chapter 2. One's loyalty should not be to any establishment, but to the one true God. If one is indwelled with the Holy Spirit, he or she would see the error of his or her ways and turn from them.

Various churches endorse secular entertainers. When this topic came up in forums and videos online, about a church group's secular affiliations, the concern was lied about, ignored, reasoned away or swept under the rug and decorated with a lot of excuses and benefits. When I personally talked with a few members of churches who welcomed secular entertainment, I too, was given excuses. Former members of secular entertainment and civic groups have gone on record stating that the one true God is not worshiped as one reaches higher levels within Freemasonry and other similar groups. Conduct a search online and put "Christians sold out to the devil" in the search engines and you will find videos and pictures of entertainers giving hand signs and symbols showing their support to devil-worshipping groups. If anyone reading this, claims to be a Christ follower or openly loves the Lord, he or she should not take or participate in any blood oaths (Jesus already shed his blood on the cross), worship any statues or pledge one's life to a group while making ungodly promises to a brother or sisterhood. If you have already done this, confess your sin and repent. God tells us in his Bible, "You shall not bow down to them or worship them; for I, the Lord your God, am a jealous God, punishing the children for the sin of the fathers to the third and fourth generation of those who hate me…" (Exod. 20:5).

These wayward leaders in entertainment have been known to covertly send cleverly hidden messages in plain sight to their owners, investors, and astute followers within their brother or sisterhoods while receiving special favors (Eph. 5:11). You can find the meaning of some of these secular group's symbols and hand signs by researching the name of the suspected association along with selected keywords related to what you have noticed. You might even consider doing an extensive search for the church leader's name, the denomination, the group affiliation along with words like "former members," "exposed," and other related words. However, keep in mind that not all criticism is valid. Satan uses his demons to destroy the reputation of those who are sincerely called by God too, so always pray and listen to the Lord.

You may have seen peculiar hand signs, symbols on clothing, or noticed signals during conversation between church leadership and members, but didn't think too much about what you saw. It may seem unimportant to research such material, but some readers must understand that not only is the tongue lethal at times when it speaks, but there are times when it can't; therefore the signs, signals and symbols speak for many deceptive groups. Before you encourage a brother and sister to join a sect or speak praises about these secular and religious organizations, know the history, who runs them and what they represent behind the scenes. As mentioned in Chapter 2, there are organizational structures you see and those you don't. Every group has a public objective or mission statement, but then they have private goals. Everyone who says, "Lord, Lord" is not of the one true God.

So what is it about that tongue that keeps the Christian masses engaged and all-too-willing to fork over hard-earned dollars to local, national and international leaders? It is none other than God-talk. One creates a recipe based on one's interests. It goes something like this: appeal to the masses by sprinkling in a little God-speak, then add personal opinions as it relates to one's difficulties, throw in a little shouting, add music, a couple testimonials, and a money basket for the full affect. Your meal is ready, now go out there and serve it to the hungry crowd. This is how Satan's followers operate when they are in need of money, fame and power.

Hanegraff wrote a book entitled, *The Counterfeit Revival* in it he talks about church leaders who manipulate the masses and use revivals for selfish gain. One minister, who the author names in his book, warned those attendees at a revival who questioned the leadership's actions. Hanegraff writes, "Dramatically he gestured toward the crowd and warned them that those like me, who would dare question that what he was doing was of God, had committed the unpardonable sin and would not be forgiven in this world or the next." He went on, "...(The church leader) labeled his critics "idiots" and warned that they were about to experience either "riot or revival."'

Now some mainstream ministers will prostitute their spiritual gifts to arouse the masses. I have seen video where bold believers called out false prophets before congregations for doing such things. What usually happens after these false ministers have put on their shows, copycat ministers arise (you may have a few in your hometown who remind you of someone). Showing off spiritual gifts, acting, boasting or doing things specifically to get an emotional charge out of the public is not what Jesus was doing when he walked this earth! Now I understand that at times we all tend to get passionate when we are sharing something with someone, but there is intentional and unintentional emotion. Everything with false ministers is intentional. Many ministers have turned into entertainers who are paid by their sponsors to get television viewers and live crowds excited. Church attendees will watch the pastor scream, shout, and pray loudly. The more visitors turned club members, the more money. Once the ministers have a steady group of followers, they don't feel the need to entertain so much. In time, people begin to lessen their giving or stop giving altogether their tithes and offerings. So the minister has to come up with something else to keep the public interested from prayer cloths to classes. All the while, no one is truly being saved and delivered. The unsaved walk into the church and come out the same way, if not worse! God sees those who are just pretending and they will be judged. For further study, read: 2 Cor. 11:15; Rom. 2:6; and 2 Timothy (whole chapter).

Pharisees exist today as they did in the past and if you are winning souls for Christ, (maybe more than the local churches,) they might have a problem with you (John 4:1). Wicked teachers are judgmental, critical and even angry that God appoints the poor, the middle class, and those they consider have no class to spread the gospel; therefore, at times you may be harshly criticized (Matt. 15:11). "How can such people call themselves prophets, seers, teachers, apostles, and leaders and are not schooled? Why would anyone listen to that 'ghetto' minister? Who does she think she is telling people what to do when she is a mere woman?" Some of you reading this book have even asked God such questions of those who he has called to ministry and his response is no response.

There are consequences when you speak negatively about those who are genuinely called to perform God's will. According to the NIV Study Bible, Miriam mocked Moses and was stricken with leprosy. Korah and his followers led the people to rebel against Moses' leadership and they were later swallowed by the earth. You can find both of these stories in the Book of Numbers. Michal despised David praising the Lord; she remained childless (2 Sam. 6). Young people laughed at Elisha's baldness and were killed by bears (2 Kings 2). There are other examples, but you get the point. We all must watch what we say about those who are called to perform God's will.

Now in the Book of Proverbs we are provided with insightful wisdom about the tongue and what it should do and not do. It argues, lies, curses, belittles, and angers people, this we know. If you find yourself frequently doing such things, you have to question whether God is in fact using you to speak to the masses. At times we believe that God is moving us to do his will, when in fact he really wants us to sit down and be quiet for a time. I know for some of you reading this, to be quiet is hard to do especially since you feel spiritually empty when you are not doing anything for God's kingdom and have many followers dependent on you, but God shows us repeatedly in the Bible where for a time his chosen men and women did not speak and used that time for prayer, fasting and other things he has called them to do. He also doesn't want us leading men and women to us, but directing them to him. In time, the student becomes a teacher and will have no need of you. Like a child grows up, those who learn more of God and his ways, are eventually set apart and used to do things for his kingdom. This doesn't mean that those who consider you a mentor will stick around to help you. God advises us to, "Study to shew thyself approved unto God, a workman that needeth not to be ashamed, rightly dividing the word of truth" (2 Tim. 2:15). The more you study, the better equipped you are to fight a spiritual war when called upon.

As I write, I hear the Spirit saying, "You are one of the chosen, Reader, to embark on a new journey—one that was created and destined to be yours alone. You need not wait on man or woman to assist you when God has already given you the green-light to fulfill his mission. Those of you who are wondering, waiting, planning, and even escaping (like Jonah,) God wants you to move on your projects quickly, quickly, quickly! You have sat quiet long enough." Now when you begin to speak those things into existence, there will be those critics waiting to silence your tongue. They will tell you that, "You are a fool! I am not giving up anything else for your ministry! Are you sure God wants you to move now? I can't believe that you read that in a book? What do you think people will say?" When God is in the plan, who cares what man, woman or child thinks?

You have been so moved to do some things in the supernatural that the enemy will not want you to commit to anything. So your critics' intentions are to cause you to self-destruct, self-sabotage, and overall act selfishly. He doesn't want you to do anything that will build yourself and others up. He wants you to speak out of turn with God-appointed leadership in your life. Satan will cause emotional and physical discomfort with your own words; others' lies, and tempt you to compromise the truth. But you must rise up my friends from your seated position and say, "The devil is a liar and I will not be shaken by your criticism! Go away in the name of Jesus!" Some of you know the power of that name Jesus and I will discuss more about his name in a later chapter so that your spirit will be further uplifted.

At this point, I believe I should get somewhat personal with some of my readers. You may have been called to marry, become a parent, relocate, and do other things, but if you don't stand in the face of resistance and stop backing down due to one's negative words, you will unfortunately find yourself missing out on great opportunities spiritually. Remember there is our time and then there is God's time, which time schedule are you on? The next time someone asks you, "What time is it?" Say it's God's time! Do what God wills for your life and stop fighting! Overcome that critical tongue inside your head!

What Does Your Tongue Say About You?

"He who guards his lips guards his life, but he who speaks rashly will come to ruin" (Prov. 13:3). Oh how we are so quick to assume the worse in others. Someone doesn't make time to chat with you it must mean they are unfriendly. Someone doesn't say "thank you" or "please" when you think they should, then they are considered impolite. Someone doesn't bother to celebrate holidays, one assumes the person belongs to a cult, has mental issues or doesn't like people. Those little remarks about a person's demeanor or inaction, without knowing the facts, will cause them to mark you. It tells the discerning, "Keep away, this person is a busybody, a trouble-maker, a gossip…"

When one generally speaks about a topic, without being asked, he or she is usually already in a defensive position if you should question him or her about it. For instance, think about the following invented scenario for a minute, a woman decides to comment about her neighbor to her husband and before long the one doing the criticizing ends up being the criticized.

"I was just wondering about our neighbor," the busybody woman says. "She used to be so cordial, but these days she barely speaks. I wonder what's wrong with her."

Her husband questions, "Who cares? Is she bothering you?" Why is the neighbor's demeanor so important to this wife? There is no right or wrong in such a discussion—that is until one begins to act like an authority on what is a seemingly irrelevant subject matter. Unfortunately, it puts one at risk of being criticized. Notice what happens in the following dialogue.

"Well I know that other neighbors have noticed the same thing. I feel like maybe she is upset because she has no money to maintain the outside of her home. I guess I would be acting distant too."

Without the facts, why would anyone make an unfair assumption about her neighbor?

Her husband cautions, "Now honey, could it be that the woman simply doesn't want to be bothered? You don't know if she is acting distant because of her house. Don't start spreading gossip to your friends. You know you have a habit of doing that!"

You can clearly see from this example, the grandmother simply has too much time on her hands. "Oh don't you start! You are always running your mouth about the neighbors. Don't start acting self-righteous, you hypocrite! You have a lot of nerve!" the wife yells.

"Watch your tone…" the husband cautions.

We could go on and on with examples of how we have all used our tongues to insult others.

The high profile business person, entertainer or someone else with a large platform may use big words, boast about achievements, and share personal experiences and even talk with witnesses to attest that he is credible enough to manage others. However, upon closer inspection, the speaker will evilly scrutinize his followers, disrespect them before others, and leave them speechless with his backhand remarks. You might recall a situation like this where you felt like you were right and the other person was wrong, but when you thought more about the conversation, you either spoke too soon, too quickly, or too harshly. It's just better to remain quiet when attacked by a wicked mocker— some fools know that much. "Even a fool, when he holdeth his peace, is counted wise: and he that shutteth his lips is esteemed a man of understanding" (Prov. 17:28).

Godless Critics Not Interested in What God Has to Say

Now that you have taken a look back and possibly thought about a few people you know from these examples, let us look forward. Shall we see the light at the end of the tunnel? What might a godless or backsliding critical man or woman do to you that would keep you from fulfilling God's plan for your life? You should know by now, he will criticize your faith. He will nit-pick. He will create doubt. He will twist Scriptures. He will justify wrong-doing. He will say that you are mistaken to follow God and will encourage you to become more self reliant.

I must ask this question, to some of my readers; do you serve God or man? Seriously ask yourself this question again. Think about it. How many times have you listened, compromised, or kept "the peace" for men and women even when God wanted you to stand for truth? You may have ignored the Lord's voice and went along with people even when you were sick, depressed, angry, and more. You gave man or woman your money, time and body when all God wanted was you! You could have walked away from man, promised to talk to him another day, gave him less time, and gave God more, if only for a moment, but no, some of you gave man ALL and then you wonder why God is not pleased and why you are battling with feelings of unhappiness in your personal and professional relationships. Then there are those believers who will criticize God when men and women fail us.

"Why God did this happen? Didn't I serve you? I am so sorry I ever laid eyes on this person! What did I do Lord to deserve this?

Some wonder if God was even listening to their cries. They might doubt whether certain people were sincerely put in their lives. To all of that, the Holy Spirit asks, "Why were you disobedient? Why did you lie with man or woman when God was calling you to the dinner table to pray? Why couldn't you have stopped doing what you were doing long enough to see what God wanted?"

Some of you have seen the damage that a tongue can do in your lives. In Proverbs 15:4 (NIV), "The tongue that brings healing is a tree of life, but a deceitful tongue crushes the spirit." Men and women have died because of a tongue. There have been people in your own family who were put in jail over a tongue. You gave over your life to someone who you love because of your tongue. The tongue is more powerful than any other member of your body. It moves and shakes. It insults and takes. It loves and it hates. The tongue can build men, women and children up and in one voice tear them down. "The tongue also is a fire, a world of evil among the parts of the body. It corrupts the whole person, sets the whole course of his life on fire, and is itself set on fire by hell" (Jas. 3:6, NIV). What do you really know about your tongue? While you are studying your critic's tongue, study yours! A man or woman's worse enemy can be self. An inner critic who negatively comments about all that is wrong with "me, I, my…" When one dislikes self, it is very difficult for him or her to like others or yield to the Holy Spirit.

Are you sincerely building, creating, and strengthening others with your tongue? Do you find that when you are emotionally upset, you break other's down with your tongue? If so, stop it! Pay close attention to your words and then call on Jesus. It is better that Jesus come out your mouth than a curse word, for he will hear and bring peace to your situation.

When you see that you are not doing what you are called to do because your inner critic or a critical person has casted a dark shadow over your life with his or her words, ask the Lord to instruct you. Ask him to give you insight as to what is your next move? Face your issues. Find out what is keeping you from being obedient to the Lord and doing things that will bring out a better you, if this is your struggle. Resist the temptation to pity yourself. The only way that you can look beyond yourself is to begin to take action. Pray and fast until you are confident that God is indeed with you. Now when it comes to dealing with external critics, usually it doesn't involve confronting a critic unless he or she is determined to keep you away from your goals. If so, correct, rebuke and encourage—these should be the fruits on one's tongue. God's word should come forth if you trust in Him to provide you with wisdom. But if you don't, you will act just as evil, if not worse, as your critic, and who knows where your negative words might lead you? Don't blame God, blame your tongue.

You may have been in circles where all seemed to be going well until someone showed up with a long list of complaints, concerns and rebuttals for anyone who spoke up against his or her conversation. The offended yells, "I am entitled to my opinion! I'm not starting any trouble! So you think you are better than me?" This complainer is all-too-ready to give someone a good tongue lashing. You have a choice: waste time rebuking the fool, keep quiet, or walk away. Most likely, whatever you choose the critic will have something negative to say. It is useless to argue with a fool. "If a wise man contendeth with a foolish man, whether he rage or laugh, there is no rest" (Prov. 29:9). A fool's comprehension is like that of a child, he is lost in the conversation, troubled because he doesn't understand, nor is able to articulate his thoughts. He is untrustworthy with wisdom and will strike at someone over the slightest infraction.

The Christian's critic is lethal because he uses his tongue as a weapon not so much directed at the person, but to strike the Spirit behind the person. One should never grieve the Holy Spirit as warned in a previous chapter. But what some Christians do is use his or her religion in such a way that it attacks rather than uplifts. A seasoned believer might mouth off many Scriptures that insult those he or she may not be in agreement. She might bombard an enemy with all things deemed "Christian" (which many things are not) never bothering to wait on God to avenge. "If any man among you seem to be religious, and bridleth not his tongue, but deceiveth his own heart, this man's religion is vain" (Jas. 1:26).

Man doesn't understand, nor does he know what God has instilled in him. Nor is he able to justify wrong-doings in the presence of the Spirit; therefore why try? A man (or woman) makes his mistake with God when he decides that he knows more than God. He shoots the messengers of God with his bitter, careless tongue speaking. Whether he speaks in an unknown tongue or in his birth language, the ungodly man boasts and brags about what he knows while participating in utter foolishness. People wag their tongues at God like they do when conversing with one another apart from the Spirit. Understand there must be a reverence for God like what Moses displayed when God showed up in the burning bush. He listened and followed the Lord's instructions. "Then said the Lord to him, Put off thy shoes from thy feet: for the place where thou standest is holy ground" (Acts 7:33). Moses didn't stand there talking about whether what he heard was really the voice of God. Nor did he complain about taking his shoes off. But what would some believers and unsaved people have done in a situation like this? Find fault with what was taking place and talk about "I" like "What I want, what I don't want, and what I feel..." rather than listen to what God has to say.

The tongue-waggers believe that the louder they speak and the quicker they communicate their requests to the Lord, he will hear and act swiftly. Who is man that he should command the Spirit to react by saying things like "Right now...I command...Do it now?" A man with such a foolish disposition, a profile similar to that of a robber, a liar, and a cheat, and he commands his Father to act by use of one of the most vilest organs in his sinful body, the tongue? This is why we need to come in the name of Jesus, because only he can make a dirty tongue clean. Remember the tongue has killed, stolen and destroyed more homes, relationships, businesses, school systems, and more because man will not commit to God-appointed people or tasks. In addition, he compromises truth to get what he wants in life, and ignores the demands of the people. Then he wonders why, he is left without a job, an income, a companion, real friends, and more, because he doesn't know how to shut his own mouth long enough to hear the Spirit speak for him! He isn't disciplined enough spiritually to turn off the tongue-waggers on the TV screen, radio, Internet, or cell phone so that he may draw near to the Lord.

How do you view yourself? Is your tongue getting in the way of promotion? Is your tongue keeping you from achieving your goals? Is your tongue creating holes in your pockets? Is your tongue crucifying the flesh or giving it everything that it wants? How is your tongue operating these days? If you were given a piece of fruit and it was ripe, would you bite into it or would you just let it sit there and rot? The fruit that God has given us is meant to be shared, not put in a basket and left to rot. A tongue that ignores what is healthy is a sick tongue. Understand that God has had enough of the tongue wagging!

Know that God is doing great things in our lives presently and he needs to put some tongues in our families to silence prematurely, because for far too many years they have caused much destruction in our households from divorces to abortions. Wicked tongues have murdered dreams, demolished peaceful settings, cause believers to stumble, and brought relationships to utter ruin. The woman or man behind the tongue is ruthless—angry, bitter, and jealous! One's mouth rages like a lunatic. It uses curses to bury the lost. It refuses to be corrected in these last days. All words of wisdom are taken as insults. Say one thing about someone's child who is committing a wrong, and the tongue is ready to lash out at you. Say one thing to someone about not doing something they know they should be doing to help someone else, and the tongue is ready to argue. "God's children are guilty of this," says the Holy Spirit as I write. We have all suffered greatly behind our tongues.

Ask God for deliverance right now from your negative tongue speaking, I'm not referring to the prayer language that you use—although some readers must stop using it for show, says the Lord. Instead, use your tongue to pray when you violate God's precepts. Ask the heavenly Father to help you have more self-control over your mouth. If you can't resist saying something to someone, at least allow them to speak first. Do not be so quick to retaliate when your enemy or friend says something to you that you don't agree. Rather, take the opportunity and learn, grow from the criticism! Know that God is in the plan.

4. Study Your Enemy

Every enemy of my faith has known more about me than I have about them. There were times I didn't even know I had enemies until God showed me things about them that identified them as such. These people anticipated what I might say and do before I did them. Some have come as a brother or sister supposedly walking in the light, but are really in darkness. The Bible specifically tells us how we can identify our adversaries, "In this the children of God are manifest, and the children of the devil: whosoever doeth not righteousness is not of God, neither he that loveth not his brother," (John 3:10). You may wonder what exactly defines a child of God, "Yet to all who received him, to those who believed in his name, he gave the right to become children of God…" (John 3:10). Those that accept Jesus are children of God.

I have observed my critics and I have listened to them create fantastic stories right before my eyes and not blink. I think of the following passage of Scripture, "You belong to your father, the devil, and you want to carry out your father's desire. He was a murderer from the beginning, not holding to the truth, for there is no truth in him. When he lies, he speaks his native language, for he is a liar and the father of lies," (John 8:44). I have heard from some so-called believers who say, "I am a child of God," yet when you mention the things of God, one's face frowns followed by a quick retort, "But I pray...I know the Lord, I walk with Jesus." Test the spirits long enough and you will find out that they are liars. They love self more than they will ever love God or his people.

Some hypocrites will successfully get away with lies with some listeners. It isn't until you make the time to study them that you can see through their false fronts. God knows the hearts of men. After careful study, I discovered that some standing in my presence were nothing more than manipulators, backstabbers, liars, thieves, mean-spiritcd, uncompassionate, jealous, greedy, unforgiving, vengeful, and many other characteristics described in my book *Face Your Foe: 28 Critics of Your Faith You Can Overcome*. I would know about this subject matter, because some of these traits talked about in the book, I could identify with since I demonstrated them more so before I got saved sanctified, and Holy Ghost filled. Now I have to fight the temptation to go back to my old, ugly ways.

I know critical people who never want to be confronted on a wrong. They prefer I do the following: pretend that I didn't see what I saw, believe that I was mistaken or had amnesia, or sit down and be quiet while they attempt to convince me that all is right with them and everything is wrong with me. You may have noticed in our society there is an extreme movement to blur the lines between good and evil and the enemy has used many church leaders to ensure that the goals of his plans will be accomplished. Think twice the next time you see or hear a minister rationalize why something that goes against Scripture is perfectly okay. Also, take a close look at the Bible he is preaching out of, chances are it isn't a King James Version. Many present editions of the Bible have been edited, rewritten or omitted text. I encourage you to purchase books that expose the discrepancies in modern bibles.

As a believer in Christ, you must anticipate that a critic who is hurting on the inside will hurt you. A sinful person just doesn't become this way, he or she molds his or herself into one by continuing to sin despite all sound advice. Foes of the faith will sit back and contemplate how they are going to get what they want, when they want, and how they want it. Maybe they want money, power, fame, a partner in crime, or maybe they have it all, but they just enjoy watching others suffer. Whatever the reason, we must remember no enemy of God loves us. They may enjoy what you do for them as mentioned in other chapters such as: gifts you give, the time you spend with them (as long as it's convenient,) and the way you style your hair, and dress your body. However, these trivial things mean nothing when an enemy is focused on achieving his or her objectives to hurt or do away with you once you have upset him or her with your spiritual conversations.

Red Flags

An enemy of your faith will provide you with signs that he or she isn't interested in you or your belief system. Seven red flag signs often used include:

1. Walk away when you begin talking about Jesus, God and the Holy Spirit.

2. Act defensive or possibly aggressive when you are responding to their criticism about the Word of God. They might also recruit and support someone else who may be against you as well.

3. Refuse to show respect when you ask the critic to stop saying and doing things that hurt you emotionally and physically.

4. Tell lies, exaggerating, being loud, or doing other similar behavior for attention.

5. Participate in destructive activities to hurt you or those you love.

6. Create distractions to keep you from serving the Lord especially during times of fasting.

7. Cause unnecessary confusion or debate when you are trying to assist someone.

One who is sincerely concerned about you will encourage you to stick with positive people and things. However, one who isn't in support of your faith will often ignore, ridicule, lie, insult, or do the kinds of things to sway you from fulfilling your higher calling in Christ. Notice, I didn't say fulfill the profession that man or woman has planned for your life. Men and women's plans are usually focused on selfish desires ie.) more money, but the one true God's plans are centered on obedience to his will (such as using one's position to spread the gospel of Christ), not to worship human beings. Judgmental people will not move you to be the best you can be when they are working for the enemy. Some individuals, who are sold out to anti-Christ doctrines will not consider messages that conflict with their dark, witchcraft-inspired paths; rather they will ignore your teaching, preaching and gifts while attempting to get you to follow them. Out of frustration, some Christians will fight back by prematurely going into areas and destroying people and things that God didn't authorize them to do. This is why some people have no interest in spiritual things because of zealous Christians that start wars that they don't have the means to win.

You must not ignore the red flags that alert you to an enemy in your camp. Watch as well as pray when you see old and new individuals in your life falling away from the Lord. When you are being criticized by your foe for calling them back to Christ, avoid the temptation to defend actions you know full well God has called you to do. The enemy just loves to anger Christians and get them to doubt that they have sincerely heard from the Lord.

Some fault finders want to be leaders, but they don't want to participate in the kinds of activities that put them in servant positions. When this happens, you have double-minded, wayward, selfish individuals who appear to walk in the light and do things that appear godly just so that they can achieve certain titles. I explain further in my book, *Face Your Foe: 28 Critics of Your Faith You Can Overcome.* As we all know, selfish individuals are only concerned about self. Some have the mindset that as long as you flatter me by saying and doing the kinds of things that make me feel comfortable and happy, I might help you. But if you don't, as I said in other sections of this book, they will attack. These godless leaders are critical of Christians and will use their influence to attack anyone who questions their authority. Before allowing yourself to fully trust someone with your money, mind, children, property, and other important things, ask yourself, "Who is this person who stands before me, really? Is this someone who I can trust when the going gets rough?" Look beyond the smile, title, business connections, and material wealth.

I recall times in my life where I was approached by men and women trying to get me involved in business ventures "in Jesus name." They felt like I would be more likely to join because they believed in God. When I didn't join their groups or didn't perform in a couple as well as they thought I should, there was no talk about praying for me or assisting me in such a way so that I could be as successful as they. Instead, they talked negatively about me to others and put unnecessary pressure on me to meet goals despite my lack of contacts, transportation and tools. Like the man who was beaten up on the side of the road and left for dead, I had to look toward Good Samaritans to rescue me out of ridiculous situations that were literally robbing me of my time, money and patience.

There are always those opinionated, bold types in most circles who use their platforms to berate others; however, choose to be one of the silent types, if you are in these circles during those challenging times when no one is open to receiving your personal opinion on a matter. Rather, seek the Lord.

If you recall, Job was put to the test in many ways in the Bible. For a time, even Job's friends came to him and shared their personal opinions that didn't uplift him. But in time, when his three friends noticed his great suffering, they didn't speak anymore. In Job 2:13 (NIV), "…they sat on the ground with him for seven days and seven nights. No one said a word to him…" Some readers must remember this passage of Scripture when one is grieving over a loss whether it is of a relative, job, game, or something else, your opinion is irrelevant during trying times. Avoid the temptation to say what's on your mind. If you must verbalize your concern, do it with those you trust. But stay quiet around those who are upset. Some loud mouth, unkind critics will spend much time talking about others while puffing their selves up. "I remember when I lost my mother, but I got over it…I know how you feel, I once lost a game and I didn't cry about it…It must be terrible losing a job, you should have listened to me years back because I could have got you a job with another company." Does any of these statements sound like someone comforting the griever?

Observe the critics' evil ways. Determine whether this person is indeed friend or foe. Critics will boldly share their feelings about various subjects even if they are less than knowledgeable. Some will communicate their concerns politely while others rudely. Foolish critics don't typically reveal much about themselves unless they can paint a pretty picture that appears as if they are wise. They may talk about a highlight in their lives, yet stay away from topics that might make them look like failures. If the critic is more successful than the listener, at some point in the conversation he will boast about how he is qualified to share his less than uplifting opinion with his protégé. If she is older and considers herself mature, she will say things that seem like they are helpful, but after putting her advice to the test, the student will quickly learn that she is no more than an old fool. If God has sincerely used a certain critic to assist or mentor you in your life goals, you will know by his or her fruit. People, who are not appointed to serve you, will not say and do things that will motivate you to be obedient to God; rather they will gradually direct you toward the evil one. But sometimes, we allow these people in our lives knowing they are not mentally or physically healthy for us. We might even be jealous of what they have, but in Proverbs 24:1-2 (NIV), "Do not envy wicked men, do not desire their company; for their hearts plot violence, and their lips talk about making trouble." Think of the many men and women who have been found guilty in a court of law for lying, torturing, murdering, and destroying others' reputations for all sorts of things including money, yet believers befriended them anyway.

A number of critics will tell false stories and enlist the help of bystanders to validate their stories. In Exodus 23:1 (NIV) God's law cautions, "Do not spread false reports. Do not help a wicked man by being a malicious witness." People like this can be found in the world and in the church. For example, there are some leaders who expect loyal church members to share embellished stories with their audiences so that they can receive more donations during Saturday and Sunday services.

Good Times Don't Last

You may have met sinful people in your life that fit all the signs discussed in this book, yet they are still fun to be around. Your relationships with sinners may have had ups and downs. You might have convinced yourself that they wouldn't cause problems in your walk with God because they "know me and I don't play." Enough with the tough talk, the enemy doesn't care about how strong, bad, dangerous, or what kind of anointing and influence a man or woman thinks he or she might have. When an enemy is offended by someone, especially one who is walking with God, he or she won't stop evil ways. The devil is using this person in the hopes to undermine God's plan—you are a part of God's plan! If we are honest with ourselves, we know that the Lord has repeatedly warned us about a particular nefarious individual's actions in our circles, but we reason that this person is "cool" and "they wouldn't hurt a flea," so what happens? God will let the enemy go ahead and have his way with us for a season until we take the rose-colored glasses off and see the truth about someone or a group.

God may have showed you things in the spiritual realm recently where there is no denying the truth! But like old shoes, you just can't seem to let certain people go for one reason or another. Good times with harsh critics never last! Today you are laughing, but tomorrow you might be yelling or crying about something they said. If God's wrath has been rendered upon a backslider or unsaved person right now, think about this, you might be spending your personal time with a person God hasn't called you to communicate with or be around! Without God in the plan, the wayward in the faith or lost just might corrupt you if you aren't strong in Christ. Avoid intimate conversation with an enemy. I think of the following Scripture, "Be not deceived: evil communications corrupt good manners" (I Cor. 15:33). God's wrath might be due to come upon the pagan, but you, Believer who isn't obedient to the Spirit, just might experience it too! You've heard the old adage, "Wrong place at the wrong time." You don't want to be at the wrong place at the wrong time with a person God intends to give a life-changing spanking. Remind yourself to pray before considering a loud mouth critic or negative person as a friend.

I recall a time when co-workers warned me about someone we worked with being "a problem" and "don't trust her." In time, the woman befriended me. Later, I learned that she was a backstabber and liar. She attempted to paint a negative picture about me, because she was jealous of some of my accomplishments at the workplace. After telling her some of what I noticed about her, she made up some excuses. I quickly cut off all communication with her.

Traitors

The late reverend, author and civil rights leader Martin Luther King Jr. said once, "In the end, we will remember not the words of our enemies, but the silence of our friends." It's not just what someone says about you, but also what they don't say about you that could possibly make a difference on how a challenging group or difficult person views you. You will know whether a person sincerely is supportive of you by what they don't do as well as what they do for you.

A critic that negatively talks about you behind your back, shares your information with an enemy and conspires with others who don't like you is a traitor. We see examples of this sort of behavior on many television shows. Judas exhibited these characteristics when he sold out Jesus. Your enemy may offer his or her opinion about your life's decisions and appear supportive to your face, but if he or she has a grievance with you, this person will take your information back to others and include his or her negative spin on it. Not only do you have a critic who is against you, but this person will recruit others not to like you. Some people might fall for his or her trick while others won't. Righteous advisors will be the ones who might warn you, as God leads, to keep away from certain individuals. I say might, because sometimes God doesn't always send someone to assist us, because he knows we don't always listen when God provides his help—for some of us we have to learn the hard way. For some believers, rather than accept warnings about an enemy from the good-hearted, they become defensive and will talk about "how they don't want your advice, need your help…" But when they are burned by an enemy, they will wish they had listened. If Christians have grievances between one another in 1 Corinthians 6:1 we are asked this question, "If any of you has a dispute with another, dare he take it before the ungodly for judgment instead of before the saints?" Avoid the temptation to take on the traitor role when a fellow believer has upset you.

Do-Good Liars

You might have decided to do something significant to help a brother or sister in Christ, but your critic will not keep his or her opinion about your servant-hood to his or herself especially if it might negatively impact the way others view you. Do-Good liars, a phrase I thought of while writing this book, will pretend as if they mean you well and talk about how good you are or how good they are, but their hearts are filled with false feelings, lies and exaggerations. For example, a Do-Good Liar will attempt to talk you out of doing something that you might feel led to do by the Holy Spirit. "I'm just trying to help…I think you are so talented and I just can't see God telling you to do that!" Whether this person believes the person he or she is talking to is talented or not, he will say it just so that it appears as if he means her well.

Do-Good Liars always want to look like the good guys and will quickly accuse others of being liars so that no one suspects their weaknesses. They do good in order to make themselves feel good about lies told and feelings hurt as a result. They encourage talk about a partner, children, a boss or someone else because conversations like these deflect from who they really are spiritually. For example, I have heard these type say things like, "Oh I just love my wife she is a blessing to me. My children are a joy. I wouldn't mind helping you on that project." Later, you hear the wife had left him and the children are disobedient and often in trouble. When these liars refuse to admit their challenges before the Lord and change their evil ways, they will use others' challenges to appear as if they are better. Some of us have been guilty of this sort of behavior. These Do-Good Liars will not keep one's spiritual experiences to themselves, because they need something to talk about to throw others off. They may even go so far as to exaggerate situations so that they look like they had something to do with encouraging someone, assisting the church leadership, helping with family matters, or financially assisting the needy even if their efforts were less than satisfactory or not altogether true. When the liar is exposed, he or she becomes very critical of those he once praised. Usually this liar has a long history of confrontations with others and personal problems. People usually have to fix what the pretender has torn down as a result of his or her mouth.

Watch for these critical do-good liar types who know much about nothing. They share information that usually has nothing to do with the topic at hand and when told that their idea is not good or their way is unacceptable, they become irate especially if they aren't mentally stable. Don't be so quick to trust them with your personal information. They can be helpful, but also very mean-spirited over the slightest offense and will use what you share in confidence in order to avenge themselves.

When you take the time to study your enemy, note your findings and pray. You will save yourself a lot of future heartache if you trust in Jesus and not in your feelings. Emotions change like the wind and will trick you into believing things about people based on what you see, hear or even eat that aren't altogether true. Think of how many people falsely trusted in people just because they were in a nice environment were fed well. Individuals, who don't love nor respect the Lord, always leave clues. It is up to you to take notice and thank your Creator for giving you insight as to whether a person means you well or not. Closing your eyes to your enemy, in some cases, just might cost you the following: your peace of mind, anointing, wealth, time or even worse, your life!

5. Wicked Critic's Strategies

Make a backsliding or unsaved critic uncomfortable by your convicting admonition, request, or statement, and now you have just made yourself an instant enemy with some people! It doesn't matter if you were polite, had good intentions, or sincerely wanted to help this person, he or she has already formulated an opinion about you and it isn't good. "What is she up to…I don't like her kind…They all make me sick, Christians!"

People don't want to feel they have done something wrong even when they know they are in the wrong! The offended will create in his or her mind, an offensive plan to get you the next time, before you get him or her again. This is how the unwise operate, like children with their parents, angry because someone advised them to stop doing a disruptive or destructive behavior.

You might encourage yourself and justify your actions when it comes to talking to people about God, "I know that He uses me. I only tried to help this person... Ain't no devil going to run me away!" But meanwhile your own feelings begin to take an ugly turn the more you see that one who has been offended by you. The devil shows up in your atmosphere trying to mess with your emotions! He is all-too ready to use man, woman or child to get on that one weak nerve. "Please Lord, keep me from hurting this man, woman or child with MY MOUTH! Why does he take my good and use it for evil!" you might say. Do you recall a moment like this not too long ago where you had to control your emotions after someone said or did something that almost made you lose your religion? Everything within, started to churn, you said something like, "But God, oh…but God…I know he's just mad…she doesn't like me because I'm right most of the time…you know that old me would have done this and said that…" Sure, you could have done a lot of things, but you didn't. You won that time by forfeiting the battle, but what about the next one?

Be prepared for what is in store for the future when dealing with people who can dish criticism, but can't take it. Your offended relative, child, or co-worker is going to search for that opportunity to launch his or her attack when you least expect it. In the meantime, you might as well feed your belly, get a good night rest, limit your phone conversations, and stay close to God, because at a moment's notice, the offended will side with Satan to rob you of your peace and joy when you least expect it. He will move on your loved one to pick out a strategy that will best suit his or her goals when you are weak. It is surprising, how we human beings can react so terribly to one another when we are the following: tired, hungry, stressed, and distant from God. Some of us act like complete fools! We start seeing things that aren't there, yelling about things that are meaningless, and ready to hurt somebody because our flesh is in need of something that we have put off. When any of these things happen, the enemy is going to put his plan in motion.

In this chapter, I share with you some of the enemy's strategies I experienced and witnessed others go through to get a believer in Christ off his or her walk with God. Of course, all tactics can't be listed, because the book would be far too long, but many of the common ones we face are listed. Prophets, ministers and other teachers of the faith, you are welcome to teach and preach about these strategies. I provide more detail about personality types behind the strategies in *Face Your Foe: 28 Critics of Your Faith You Can Overcome.*

As I have mentioned in an earlier chapter, I realized there will be those readers, who will not believe that a supernatural enemy with many names exists in their circles. Nor, will they believe that this enemy has the capability to tempt men, women, children, and animals to do evil things; however, in spite of one's assumption that it's all a myth, know the enemy that I have spoken about throughout this book is very real. But let me remind you, "For God hath not given us a spirit of fear, but of power and of a sound mind" (2 Tim. 1:7). You can't fight a spiritual war if you know nothing about the enemy! Had I took my own advice, many years ago, I could have saved myself a lot of regret for having made some foolish decisions in my life. I would have known about deceptive enemy schemes and been better prepared had I not been so fearful of the devil, his literature and his workers. If it wasn't for God's mercy, I would not be alive today to write this book.

Some readers, who aren't convinced that an enemy exists, must also study why God would warn his followers about things like: witchcraft, divination, mediums, spiritualists, and other occult related things if there is no evil entity. If these mysterious works aren't harmful and influenced by a demonic presence, then why would God bother to tell believers to keep away from them?

There are also those reprobate minds, faithless and free thinking skeptics in our society that will fight about why they believe God doesn't exist or isn't concerned about our lives, but when you say, "The devil…" some will acknowledge his existence and believe he has a hand in their successes. I found in my experiences with people, who have such a reverence for Satan, that they usually consider themselves to be their own gods and do not give the devil his credit. These individuals are not interested in acknowledging a Creator who would denounce their selfish lifestyles and do not believe that the devil would help them destroy their or others' lives.

Just because one does not feel he or she has had a personal encounter with the one true God, angels or Satan and his demons in this life, doesn't mean that these entities do not exist! According to Ephesians 6:12 in the Holy Bible, "For we wrestle not against flesh and blood, but against principalities, against powers, against the rulers of the darkness of this world, against spiritual wickedness in high places."

Think of the times when no one could give you a satisfying explanation for an evil committed against you. What about those times when you felt an unexplainable "something" occurred in your life. Just on those experiences alone, one should desire to ask the one true God to assist him or her in sorting out some of those personal experiences from the supernatural ones; rather than, putting them all away and calling them, "Nothing" or "Coincidence." But that's what typically happens with some people, and because they don't bother to get further understanding about their spiritual experiences with the Creator, they are critical of others' faith. Even if one doesn't recognize a personal experience with the one true God and an evil entity, he or she can still do the following: turn on the television news, connect to the Internet, leaf through magazines and newspapers, view disturbing faces, watch for odd symbolism on clothing and bodies, listen for strange word phrases, and more that prove something good as well as evil does exist in this world! Yet, if one is desensitized to both righteousness and wickedness and has never been taught what is good or evil, then this person will be unable to see or feel either—no matter how much you point out what's right or wrong to them. During these last days, we are warned in Isaiah 5:20. "Woe unto them that call evil good, and good evil; that put darkness for light, and light for darkness; that put bitter for sweet, and sweet for bitter!"

So how do we combat this enemy who I call, "The Christian's Critic?" We must, "Put on the whole armor of God that ye may be able to stand against the wiles of the devil..." Ephesians 6:11. I further explain this Scripture in a later chapter as it relates to fighting a spiritual battle with our critical adversary.

Believers should avoid taking instruction from pessimistic, backsliding or unsaved critics as mentioned in other places in this book; rather go to God with your concerns! Seasoned believers know if a new believer should turn away from the Lord, so soon after declaring his or her belief in him, chances are, this person may have wicked critics around him or her providing words of discouragement. If we can see this in others, surely we can see this same thing occurring in our circles. Mature Christians would not encourage new believers to have intimate relationships with the carnal minded. They would not advise a babe in Christ to permit worldly influences to dominate one's mind. Those of us, who are guilty of having wicked people in our circles, should not shoot the Christ messenger with our words for warning us of wrong behaviors. Instead, make changes and do what is right!

There are many churches that have programs in place to keep believers interested in God's Word and will often invite Christians to special events and Bible studies. The church hopes believers will not desire to return to their former lifestyles. Yet, many of these church worship services (particularly the large ones) and biblical classes, do not equip the saints with the kind of study that can be used to fight Satan and his demons. Instead, some group meetings are designed to keep one dependent on the leadership while evoking demonic spirits. If one is focused on weak leadership, how can he or she be listening to what the Spirit says when he calls? Is he or she going to answer God with, "I have to check with my pastor?" The church may be doing some nice things, but are the saints really equipped? "So then because thou art lukewarm, and neither cold nor hot, I will spue thee out of my mouth" (Rev. 3:16).

The focus at these "lukewarm" churches is placed on biblical stories that may or may not relate to one's present spiritual condition. Eventually, some new believers feel at a lost and will then lose interest in studying the Word of God. If no one is guiding babes in Christ to passages of Scripture that teach them how to crucify the flesh, learn more about the Holy Ghost, bind the enemy, or walk and talk like Jesus, how will they know what to do when the enemy tempts them? The church must take the time to meet the people where they are! It's unfortunate, but in time, for some new saints, church fellowship becomes routine, members appear increasingly judgmental, and God seems distant in a building supposedly consecrated to Him.

So in the forthcoming sections of this book I will share popular strategies used by saints and sinners who are doing more listening to self and others (like demonic entities); rather than the one true God. Those critics of your faith will attempt to knock you off your journey toward your high calling simply because they know that you will do the following: be a threat to their operations, impact their wayward lifestyles, and possibly win them to the Lord. None of which Satan wants to happen so he will motivate the atheist, agnostic, backslider, and other worldly individuals to perform wicked strategies to cause you to lose interest in the Father, Son and Holy Ghost. The Holy Spirit's job is to convict men and women of their sins. Jesus said prior to going to be with his Father about the Holy Spirit, "When he comes, he will convict the world of guilt in regard to sin and righteousness and judgment: in regard to sin, because men do not believe in me; in regard to righteousness, because I am going to the Father, where you can see me no longer; and in regard to judgment, because the prince of this world now stands condemned" (John 16:8-11, NIV). As you read these forthcoming chapters, you may recognize people you know. Recognize that God doesn't want you to sound the alarm on these individuals, at least not yet anyway, until you learn more about them. In my book, *Face Your Foe: 28 Critics of Your Faith You Can Overcome* you will get further insight on defining each personality and how to approach people who use such strategies.

Oftentimes when preparing for battle, prayer warriors must not give the slightest warning to people in their circles that they know who their enemies are. This is what I mean by "flying under the radar" as mentioned in a previous chapter. By revealing what you know prematurely, you could be putting yourself and others at risk of further emotional harm and physical abuse. Notice in Genesis 42:7, Joseph didn't reveal his identity to his brothers right away. Remember his own relatives had thrown him in a pit when he was a child, so he had to be cautious and trust in the Lord's guidance. "As soon as Joseph saw his brothers, he recognized them, but he pretended to be a stranger and spoke harshly to them. 'Where do you come from?' he asked."

During one of my prayer times, I heard the Spirit say that there are Christians who are called to "fly under the radar." A term used when one is flying an aircraft without detection by air traffic control. In God's kingdom, you are flying under the radar at different times so that the enemy can't detect you right away. It isn't in any Christian's best interest to brag to the world that he or she is in Christ. Nor does this person want to reveal God's intentions to anyone unless he or she is called to do so. If the Lord does move on one to share spiritual knowledge, you must be wise when doing it and focused on listening to the Lord—much prayer and fasting will help you receive a Word from our Creator.

So what might the rebellious critic do to get to know you? How might he or she attempt to conquer you before God intervenes? A listing of your enemies' wicked strategies follows.

1) Achieve Your Trust

There was a time that I would have never considered anyone I know a personal foe. But once I accepted Jesus into my life, that all changed! I saw things in people I had never saw before. They actually were disappointed that I didn't remain my devilish self. They didn't want me to come up higher unless money was involved. These secular critics were conditioned to believe that God doesn't take you out of the limelight and place you in the backroom, that he doesn't rearrange your life in such a way that makes you less than the world's definition of success, and he wouldn't, couldn't or any other "not" according to their views. But we see God doing many things in the Bible that isn't politically correct, not deemed successful, beautiful, or wonderful by today's standards, right? Therefore, in order for an earthly minded critic to get you to listen to him or her while attempting to keep you from the Word of God, he or she has to put his or her spin on the Scriptures along with his or her personal phrases of disappointment to make you feel guilty about walking the righteous life. Your unspiritual critic can't get away with such things unless you trust in his or her personal opinions. Remember the unsaved or lost person's view of God is usually biased and centered on childhood rebellion, mental dysfunction, past failures, anger, bitterness, and selfishness.

Think about a time when a stranger approached you on the street, while riding a bus or plane and he or she made you feel comfortable whether in the natural or supernatural world. This person reminded you of someone. But it wasn't long before your "gut feeling" warned, "You don't know her, so why are you telling her so much about yourself? This spirit is not who you think it is." I guess those inner alarms wouldn't sound off if in fact the person or spirit we were communicating with was a child of God, right? Keep in mind, the devil will also use similar warnings to keep you from listening to God's appointed messengers.

The enemy may know your name, know a secret from childhood, and could even tell you what you are going to do in the next five minutes without you telling him or her, but just because this person knows a little or a lot of information about you, doesn't mean you should drop your guard, and it definitely doesn't mean that this person or spiritual entity is a friend whether seen or unseen. Remember people can easily check the Internet nowadays and find out about you without help from God or Satan.

Eventually, this stranger says something that leaves you feeling uneasy. He or she may even boldly criticize you about something you may have shared. What do some Christians do when listening to one's criticism? Feel angry and wish they never said anything to people about spiritual things. Now and then wicked critics will act helpful and offer to assist us when we are stressed, grieving, or have some difficult challenges we are facing in our lives. These people may suggest using various kinds of worldly meditation and visualization techniques. They may even offer to help us with our children, household or events. Know the difference between one being used by God and one who isn't. It is only a matter of time that those individuals used by the enemy will show who they really are causing more harm than good. For instance, a loved one has recently died. One who doesn't respect God or follow his precepts may suggest seeking a spiritualist, medium or witch to learn more about the deceased. In 1 Samuel 28, Saul, who could no longer hear from the Lord, did just that and he was upset about the information he received. He wanted to know what to do to win a war against an enemy. Rather than listen to the prophet, Samuel, while he was alive, he consulted with him in death. Saul learned that both he and his sons would die. You may have noticed in your own life how easy it is for the Christian to fall into the temptation of participating in divination, sorcery, witchcraft, and other dark magic—these are all things that God prohibits. (See Lev. 19:31, 20:6, 27 and Deut. 18:9-14). Wicked critics who don't respect God or his warnings will be used by the enemy to get you to fall away from the Lord.

Now maybe this person isn't into the occult, but simply suggests you drink alcohol or do drugs to get over your grief, you should know that this person is definitely not one who is sold out for God, common sense would say, "Keep away!" Before long, a simple offer to drink and share how you feel, might end up causing one to do something he or she later regrets. Once the enemy has gained your trust, he or she knows that you are open to doing whatever the individual wants whether good, bad or otherwise.

2) Make an Offer You Won't Refuse

When critics are in the wrong, they must save face. So they will say some things hoping to make wrongs right. How about an offer that you can't refuse for starters? There is no enemy who desires to get something from you that will not offer you something in return particularly when they know you don't trust him or her. Even the Messiah was put in tempting circumstances. "Then was Jesus led up of the Spirit into the wilderness to be tempted of the devil" (Matt. 4:1). I think of leaders in ministries who go out of their way to help people. But I also think of those who do good things only so that they can make those uncomfortable feelings of acting sinful (behind closed doors) go away. They use tactics while acting critical of others to deflect from their own personal weaknesses.

On occasion the worldly minded critic provides his or her tempting offers in the hopes that a Christian might change his or her mind on an issue or keep the believer around to be used for a time to better him or her. The naughty critic will even attempt to get the upper-hand on a situation by using flattery and unconstructive criticism of God's appointed so that the attention is no longer placed on the critic's evil ways. So the naysayer reasons, "If I tell him I am going to give him something, maybe he will leave me alone about what I said...If I tell her I would do this thing for her, maybe she won't get back at me for what I said." For some people, they never recover from critical words. "Reckless words pierce like a sword, but the tongue of the wise brings healing" (Prov. 12:18). This is why we must be mindful of what we say to both the spiritual and unspiritual.

3) Lay a Trap

A hunter can't catch his prey without a trap, the same holds true of the devil. In order for him to convince you to do wrong, besides making an offer, he also plans what trap he will use to get you and keep you in his grip. The Bible confirms this in 2 Timothy 2:26, "And that they may recover themselves out of the snare of the devil, who are taken captive by him at his will." People lay traps daily from using telephone recording devices to hiring private detectives. Think of this scenario, a backslider wants you to go out to a nightclub, but you are busily working on something else. How does he pull you away from your work? How does he get you to fall for a trap without you knowing that you fell for a trap? Our adversary appeals to our senses—that old carnal nature, he tries to make you feel good by saying and doing something that you like. "You are always working, take a break. You don't make a lot of money at what you do, try doing this..." he says. Once this psychopath (that's what most wicked critics are) lays his trap, he will then take what he wants and then on to the next one. If you have already fell in one of Satan's traps, then confess your sins before the Lord in Jesus name and repent. Also, forgive your enemy, and refrain from doing the kind of things again that grieve the Holy Spirit.

4) Look for Trouble

You may wonder why some individuals would look to make trouble with you. I would have to answer, because some people can't live without drama. When times are peaceful and quiet, they don't know what to do with themselves.

How many times have you heard someone say, "I just wanted to have a good time but then…I didn't think anything would happen…I was doing my own thing when…" As mentioned before, when someone hasn't overcome something that is bothering them, they look for others to hurt. The Bible warns us to, "Be sober, be vigilant; because your adversary the devil, as a roaring lion, walketh about, seeking whom he may devour…" (1 Pet. 5:8). Think about this, what do lions do when they are hungry? They roam, seek prey, and then wait for the opportune time to strike. If any animals should attempt to feast on the lion's meal, the lion will roar and most likely turn on them. You might be one of the good guys trying to take what's left of a broken person who is still in Satan's grip, if so, our enemy will not let go without scaring you with words first, keep going around him, and he will orchestrate his physical attack.

Whatever you do, don't give into temptations. They hold your mind and body in captivity especially if you have an addiction. Should you fall into sin, then you won't have enough strength mentally and physically to oppose the offending critic when he or she strikes again.

5) Provoke You to Anger

Whether you become angry at the one tempting you to do wrong or angry about something else, the point is the critic is distracting you from whatever God has willed for you to do. Occasionally we get ourselves into trouble by socializing with angry unbelievers in an intimate way. "What harmony is there between Christ and Belial? What does a believer have in common with an unbeliever?" (2 Cor. 6:15, NIV).

A person who is emotional about something will not focus on enemy strategies; instead, he will be more concerned about how someone or something has negatively impacted him. The Holy Scripture reads, "Be ye angry, and sin not: let not the sun go down upon your wrath: Neither give place to the devil" (Eph. 4:26-27).

6) Prey on the Novice

Many people falsely assume that Satan won't use a fellow believer, baby, child or senior citizen to perform his work particularly one who works for the Lord. As mentioned in an earlier chapter, children and adults can be programmed to commit despicable acts on others. We are all susceptible to being used by the devil especially those who should know better. In 1 Timothy 3:4-7, there are specific instructions on the kind of people who should be leading the church, "One that ruleth well his own house, having his children in subjection with all gravity… Not a novice, lest being lifted up with pride he fall into the condemnation of the devil…" The enemy fattens his prey with flattery then slaughters him when he's not looking. Too many immature people who don't have their flesh under subjection are: leading youth, babysitting children, and teaching groups; therefore, they are easy prey for the devil and his demons to attack psychologically and physically. Therefore weak-minded followers are taken captive by everything from sexual abuse to illegal activities by them.

7) Tempt You Again

Although you may have been tested by a critic in the past, and stood strong like Jesus, it doesn't mean that the devil will not return. We know this to be true in Luke 4 which was mentioned in an earlier chapter. The key is to stay guarded every time someone or group comes around with an offer, a question, a favor, a gift, etc. it doesn't matter if the person is saved, sanctified and Holy Ghost filled. Just like you prayed before you opened this book, pray before you pick up that cell phone, turn on your computer to check your email, and other things you do. God isn't through with you and neither is the enemy.

8) Pretend to Love You

Have you ever watched critical people act like they love others? Notice how they behave with those they really like and those they don't. The smile isn't right. Comments lack substance. Eyes wander around. These people are quick with their responses and short-tempered. But they have to keep up the act, don't they? Critics who pretend to love others will appear kind and do favors before they unveil who they really are. By the time they are done giving you everything they think you want or need, you are indebted to them.

Many celebrities act like they love their fans. But if you see or hear them off camera, you probably wouldn't like some of these people anymore. You can uncover some interesting information about a number of these pretenders if you dig for the unflattering news instead of accepting whatever mainstream media allows you to see.

A follower of Lucifer (Satan) told me that you can attract a bee to honey. He read Satanic books that provided him with tactics where he could persuade others to serve him. This Satanic follower, who believed him self to be his own god, was very eloquent and kind when he wanted someone to do something for him. You would never suspect in a million years he followed Satan and had little, if any, love for people. We often assume people who claim to love God will also love their fellow brothers and sisters in Christ. God knows the heart, ask him to reveal whether that one who you are about to trust your money and time is really in love with the cause, the ministry, the job, you, or something else. Some people don't like the idea that they have to act distrusting or defensive when it comes to dealing with someone they are fond of despite knowing that this person is an enemy. They will reason that they should love their enemy. Of course, you should, but, one should also be prayerful and watchful and "Give not that which is holy unto the dogs, neither cast ye your pearls before swine…" (Matt. 7:6).

9) Use Those Closest to You

Every so often when we are faced with challenges, we tend to go outside our circles to find out what is causing us trouble, when in fact the issues could be coming from the person to the left or right of you. Jesus knew who his enemies were and called one “a devil.” According to John 6:69-71, “And we believe and are sure that thou art that Christ, the Son of the living God. Jesus answered them, Have not I chosen you twelve, and one of you is a devil? He spake of Judas Iscariot the son of Simon: for it was he that should betray him, being one of the twelve.”

Rather than admit one has an enemy, especially when that person is a relative, he or she ignores this person and oftentimes their evil ways, behaving in this way is foolish. It is clear from the passage of Scripture that Jesus had his eye on his enemy and not only that, anyone who carefully watched Jesus at the dinner table could have easily identified who would betray Jesus. I don’t encourage people to go around naming everyone who is an enemy (in some circles that might get you killed), but I do think one should pray and ask God for guidance when you are in a position where you just might have to let those in your circle know about your Judas.

In Deuteronomy 13, God spoke of those who attempted to turn his people away from him by worshipping other gods. If one did this in the Old Testament, they were put to death. What’s interesting, God specifically speaks of relatives and friends, “If thy brother, the son of thy mother, or thy son, or thy daughter, or the wife of thy bosom, or thy friend, which is as thine own soul, entice thee secretly, saying, Let us go and serve other gods, which thou hast not known, thou, nor thy fathers… Thou shalt not consent unto him, nor hearken unto him; neither shall thine eye pity him, neither shalt thou spare, neither shalt thou conceal him: But thou shalt surely kill him; thine hand shall be first upon him to put him to death, and afterwards the hand of all the people.” *Thank God for mercy through the shed blood of his Son Jesus in the New Testament!*

10) Act as if He/She Knows You So Well

One of the things that sneaky critics like to do is act as if they know you in order to get you to reveal more about yourself. Before a devious critic hurts you with a personal opinion, he or she must act or say things that remind you of others which will make you feel at ease. This person will carefully observe your attire, listen to you converse with others, then use your information to appear like he or she has something in common with you. The devil's workers tend to lure Christ believers into witchcraft practices for a number of reasons such as monetary gain, notoriety, ideas, wealthy business connections, or just a general disdain for Jesus and his followers. The Bible reads, "And when they shall say unto you, Seek unto them that have familiar spirits, and unto wizards that peep, and that mutter: should not a people seek unto their God? for the living to the dead" (Isa. 8:19)?

As mentioned in this book previously, the enemy will use family and friends you already trust as well as strangers who look and act familiar in order to get you to feel at ease. You may want to think twice telling so much about yourself both on and offline. Allow God to lead you when sharing information about yourself and others. This way the enemy and his workers don't have a foothold in your life.

11) Try to Convince You that Evil is Good

You might have stopped drinking; fornicating and acting foolish since walking with the Lord, but that doesn't keep an unreligious person or group from tempting you to sin. When one is caught in a transgression, the unspiritual don't feel ashamed about his or her devilish acts or asking others to participate. The individual may try to reason that certain actions are good if you should call them evil. Too much talking about some- one's negative ways and reactions to the gospel will give him or her more and more ammunition to use against you including bringing up your past.

This unbelieving person most likely will say that you don't know what you are talking about and claim that you are not hearing from God. "In whom the god of this world has blinded the minds of them which believe not, lest the light of the glorious gospel of Christ, who is the image of God, should shine to them" (2 Cor. 4:4, AKJ).

Wicked critics who insult the people and things of the Lord will distract you mentally by bringing up the past. When dealing with a critic such as this, don't allow what you did in your former life to dictate your future. Keep walking with the Lord without giving money or time to rebellious individuals and their unholy causes. "The Spirit clearly says that in later times some will abandon the faith and follow deceiving spirits and things taught by demons" (Jude 1:18, NIV).

12) Create a Plan that's Void of Jesus

Whether an evil critic's intent is to insult you with a question, comment or physically harm you, your foe always has a plan to steal, kill and ultimately destroy your relationship with Christ. Many Christians sit in jail, paralyzed, depressed, and more because they did what they thought was right and left Jesus out of their decision-making. The "Good Guy" just wanted to help a "Bad Guy" in need who would later kill him. The new Christian mother of two just wanted to keep the peace with the father of her children and now she is locked up because she waited too long to leave her abuser. The manager desired to make a better worker out of an employee only for the person to turn on him and get him fired. What all of these "nice" people have in common is that they did things they thought were right without consulting the Holy Spirit first. Jesus left behind the "Spirit of Truth" for our own good (John 14:16-17). These individuals in the previous examples permitted others to dictate how things would go despite having a faith in God—they trusted self, man or woman rather than Jesus. In an article entitled, *Top 12 trends in American Christianity* (Seth-Barnes.com), "Large majorities of the public claim to be 'deeply spiritual' and say that their religious faith is 'very important' in their life, (but) only 15% of those who regularly attend a Christian church ranked their relationship with God as the top priority in their life." According to the Bible, "For the time will come when men will not put up with sound doctrine. Instead, to suit their own desires, they will gather around them a great number of teachers to say what their itching ears want to hear" (2 Tim. 4:3, NIV). This isn't to say that God doesn't use the most unlikely people to fulfill his will at times, because he does, but we have to be tuned into the Lord before listening to what others believe is a good deed or "the right thing to do," as some like to say especially when one knows that many don't believe that Jesus is the only way to the Creator.

Do you have a plan for that time you will one day be approached by someone who wants to get you involved in something that God may not approve? Your critic will be ready to bully you into making a decision in order to get you to give up money, time, connections, or things. What will you say or do when the critic shows up attempting to pressure you to go against God's will?

Since most, which are closest to you, know that you are a believer they unfairly assume that your role is to help any and everyone that comes in your path. When you refuse to assist one, two or more, the family questions, "What kind of Christian wouldn't pray, assist or show love to their mother, grandmother, cousin, best friend, or mentor?" Yet, what the critic fails to understand is that if one is Holy Spirit indwelled it doesn't matter what man or woman thinks a Christian should or shouldn't do, when God is in the plan, he has the final word. "Blessed is the man who makes the Lord his trust, who does not look to the proud, to those who turn aside to false gods" (Psalm 40:4, NIV).

13) Test Your Belief System

Your backsliding or unsaved critic hopes you have a short memory when it comes to God's instruction. If you aren't praying or surrounding yourself with spiritual things on a daily basis, you will eventually forget about God. When you do, your enemy will test you hoping that your faith in Jesus is faulty so that he or she can misuse, abuse or upset you. Be sure you know why you believe what you believe. "Let not mercy and truth forsake thee: bind them about thy neck; write them upon the table of thine heart…" (Prov. 3:3).

14) Use Fear to Keep You Bound

"If you don't do this, they may not help you…If you say that, they won't give you what you want…" the wicked critic advises you to compromise who you are so that you can get certain perks in life. If you don't, there is an "or else" clause to the contract. Some who have sold their souls to the devil awake each day to the worry that someone will be murdered close to them because of manipulative teachings and contacts made with dark entities. Many rappers have revealed in their songs that they had sold their souls to the devil. There are those materialistic believers that are deeply concerned their money and power will be lost if they should stir any trouble with Jesus talk, so they suppress their beliefs and pretend to go along just to get along.

When the critic isn't ready to disconnect from you, yet you are adamant about severing the relationship, this is when the evil critic will use all sorts of tricks to keep you bound to him or her, self or the group using things like name-calling, guilt trips and threats. Whether your critic threatens to uncover a dark past, expose lies you told, or exploit events to win you to his or her side, this person will do almost anything to keep you close to him, her or the group just because he or she is not ready to let you go.

There were rulers in the Bible (ie. Pharaoh in the Book of Exod. and King Saul) who couldn't love others due to cold hearts. In addition, these kings didn't want their kin and workers to love, interact or help the people they considered enemies. When people didn't follow orders they were threatened or worse murdered. The Lord reminds us, "Thou shalt fear the Lord thy God; him shalt thou serve, and to him shalt thou cleave, and swear by his name" (Deut. 10:20). When we dedicate our service to the Lord, we need not be concerned about what man or woman personally thinks or feels about us.

15) Stop You from Guarding Your Heart

Gullible believers will give their hearts away to anyone begging for their pity. Most likely someone who is against what you believe will attempt to get you to stop being guarded with your inner thoughts, future plans, and wisdom from God, so that he or she can benefit. When you refuse to share the deepest parts of yourself, you are accused of being mean, not a good person, unloving, cold, and more. Some who are trained in biblical study may use the Bible against you. This is their way of getting you to drop your defenses with them. Allow the Lord to minister to your heart in such situations and do not be tempted to take your eyes off Jesus to follow man or woman. "Keep thy heart with all diligence; for out of it are the issues of life" (Prov. 4:23).

16) Avoid the Truth

Offenders, who smile after you have told them some absolute truths about their spiritual condition or a wrong they have committed, definitely can't be trusted! The normal reaction from one who doesn't like Christians and Christ teachings is not jovial or kind. No one likes to be told what to do and how to do it unless they feel burdened to want to make a sincere change and are taking steps toward doing some things very differently in his or her life.

People who consider you to be an enemy will not react positively to biblical truth or any truth for that matter; therefore, you ought to be sure God has your back when you talk to them! There is a lot said when one smiles even when he or she is in the wrong. This person might gradually create distance from you or look for an opportunity to share what he or she thinks is a truth about you to others. Ask God to guide, help and protect you and your loved ones from a smiling enemy who doesn't want to receive the truth no matter how important it might be to one's situation. Refer to Psalm 91 during your prayer time.

Some of these "smiling" critics may prophecy. But according to the Bible, even prophets will lie, in 1 Kings 22:23, "Now therefore, behold, the Lord hath put a lying spirit in the mouth of all these prophets, and the Lord hath spoken evil concerning thee." In 2 Chronicles 18:22, God puts a lying spirit into the mouths of prophets here as well. Although God has specific reasons in both cases, understand that God tests his people and those who follow them. Leave yourself open to the enemy and he will use a person, who appears trustworthy, to gain your trust. Always take the time to pray before verbal and physical interaction with others.

17) Make You Feel Uncomfortable

Once a foe has won your trust, he or she will say or do something (usually not intentionally) to offend you or make you think differently about her or him, a person, organization, your beliefs, or personal situation. He or she may also reveal sensitive information you may have shared with him or her with others so that this person can get the group to help out in making you doubt what you believe.

I recall a bible study group had used this strategy on me. The group's plan was to get me to feel uncomfortable about my current lifestyle so that I could begin to depend upon them. As much as they preached Jesus, there was more of a concern to win followers to help the minister with his personal goals than to help others outside of the community walk with Jesus. If I had permitted their criticism of me to negatively influence my personal faith, I would have felt low and looked to the group to make me feel whole. I learned very quickly that Christian fellowship doesn't mean that you re-create who you are in order to meet the church's standards.

The group also combined their tactics of making me feel uncomfortable with giving me that offer they hoped I wouldn't refuse. The plan was to pay for some of my expenses in exchange for church service. Of course, I would have to sit through a few more so-called Bible study sessions listening to how bad I was and how I was going to hell. After a couple months of that, I left. Had I been desperate for friendship, who knows what else they would have put in front of me in an effort to mentally break me down so that I would solely rely on the group for everything? In time, I know they would have made me feel like I owed them my life. I learned later from a friend in the group that is how she felt about the members and because of her dedication she was overwhelmed with church responsibilities. I brought up my concerns when we were alone, but she only sang praises about the organization never bothering to address my concerns.

When the issue of making one feel uncomfortable in order for a person to behave the way the group wants comes up, red flags should be raised. Some critics as well as hypocrites will create what sounds like a logical rebuttal when questioned about their antics. They will also develop an even bigger smokescreen to keep you off their trails if they suspect you are a trouble-maker. Lastly, they will expose some weaknesses about themselves so as to appear transparent which leads me to my next point.

18) Expose Thoughts, Secrets

Stay in the presence of a pessimistic critic long enough and he or she will show you his or her "true colors." Ask yourself questions when thinking of a possible enemy, such as: "What do others say about this person? Does he or she have a long history of lying, stealing or compromising the word of God to get what he or she wants? Does this person sincerely pray, worship and fellowship with other like-minded believers?" In time, an enemy in darkness will one day address your concerns without you having to mention them. This person might share a little bit about his or herself so as to appear trustworthy before exposing you. He or she may have already informed others about who you are, what you do, your beliefs, and whether you are a person worth getting to know. Be aware your enemy may record phone conversations, have others listening in, take notes about you during meetings, and encourage you to talk about your personal challenges just so that he or she can get the upper-hand on you! Whether this person's opinion is wrong or right about you, it will be hard to change made up minds and even more difficult to take back information you shared in confidence with her or him. "A gossip betrays a confidence, but a trustworthy man keeps a secret" (Prov. 11:13).

19) Test You per God's Instructions

Read enough biblical Scriptures and you will begin to notice that God, at times, allowed his followers to be conquered by an enemy. A critic takes great pleasure in being proven right. "I told you your husband was no good…I knew that she would fail…Didn't I warn you, you were making a big mistake with that one!" When one is being tested by critics, God might allow Satan to have his way with the individual in order to get him or her to: become more humble, change something about his or herself, and draw nearer to the Lord.

Sometimes a difficult person is not altogether sound in mind, body and spirit. God might use the believer to help this person out during a challenging time in his or her life. We see an example of this in the following Scripture with King Saul, “And it came to pass, when the evil spirit from God was upon Saul, that David took an harp, and played with his hand: so Saul was refreshed, and was well, and the evil spirit departed from him” (I Sam. 16:23).

When God’s people disobeyed him, in the Bible, they paid a dear price. People were inflicted with illness, wars were lost, entire families died, land was taken away, free people became slaves, etc. and more—God was in control of it all. For example, Adam and Eve, the Psalmist David, and the priest Eli all lost sons, and in each situation someone was supposed to have listened to God, but refused. Disobedience leaves people open to Satan’s attack.

Demons are critical of God’s people and don’t want them to listen to the Lord; therefore, they will put up all sorts of tempting situations. These trials (which God allows) will either teach us to draw nearer to the Lord or move us toward Satan—our choice. “Don't have anything to do with foolish and stupid arguments, because you know they produce quarrels” (I Tim. 6:4, NIV).

When we know we are in the wrong or have been for days, weeks even years, why ask why? “Why does God allow bad things to happen to me?” a mother might cry out after years of protesting wisdom. Then there is a father who turns his back on God when his son dies, but yet forgets how many years he sinned against God and never repented. “Let the iniquity of his father’s be remembered with the Lord; and let not the sin of his mother be blotted out” (Ps. 109:14). Rather than pity yourself, ask God this, “Why do I not listen to what you have to say Lord? I ask that you have mercy on my soul and bind generational curses in Jesus name over my life and children.” If there is any critic we should listen to when we are afflicted, let it be a wise one.

20) Create Distractions

Believers, unbelievers, backsliders, and others can be easily distracted by enemy schemes. Influenced by unbelieving critics, they will not listen to the Lord or his messengers. Much of celebrity television is nothing more than mere distractions to keep us from spending quiet time with the Lord and studying his Holy Words. We must minimize our distractions when we know God is calling us to perform his will.

At times, believers belonging to the church and related associations will distract you from hearing from the Lord by assigning you tasks that you didn't think about asking God. Meanwhile, your assignment is put on hold so that you can follow others. We have to pray before committing to projects, because some people are nothing more than distractions put in place to keep us from being obedient to God. "See to it that you do not refuse him who speaks. If they did not escape when they refused him who warned them on earth, how much less will we, if we turn away from him who warns us from heaven?" (Heb. 12:25).

21) Convince You to Accept Godless Opinions, Lifestyles

A wicked critic will not stay where he is not welcome; therefore he must do some things to get you to accept him or her. Whether it is an ungodly lifestyle, wicked behavior or something else that would turn people off in your inner circle, the critic will attempt to persuade you to reconsider your righteous stance on all that is wicked. "God loves all people," she says. "Don't judge…it's not like you are so wonderful, you know?" Now if you were to change your way of thinking to suit the wicked critic, and let's say, do something like the following: agree with his or her ungodly lifestyle, play ungodly music, watch ungodly television programs, and participate in ungodly activities, not only would you be compromising your faith but you would also be ushering in the presence of the critic's boss, Satan, and his minions.

When you take a stand against your critical foe, he or she will not want to stay in your presence. However, if you feed into a loved one's negativity, he or she will continue to bring you more challenges while hoping to stir fierce emotions within you. Allowing a person like this to take up most of your time manipulating and frustrating you will only lead you into committing actions you may later regret. You will not only find people like this in your family, but on your job and elsewhere too. These people will use what appears to be friendly conversation to get close to you as mentioned earlier. After talking with them for awhile, you learn that you have nothing spiritually in common with the unrighteous. However, they may find that you are a valuable addition to their lives and will continue to come around, carrying their personal demons with them, as long as you let them.

22) Act Controlling, Stifle God-Inspired Creativity

Try telling someone, who doesn’t like you or what you are doing for God, about an idea. Watch his or her mannerisms. You will notice this person will say or do things to discourage you and will even go so far as to take over your God-inspired concept. He or she may talk over you when you are trying to explain what God has laid upon your heart. This person may redirect your attention to other things and attempt to get you to doubt what God has been saying to you, because he or she thinks they know what is best. Your wicked adversary might embarrass you by talking to others about your weaknesses so that you will lose your faith. The individual might also blatantly tell you that he or she will not support you on your God-inspired endeavors hoping that you will become sad and needy; therefore making yourself come back to him or her for assistance.

Controlling types often talk positively as well as negatively to others about those who they are secretly jealous of. Wicked conversations are used to try to enlist some help from others on how to stop you from performing God’s will especially if what you are doing should affect anything that you might be doing for them.

Critics don’t like people who may appear smarter, wiser, more successful, or happier than they. When you pick up on a jealous critic, ignore this person and most of all don’t conduct business with such a person. If you are experiencing jealous feelings, remember the following, “Do not let your heart envy sinners, but always be zealous for the fear of the Lord” (Prov. 23:17).

23) Try to Confuse You on What is of God and What Isn't

Counterfeit miracles, signs and wonders abound amongst false prophets in churches and secular organizations. In the book of Exodus, we read about symbols and actions that leave witnesses in awe concerning magicians and sorcerers. Many of which were similar to what God called Moses to demonstrate before the Pharaoh. The counterfeit's goals are simply to obtain more money, power and fame from followers as discussed in an earlier chapter.

Someone may have invited you to an event that made you feel all warm and fuzzy on the inside. You may have paid close attention to what was of God and what wasn't at the event you attended. Meanwhile, others just enjoyed the show and didn't think too deeply about it. Many so-called Christian events look and act like the world, because some speakers have studied the ways of witches, warlocks, mediums, and spiritualists. The Bible warns, "Even him, whose coming is after the working of Satan with all power and signs and lying wonders" (2 Thess. 2:9).

Unfortunately, there are far too many people who don't think about too much of anything except money, bills, children, and what should they eat and drink the next day. They have fallen away from God by getting involved with the wrong people and doing the wrong things. Many are in relationships where they have committed to an unbelieving spouse and are supporting him or her with things that God never called them to do.

If you would like to find out whether someone you listen to via radio, television or watch on the Internet is practicing divination, simply put the person's name, their ministry and "witchcraft hand signs, occult symbols, witchcraft exposed…" or something related in the search engines. Always pray before you accept an offer to go anywhere locally, nationally or internationally. Ask God for spiritual discernment.

24) Use Others to Transfer Spirits

Some believers don't think spirits can be transferred from one individual to another. This shouldn't be a concern if one is sold out for the Lord, but for the wayward believer, unbeliever, ignorant, or unsaved, they can all be subjected to demonic entities wanting to inhabit their bodies.

I have watched Internet videos where people involved in heavy witchcraft have admitted to performing spells on people in order to influence their atmospheres. For some witches and warlocks I viewed, they were able to move demons to inhabit unsuspecting people.

If you don't believe that one has the power to send demonic activity to someone else, feel free to study information provided by former witches who are now born again. There are plenty who felt so bad about all the mayhem they have caused in their victims' lives that they expose some of the witchcraft they used and what resulted in the following sources: books they have written on the subject, on websites (such as blogs and video), and at offline gatherings.

During a phone conversation, a person (who I will keep anonymous for privacy reasons) revealed to me that her body had been attacked by a devil entity that wanted to "come in." The "thing" proceeded to moan and lay on her body she said. When I asked her what she had been doing to cause this "thing" to want to enter her, she said she had been masturbating earlier that evening. I questioned whether she thought her actions may be triggering such an event? She believed that they could be responsible because she had been doing it for years and watching porn.

Another person shared with me a story about a Pennsylvania woman he witnessed confiding in his mother, a minister, about being attacked by a demonic entity who left scars on her back.

Have you ever heard someone use the phrase after acting out in a rage, "I don't know what got into me?" If one is not Holy Spirit indwelled, then the enemy will temporarily inhabit one's body to fulfill his selfish will. We know this to be true by the examples in the Bible that talk about those who were demon-possessed. If you are Holy Spirit indwelled, a demon can't very well live in your body, but he can manipulate your atmosphere (with God's permission of course) to get you to do what he wants. We know this to be true when we read of those individuals in the Bible who God allowed Satan to tempt, test and murder.

Casting demons out of humans was not foreign to Jesus and it shouldn't be to us if we say that we are new creatures in Christ.

We are to study and learn what to do when we see the demon-possessed we are not to fear them. Apparently there is something that people do which encourages the demons to want to inhabit them. When they show up, they curse, insult, lie, fight, and more. There are passages of Scripture where demons were living in men, but when Jesus showed up they knew they would be casted out. In one story, the demons asked Jesus if they could enter some nearby pigs. (I talk more about casting out demons in Chapter 10). Notice, the demons desired to go elsewhere before Jesus called them out of the men. This proves that demons need a host in order to keep up their activity. In addition, they don't stop bothering others just because they have left a body.

When people partake in things that increase demonic activity, the demons must find someone or something to enter in order to fulfill the devil's will. For some of you, don't be fearful about studying more about what Jesus did when he was in the presence of those demon-possessed, because you never know when God is going to call you to pray for one battling with a demon.

25) Involve You in Drama Unrelated to You

Despite being critical of you, it doesn't keep a critic from sharing his or her personal conflict while hoping you will help. In Proverbs 26:17, we are warned, "Like one who seizes a dog by the ears is a passer-by who meddles in a quarrel not his own." When you choose not to help a wicked critic (or simply someone who just expects you will do for him or her), the desire for your assistance only increases within him or her. The critic will find ways to get you involved in their personal dramas (or someone else's) even if you rather not. I think of the following personality type described in Proverbs 7:11, "She is loud and stubborn; her feet abide not in her house..." The wayward believer wants you to get mad about the same things that upset her. An uninterested response will infuriate the emotional critic. Be prepared for this person to tempt you. He or she will be unhappy that you don't seem to care or will not offer you assistance. "Some Christian you are!" says the critic. Don't fall for the sobbing when you know that God is not with this person! You will know because his or her lack of fruit will show it.

26) Try Using the Silent Treatment to Annoy You

Your critic is bothered by not only your faith, but the way you act or react toward his or her sinful behaviors. Like a child, this person will try to get your attention by saying nothing at all even when you are talking to him or her. He or she will act as if you don't exist. The silent treatment is one of many strategies Satan uses to deceive individuals in order to get them to conform. Those who are desperate for companionship, obsessed with pleasing a partner, or desire some things from certain individuals will break under the pressure of the silent treatment.

27) Twist Scripture to Suit an Agenda

Anyone that wishes to control you will use the Bible in order to suit his or her plan. Most people would not go along with anyone's twisted doctrine if they were just told to follow instructions or else. Therefore, Satan has to dress his messages up with spiritual experiences, persuasive words, music, promises, and other things that tickle wayward believer's ears. Whether the Prince of Darkness appears as an angel of light or a beautiful woman, he knows that he has to mix biblical truth with a lie to convince others to be their own god and follow him. Watch reading books, listening to music, and speakers that give very little biblical truth. Many provide much personal opinion that often conflicts with God's Word.

Your critic may have studied the Holy Bible before he or she approached you with a concern or request so that this person appears more knowledgeable. If you should raise a concern, this person will find a Scripture to validate his or her actions. For instance, an abusive husband may reinforce all Scriptures related to how women should act with their husbands so as to make her feel guilty. Watch how some people who claim to uplift and encourage people, use the Bible to ultimately get what they want and not what God wants.

28) Lie and Deceive to Hurt Others When Feeling Offended

Ananias and Sapphira, believers located in the New Testament (Acts 5), showed that they really didn't want to part with monies from their property sold. When in the presence of disciples, they acted as if they gave all their money to help others so as to look good. But the truth was they held back part of the money they got from the sale of their land and because they lied, they died. Lying to the Holy Spirit is not taken lightly from this example and since some believers might not be sure who is friend and who is foe, it would make sense not to lie in the first place.

All deceitful critics will not hesitate to come up with false stories and exaggerations in order to get listeners to go along with their opinions. For some, it is a classic tactic of retaliation when one is offended by statements of fact. "I don't know what you are talking about…I did everything you asked…I never said that! You're the liar. You're crazy!" the liar says. You can't trust these manipulators once they are found out. When they know that their criticism is not working on you to get you to go along with their program, they will say the kind of things that they think you either like or dislike depending on what makes them feel good and how what they say might benefit their situation. Remember your enemy has studied you, so he or she tends to know your personality type, need or want. In the case of Ananias and Sapphira, they knew Peter, the disciple, but they underestimated the Holy Spirit behind Peter.

Once the critic has your attention, he or she may reveal some truth to the story behind the story. But keep in mind, the critic creates many layers to a story because he or she doesn't care about, nor respect the truth—especially if they don't see any benefit in telling the truth. Therefore, you may never hear it, or anything else you may find important in a relationship, friendship or business partnership. Insist on the truth anyway! When you don't get it, walk away, ignore, or cut off this person as God leads. Look for other people, places and things that will lead you to the truth after much prayer and fasting. As much as it can be a temptation to lie, name-call and do other things to retaliate because this person has done these things to you, don't do it! Colossians 3:9 (NIV) instructs, "Do not lie to each other, since you have taken off your old self with its practices."

29) Warn God's People of Some Evil, but Still Has Ill Intentions

Your foe is a traitor. He will walk with you, talk to you, show you some affection, and even swear he would never betray you. He might even warn you about other enemies. Notice what Judas did when he gave Jesus up to his foes. "Now the betrayer had arranged a signal with them: 'The one I kiss is the man; arrest him and lead him away under guard'" (Mark 14:44). The person who has your ears may provide you with some sound doctrine and appear to be helpful and kind. But in time, what's in his or her heart shows up especially in the presence of others who may not like you. Unfortunately, he or she may have been the one to conjure up the chaos in the first place!

In the book of Esther Chapter 3, Haman plotted to kill the Jews especially Mordecai, a man who reported a past plot to kill King Xerxes. Haman wanted the brave man dead because he refused to bow down to him when he passed, but in time planned to have all his people murdered because they were Jewish. Despite having a good reputation with the king, Haman wanted Mordecai dead. However, despite his murderous resentment, Haman had to obey the king's orders and honor Mordecai for his past service. This is a clear example of how someone can act polite and respectful, yet have evil intent harboring in one's heart.

From time to time, God used an enemy to fulfill his will in different situations in the Bible; however, this doesn't mean that just because there is a history of this, a foe can be trusted. One, two or many nice deeds someone does for others don't mean that he or she is one of the following: a worker for the Lord, a potential mate, or "the man" or "the woman" for the job. We tend to put too much trust in people because "they are nice." Learn more about them besides how nice they treated you during a one-time meeting of exchanging pleasantries.

Remember to keep your eyes open for false prophets both in and out of the church such as: talk show hosts, speakers, rappers, and anyone else who has a large platform created to influence the masses. "For such people are not serving our Lord Christ, but their own appetites. By smooth talk and flattery they deceive the minds of naive people" (Rom. 16:18, NIV). As I have said many times in this book, watch relatives too who claim to love you, but have selfish interests.

30) Study the Competition with Plans to Conquer

The world instructs those in business to study the competition and this is just what the godless critic is going to do before she starts talking about how she doesn't need God, want God or thinks he doesn't care. This person may offer a personal opinion that is informative, wreck-less, or ignorant. The critic may be coveting a certain position or audience but you might stand in her way of achieving goals. This clever individual will watch you closely in the hopes that she will learn some things about you to get you to one day conform to her way of thinking.

Once an enemy has you on her side, this individual will find any contradictions you might display in your beliefs, then use them against you (usually when you have offended her with truth). This is another good reason why you should never tell everything about yourself to everyone, especially those who are close to your enemy and definitely don't trust them to give you advice. "Blessed is the man that walketh not in the counsel of the ungodly, nor standeth in the way of sinners, nor sitteth in the seat of the scornful But his delight is in the law of the Lord; and in his law doth he meditate day and night" (Ps. 1:1).

31) Use Children to Change Your Mind, Disturb Your Spirit

The last thing we would ever think is a critical person influencing a child to criticize us. But there are those wicked critics who will do just that! God tells us to, "Train up a child in the way he should go: and when he is old, he will not depart from it" (Prov. 22:6), but it doesn't say train children to conspire, manipulate, lie, or dictate others. Satan has always used children to do things to disrupt the Christ followers' faith. I know this to be true because out of the mouths of babes (speaking of my own children) I was told that "some ugly thing, mean voice, shadow, devil dog" or something else told them to do something bad. Then there were those children, I had watched for others, share with me some of the mean things their parents said about others; therefore the child would do nothing more than act like the parent and carry out his or her ignorance and evil speaking when interacting with others. A mean-spirited parent influences a child to act ungodly; therefore giving Satan a foothold in the child's life.

Evil adults will take advantage of the innocence of a child in order to do the following: obstruct one's view of God, create pandemonium, cause intimate relationship problems and satisfy fleshly desires, cast revenge, and more. This is why one must be cautious even of children because you never know what evil they have been exposed to at such a young age. Remind older children of James 4:7, "Submit yourselves, then, to God. Resist the devil, and he will flee from you."

A kid may cry, whine or act out during a time when all an adult wants is to pray. This is a popular challenge that most parents face while raising children and making time for the Lord. Children are not only blessings to most parents, but they are also major distractions if one doesn't set aside time for both God and children. A parent must also be aware and prepared for children to be used by adults (as well as spirits) to question or doubt the existence of God and all things spiritual.

In addition, a parent must be mindful that a young person will play a guilt trip to get him or her to go along with something most likely devil-inspired. Look at the sheer number of dark games, movies, music, and entertainers advertised in print, on TV and over the Internet specifically targeting young people. The teenager yells, "You don't let me go anywhere! You never help me…You don't care about me…You are a bad parent…I hate you!" just because you won't let him or her stay up all night talking to someone who is negatively impacting him or her or letting the young person hang out with friends past curfew on a daily basis. No parent ever wants to feel like he or she is not doing what's best for his or her child, but some sons and daughters might make you feel that way. When we know an enemy is using a child to get to us emotionally, physically or financially, don't fight with the child, instead consider the source. Where is the evil coming from? Cut it off by examining yourself, influences, past decision-making as it relates to your children, and other things you may or may not be doing to give your child the best example. Show the child love and listen to his or her concerns. Be the best role-model you can be and hopefully all the negativity that someone may have heaped on a child concerning you or others will go away. When a child is convinced that you care about him or her, the enemy can't do anything but retreat.

32) Turned Off by Your God Talk and Walk

A foe will warn you about "talking too much about God, doing too much for God" and other spiritual actions as mentioned in previous chapters. He or she does this so that you will slow down and think more of yourself and less of God and helping others. Some church-goers will be critical of little things you do for God's Kingdom so they too might be guilty of trying to oppress you and your faith. They may be jealous or fearful you will overshadow them with all your God talk.

When you see a negative display of behavior from those around you, ask your Creator to first show you the truth about yourself and why people may be reacting negatively to you. Study more of God's Word, find more answers to your questions, seek God on the direction of your ministry, entrust God's appointed to help you with whatever God reveals to you, and most of all listen to God and his messengers. However, if you have done all these things and still people are reacting negatively and attempting to shut you down, consider asking God to move you elsewhere. He will. "I am a witness!" When one tempts you to talk about things that are obviously not of the Lord and has Satan's stamp of approval (so to speak), bear in mind 1 Thessalonians 5:5 (NIV), "You are all sons of the light and sons of the day. We do not belong to the night or to the darkness."

33) Disrupt Your Plans to Forgive Someone

A bitter Christian critic knows there is liberty in letting go and letting God, ye t chooses not to do this. He or she would rather attempt to derail your efforts to ask others for forgiveness—particularly if your actions will make you look better than the critic. Miserable relatives and friends are good for keeping you from making peace with people they consider their enemies. They do this, because they just can't seem to forgive their foes. You might one day have to make a choice between your faith or your beloved partner, relative or friend, choose wisely. Those that criticize you for forgiving someone, must have overlooked the following Scriptures, "And the fruit of righteousness is sown in peace of them that make peace" (Jas. 3:18). "And the work of righteousness shall be peace; and the effect of righteousness quietness and assurance forever" (Isa. 32:17). I don't know about you, but I wouldn't want any future mental wars within myself because I couldn't receive the kind of peace God gives "which transcends all understanding" (Phil. 4:7, NIV). Now forgiving someone who may have hurt your family doesn't mean that you are choosing that person over your family, rather you are freeing yourself of personal feelings toward that person. God showed me this when I looked back on some things in my life that was keeping me emotionally bound just because other people were still harboring ill feelings toward a foe. I have since let certain relatives and enemies go in Jesus name!

34) Lead One Astray by Involving Him or Her in Something that Contradicts the Word of God

Watch out for people who seem to act far too excited about you and your ideas, chances are they have a plan up their sleeves that may not have anything to do with God or helping you. Imagine joining a group that claims to assist people in need only to find out later that they are really robbing people of hard-earned money and time. When you speak up about the group, members start warning you to, "Be quiet, or else." But you only get louder and talk about how everything they are doing is contrary to the Word of God.

Many Christians are recruited into civic groups, businesses, or nonprofit organizations that have unethical practices and if one threatens to expose, he or she is quickly put to silence. Before signing the dotted line on a contract, conduct research "And have no fellowship with the unfruitful works of darkness, but rather reprove them" (Eph. 5:11).

35) Unbelieving Critics Ignore or Keep Away from Believers

There will be those times in our lives when we have no choice but to work with someone who is critical of God and his people, but just because we have to be around them doesn't mean that we have to answer their questions, be lulled into a debate about the works and teachings of God, and do anything else that will give the critic an excuse to demean us with their comments. When on or offline, I have to often remind myself, "Don't cast your pearls to swine." (Matt. 7:6) Whether critics have had bad experiences with Christ followers or they just don't have any interest in spiritual things, these unconstructive people usually don't like being around religious people (unless they can get something from them) as mentioned previously in this book.

36) Create a Mind-Controlled Slave Out of a Man or Woman

This is the most explained tactic of all of them in this chapter. I felt I had to be more descriptive with this one, because of the many badly informed Christians who unfortunately idolize pop culture and put much faith in the American media.

Some people with lots of money and talent unfortunately use their skills not to uplift others spiritually, but to break the unsuspecting down mentally and physically over time. There are many elitists of our society who are connected to individuals and groups who are specifically trained to get the masses to change their way of thinking. They use the impressionable to control others in order to get both legal and illegal things done. What I am describing is mind control, also known as brainwashing. This is done through: television news, movies, print media, radio and even many churches use brainwashing techniques both online and offline to get you to do the following: vote a certain way, buy someone's product, influence others to get them to support a certain agenda, or attend a church service. The information is tremendous on this subject of mind control. You will quickly discover that mind manipulation tactics are used often by our local, national and international governments, entertainment industry and in product advertising.

Kent R. Rieske, B.Sc., and Bible Life Ministries (Bible-Life.org), warns believers on their website about church bondage. "If you hear a pastor or television evangelist say, 'God told me to tell you,' hold onto your wallet and run. These are the modern-day money changers similar to those who Jesus threw out of the temple." They go on to describe some of the brainwashing techniques used to get people in the church to do the leadership's will. "The modern Christian churches use brainwashing, mind control, indoctrination, oppression, coercion, intimidation, legalism, false teaching, guilt, shame, peer pressure, and other bondage techniques to control members, increase church attendance, and obtain more money. The goal is said to be 'winning souls to Christ,' but the underlying agenda is the desire for more power, control, and money. These mind control and bondage techniques are not needed to win souls to Christ. In fact, they are very counter-productive to soul winning," said Rieske.

If you have ever watched movies whether fiction or nonfiction related to crooked ministers, notice the story pattern in many of them. The church is in need of money. The pastor doesn't know what to do, so a business professional (who usually isn't righteous), offers to help the struggling ministry. Later, the pastor learns that the man or woman is crooked and now he is faced with trials that tempt him to do evil. Could it be that this screenplay is frequently being demonstrated in many churches all across the land in reality? What might some of the tactics be that unsaved, worldly business professionals might use on an unsuspecting believer who might have something that interests them like a large following, a massive income stream and powerful connections. First, the individual or group would present an appealing offer. Maybe the church has some financial issues, a building in need of maintenance, or other challenges that may not be tended to at this time. Next, the wolf in sheep's clothing might recommend some "experts" to assist the believer's struggling ministry such as: financial advisors, business planners, shady psychologists, psychiatrists, other sell-out church leaders, crooked police officers, and similar people in authority who are instructed to treat him or her "like gold" in order to recruit church leadership to go along with the wolf's program. This deceptive helper, also critic, is meticulous and may gradually encourage certain church leaders and members of the board to denounce core beliefs in the one true God, Son and Holy Spirit so as to get assistance from the wolf's affiliations. Offers of money and material wealth usually help facilitate this wicked critic's goals. Before long, the pastor is no better than the wolf; he or she has sold out his or her talents, business, church, connections, family, and more. Some wayward or cold-hearted ministers might receive temporary worldly success that may not be typically offered to "commoners," specific genders, and ethnicities depending on how much they have sacrificed their lives for the deceptive group or individual.

Crossbearer Brian O'Connell, an evangelist for Christ who manages a website called, Crossbearer.net, shared on the site how he was given "a personal testimony from a Pastor who had been approached by Masons attempting to "buy the church"! He writes, "Once the Masonic Lodge 'builds' the church by buying out the Pastor, the Pastor becomes a servant of the Masonic Lodge and a 'worshipful master'—that is Not Jesus Christ!" He then quotes the biblical Scripture, "No man can serve two masters: for either he will hate the one, and love the other; or else he will hold to the one, and despise the other. Ye cannot serve God and mammon" Matthew 6:24.

For years, televangelists, as well as local ministers have benefited from the secular world. Some started off with nothing more than a Bible and a room then evolved into huge congregations, thanks to worldly individuals and groups. These pastors are then decorated in the best of everything including personalized logos while signaling their respect and appreciation to their ungodly affiliations. These same ministers have used various marketing programs that changed business as usual into what many researchers call a paradigm shift (which means a radical change in beliefs). An example of this kind of teaching has become a popular movement in many non-denominational churches. It is called the Word of Faith Movement. Many websites report the errors of this gospel including false teachings that deceive people into thinking they are little gods and have power over stuff like places and things. They believe that by simply naming and claiming something while believing that God will give it to them, they are entitled to financial abundance. This kind of thinking puts man on the throne and God at his feet. "As we said before, so say I now again, If any man preach any other gospel unto you than that ye have received, let him be accursed" (Gal. 1:9).

One must be careful following after secular or "supposed" Christian leaders who brag about their successes in life, because you don't know what they had to do (behind the scenes) in order to obtain wealth—
they did more than just speak things as though they were. Recently, I came across a former minister's wife speaking on a radio program about her husband who was homosexual and how he was able to deceive many including her with his assumed heterosexual lifestyle. She never questioned how much time he was spending with the same sex. Many secular civic groups have a long history of homosexual rituals. Some are nothing more than sex cults. Be prepared in advance before you are approached by one. Learn more about their historical truths by searching any group you suspect on the Internet and add keywords like "cult," "exposed," "homosexual" "gay" and other similar words in various Internet search engines.

Oftentimes carnal minded business moguls (or so-called God-appointed leaders) participate in activities that go against God's Word. I recall one day stumbling across a website that listed many ministers who were affiliated with secular organizations that participated in ungodly oaths and ceremonies. Right away, I knew something was wrong and thought of the Scripture again about, "…You cannot serve both God and money" (Matt. 6:24, NIV). I was also reminded, by the Holy Spirit, of how much God detested idols. Many members of both secular and religious groups tend to idolize one another and have ungodly sculptures and other items that they highly esteem. So while many church leaders criticize followers for behaving ungodly, many forget that they too are participating in groups and activities that recruit both children of light and children of darkness to promote evil works and despicable lifestyles while revering idols. These church leaders know how to cover themselves well from public scrutiny once a few vigilantes threaten to expose them.

Various media outlets reported that Bishop Eddie Long settled out of court back in 2008 for millions. He had been accused of engaging in intimate sexual acts on four young men back when they were teenagers. "Long's attorneys deny those allegations and maintain that the pastor was attempting to be a father figure to the youths by providing them with financial assistance and encouragement," according to an article by John Blake, titled *Bishop Eddie Long Settles with Accusers* (CNN.com). Since then, the Bishop's wife divorced him, but his church still supports him. In a video which appeared on a website called, TheGrio.com, Bishop is crowned king in God's government at New Birth Missionary Baptist Church by Rabbi Ralph Messer who wraps a 312-year-old scroll which he claims is from Auschwitz after World War II.

For some of you, what I just mentioned might sound all too familiar to you if you research and expose similar events involving priests and choir boys and other scandals of ministers as well as those who are not in religious organizations, but in businesses and schools ie.) the Penn State scandal involving a staff member participating in sexual acts with minors. Now when someone is in trouble, who is beloved by all, their affiliations might help or hurt them depending on the circumstances and whether or not this person might be a threat to the pyramid structure behind the scenes as discussed in Chapter Two. You can study more by carefully analyzing the history of secret societies and how they are connected with national as well as international governments.

From multi-level marketing gurus to government funded groups when favored leaders mess up, no worries, if you have the right worldly connections, someone somewhere will save your reputation or failing business. Critics are quietly controlled through distraction by individuals and groups with the most money and prestige while mainstream journalists are used to help ensure that a once-popular story of a celebrity is place in front of the public's eyes at the right time, and then put on the back-burner when inconvenient. Find out about public relations tactics used to control public criticism by researching subjects like media manipulation, mind control, subconscious manipulation, and sensationalism. Take a look at American history and you will notice former workers in certain industries who exposed wrongs committed against them and others by superiors had unfortunate things happen to them. Whistleblowers suddenly come up missing, become deathly ill, wounded due to an unfortunate accident, go to jail or worse, murdered. It is in their stories that the truth is revealed. No one who is currently being fed by a corrupt system will bite the hand that feeds them unless they have a death wish whether in the metaphorical or literal sense. So if you are in search of truth about a certain industry, business, celebrity, law or even a religious doctrine, you won't usually find it coming from a satisfied employee who is receiving a paycheck from the organization in question.

One hit wonders in the entertainment industry, failed business moguls, and guilt-ridden sell-out Christians have a lot to tell particularly if they are still bitter about the years of criticism they received by those around them. The questions that should be asked when listening to their "rise to fame" stories are: "Why didn't someone come to their rescues when they failed? Could it be that they became a nuisance, threatened to expose someone or simply got tired of the false fronts and the condemnation from bosses, assistants, media, family, friends, and fans? What did these former "stars" have to do in order to save their reputations and have a place on a pyramid structure in their industries? For some, one-hit wonders, retirees, and troubled stars, they returned to their industries after years of being out of the spotlight, while claiming to love the Lord, only to die soon after. When people have a history of selling out, acting like traitors, it is hard to trust them especially when they are blatantly worshipping a sun god, human god, mother god, animal god, or many strange gods related to Lucifer for various reasons. The backslider will eventually experience the one true God's wrath sooner or later. We see evidence of this with the many kings, prophets, tribes, and others in the Bible who didn't remain faithful to God or his words.

A dangerous critic who is paid to attack someone for a variety of reasons will do many things to get someone to conform to whatever agenda of the day it is. I think of those celebrity handlers who have been accused of encouraging risky surgeries, acting irresponsibly, assisting with accidents, creating harmful settings, using tactics to evoke split personalities, ordering drugs both legal and illegal, and more so that they can keep certain celebrities under control while the industry makes money off of them. Many viewers leave their share of negative feedback never bothering to investigate the story behind the story. As I write, what comes to mind are the sheer number of celebrity melt downs and split personalities that show up during stars' interviews, guest appearances, music, movies, videos, and concerts.

In a book titled, *The Illuminati Formula Used to Create an Undetectable Total Mind Controlled Slave* by Cisco Wheeler and Fritz Springmeier, the authors share various tactics people use to control others emotionally, physically and morally in many different industries from religion to entertainment. Springmeier explains, "Over the years, I have spent thousands of hours studying the Illuminati, the Intelligence agencies of the world, and the occult world in general. The centerpiece of these organizations is the trauma-based mind control that they carry out. Without the ability to carry out this sophisticated type of mind-control using (multiple personality disorder) MPD, drugs, hypnosis and electronics and other control methodologies, these organizations would fail to keep their dark evil deeds secret." He goes on, "When one of the mind-control programmers of the Church of Scientology, who has left Scientology, was asked about MPD, he said, "It's the name of the game of mind control." Some would say after reading this, "I always knew the Church of Scientology was a cult." Of course, but we have to also examine local and national Christian associations and denominations who might be guilty of doing the same thing. Investigate them like you would a known cult. Check other industries as well: sports, health, publishing, and civil government just to name a few. These groups are not exempt from leaders using mind control devices and tactics on employees. There is a long history of professionals speaking out against mind manipulation. In addition, we have seen countless movies portraying individuals and groups brainwashed based on real events. Sure some of the movies might appear to be far-fetched, silly and even peculiar, but there is always a little truth sprinkled amongst exaggeration and lies. By the time discerning individuals catch on to the manipulation and share what they have learned with others, the critics have already created a false front that keeps truth out.

Evil workers in various Christian denominations will say belittling things about one's body, mind, spirit, well-meaning actions, and God-ordained gifts as a means to mentally breakdown followers so that they can be better servants and easily controlled. Some will use the pulpit to sway the masses to vote for a certain candidate, invest in a business venture, join an affiliate group, talk and even dress and style one's hair in particular ways. None of which have anything to do with spreading the gospel of Christ. If you are a man or woman of influence (with a large following) and should choose to do something Holy Spirit inspired which conflicts with the wants of the church board, then there will be a critic or a group of naysayers that will tell you about yourself and how your actions "aren't of God, not good, unpopular, worthless, bad, crazy…"

The handler (often described in Springmeier's book) also known as "the help" in some circles will encourage abuse and misuse of man-made substances, as well as manipulate one's environment in an attempt to make a person feel as if he or she is going out of his or her mind. All of these scheming tactics continue to rip away at one's spiritual hindsight. For instance, a handler (someone who you might respect or admire) might say, "Oh that's a dream—it doesn't mean anything. So what, you got a bad feeling!? You are crazy, you believe in that stuff? God doesn't care about your issues. Believe in yourself because that's all you got!"

Once a critic sees you are doing things that cause you to stumble, (because your backbone of faith has been broken) he or she will continue to discourage you from walking with God, yet encourage you to run into the arms of men and women because "It's too hard to do things on your own…You don't need God that's why he gave you a mind…You are better than that…What will your fans think, you don't want them to say, 'You are a Jesus freak,' do you?" What usually ends up happening, the backslider or lukewarm Christian starts making his or her handlers' gods. When they are displeased, the victim cries out, "I can't do anything without you! I need you! Don't leave me! I will come to ruin…please help me." Think of some of the autobiographies you may have read or watched where this sort of behavior took place with America's beloved entertainers. After being called a few chose names, given a list of requirements and consequences if the entertainer messes up again, the handler says, "I'll help." If the mind-controlled slave steps out of his or her programming (or no longer serves a significant purpose), he or she is gradually faded out of the spotlight or worse loses his or her life because he or she may be worth more dead than alive. This I have noticed after reading: articles written by entertainment researchers, Springmeier's book, and noting my own personal observations.

The once believer turned backslider turned believer again is eventually annihilated once more by his or her own personal weaknesses and critics. I believe the "I told-you-so" crowd and the weak-minded (who hang around everybody from public figures to the girl next door), help influence personal demons and force them to go over the edge especially if one is jealous. Many entertainers, as well as others, talk about their faith, but rather than remind people about our Creator and his son Jesus, they destroy their adoring fans with careless words, ridiculous fashion sense and weird philosophies.

A sincere believer, especially an influential one with a massive platform, must not ever give God a break or in other words, fall away from the faith by making compromises with wicked people and groups, otherwise he or she leaves self and family uncovered and subjected to demonic attack. "What good is it for a man to gain the whole world, yet forfeit his soul?" (Mark 8:36, NIV).

37) Attempt to Make You Distrust Those that Bless You with Purpose, Joy and Freedom in Christ

Selfish, jealous critics will put thoughts in your mind about people who mean you well. They will not be excited about those in your inner circle who encourage, inspire or move you to be a better individual. These people will find fault with those you like from their skin tone to how much time you are spending with them. When you share the good things that are happening to you as a result of certain fellowships, the critic will tell you all sorts of negative things to get you to not trust your God-appointed friend or group. I say God-appointed, because there are those people that God entrusts to act like a support group in our lives while the enemy has his select individuals to come into our lives to cause disruption. Ask God to reveal your critic's motives.

No critic of God and his people is happy with your choices. This is why unsupportive critics aren't readily accepting of what a Christ follower has to say. The backsliding or unsaved critics feel that your new connections might impact their relationship with you. The selfish critic thinks, "If she connects with them, they might take all her money, so she won't be able to help me. I don't like those people, and I don't want them asking me for anything. I won't start attending any church, because they will want me to start helping others..." Children of God are threats to the critics' lifestyle, belief system, and more. Satan and his demons know what believers do to get evil people to turn from their wicked thinking. This is why you experience a spirit of resistance when it comes to trying to lead someone toward a righteous path or wise instruction.

We know our purpose in Christ and we are happy and free doing what we know to be right. Therefore, we can continue to work with the Spirit of God on his will for our lives. We can also pray that our enemies will one day be one of the chosen. Hopefully, they too will come to the realization of God's truth. For the Bible reads, "For many are called, but few are chosen" (Matt. 22:14). In my book, *Face Your Foe: 28 Critics of Your Faith You Can Overcome*, I explain more about many of these critics described in this chapter. Now that you have over 30 different strategies a critic might use to get you to go outside of the will of God, here is one small piece of advice, keep your eyes on Jesus! The enemy would just love for you to focus on him and only him, but don't give him (or her) that satisfaction.

When the next battle comes, and it will, be prepared by wearing your spiritual body armor. The critic always has an arsenal of verbal insults, blaming statements and more so that you will spend more time focusing on what he or she said, and less time focused on what God says.

For you, who do the kinds of innovative things that flip rules, situations and establishments upside down without listening to God first, remember the following: "Whoever digs a pit may fall into it; whoever breaks through a wall may be bitten by a snake" (Eccles. 10:8). So be sure God has your back when you are attempting to change, rearrange and motivate others to do something different! Sometimes we invite unnecessary criticism.

To know your critic doesn't mean that you know so much about him or her that you lose sight of God, but to truly know your critic is to be prepared when this person attempts to shatter your faith. Be ready to run toward the loving arms of God, rather than away from him!

6. When the Critic Attacks

Sometimes you end up living in neighborhoods, working in towns, and participating in events where people just don't like you because you're not like them. You may not be a social butterfly, a town gossip, a drinker, or someone who believes in someone or something other than God. When you are one of "those types," you are labeled, talked about, and eventually approached by one who wants to challenge you on why you do and say the things you do. There are many people who have no problem co-existing with others who aren't like them; however there are those who just can't seem to get along with anyone who isn't what they are ie.) rich, poor, black white, young or old. We see evidence of this from the local church, who has attendees who are primarily one ethnicity or another, to congressman who only vote one political party or the other despite views that may be different from theirs. Problems begin when an individual decides he or she is going to say or do something that changes the current way one thinks or operates. Regardless of whether it is valuable information or not, any change to one's circumstances most likely will be met with objection.

One Muslim group didn't like the new pastor in the neighborhood. So what did they do? In an article that appeared on the Voice of the Martyrs website on January 2009 titled, *Pastor Attacked, Wife Gang-Raped,* they decided to make life difficult for him and his family. The group tied the pastor up and blind-folded him while his wife was gang-raped in their home located in Bangladesh, Asia. The couple was Christian Baptists. The article makes no mention of children. The assailants, Muslim, looted the couple's home and defecated their church. When the pastor managed to untie himself and remove his blindfold, he noticed his wife was unconscious. He contacted police. In the police report, facts were changed so that the Muslims who attacked the couple were left out the report and instead it said thc couplc was attackcd by two Christians and a Hindu. It is not mentioned in the article whether this couple remained Christian. Since the attack, they live with relatives. The article also doesn't mention whether their families are Christian or Muslim. If the relatives have no faith or believe very little, what is the likelihood that this couple will be criticized for their beliefs? What might someone say to them? "If you weren't Christian and talking about God to everyone, this wouldn't have happened to you."

Although many of us have had our share of personal attacks for our beliefs, there are those who are physically wounded and suffer for years as a result. We must stay in prayer for Christians who are in danger for their faith. Unlike most of us, our lives are comfortable. Sure many of us have those moments where we are verbally assaulted for telling someone the truth about themselves, but for the most part, no one is torturing us because of it. There may be someone in your circle who suffered a tremendous loss, experienced a disaster or in much pain due to an attack made by someone who doesn't like them. For some victims, they lose sight of God while others draw closer to him.

The most important thing that all of us believers can do is prepare ourselves before the enemy strikes as best we know how to do. Keeping in mind that God will help us, but he will also test us. It is only a matter of time that something will happen to cause any one of us spiritual upset in our lives. If we stay close to God and ask him to keep our minds intact through life's storms, he will. God uses difficult people, situations, things and places to enlighten us. We rejoice when our stories of heartbreak end with how we overcame. Losing material wealth, health, loved ones and more, some can just look at the pros in the fight for justice, love, freedom, new locations, money, time, and most importantly faith. Sometimes we will pray for God's protection; yet, things will happen anyway. Looking back on your struggles, did you remain faithful? For some of us, we did during one trial, but fell off the wagon when it came to others. When this happens, it's usually because we let some of our critics get next to us.

In March 2009, CNN reported a pastor was killed in Illinois during a church service by a gun man. Words were exchanged between the gun man and the pastor prior to his death, but there was no mention of what was said in the article. Most church attendees were crying and praying while the shooting was going on. However, two members tackled the gun man who also had a knife. The attacker survived. In a tragedy such as this, what might have gone through the minds of those who may not have been strong in their faith? I'm sure they questioned, "Why Lord, I prayed?" Are you prepared to answer a new believers "Why" questions? How would you have encouraged yourself and others during a difficult time like this?

Critics will also attack you about the blogs you write, websites you create, and comments you post on the Internet as mentioned earlier in this book. Are you prepared for possible imprisonment, on and offline attacks such as your site being shut down or your account being canceled, or even worse physically threatened, wounded or killed for the things you say over the Internet? There are places in our world that do not allow their citizens to simply post how they feel about an issue or expose injustices.

According to an article entitled, "*Imprisoned, Attacked & Dead Bloggers Increases Worldwide in 2009* (ReadWrite-Web.com), a report by Reporters Sans Frontières showed a "number of bloggers around the world arrested because of their online work (which) jumped from 59 to 151 between 2008 and 2009, an increase of 155%. Additionally, one blogger died in prison and 61 were physically assaulted." A recorded number of these cases happened after a leader in Iran was re-elected.

Over the years, we have read and watched television shows where whistleblowers mysteriously came up dead for uncovering truth, exposing truth, threatening to share truth, and participating in campaigns for truth. Right now, I hear in the spiritual realm that many well-known names will be coming out of their mind control programming to share truth and many celebrity worshippers are not going to be able to handle it all. Therefore, many celebrities will die unnecessarily due to a lack of support. We have to keep in mind that truth goes beyond just the Holy Bible. God wants us to share truth. "These are the things you are to do: Speak the truth to each other, and render true and sound judgment in your courts; do not plot evil against your neighbor, and do not love to swear falsely. I hate all this," declares the Lord (Zech. 8:16-17, NIV). Exposing truths so that we can help others will cost some of us our lives. So for those of you out there treading dangerous waters or about to, you might as well prepare yourself and loved ones. "For every one that doeth evil hateth the light, neither cometh to the light, lest his deeds should be reproved" (John 3:20). If they hate the light, critics will hate you. Think about this for a moment, Jesus said, "If the world hates you, keep in mind that it hated me first" (John 15:18).

We can act like Jonah all we want when God is moving us into areas of ministry that we really don't want to go into, but there are consequences when God wants you to do something, but you refuse to listen. The Lord will put in you the courage, the motivation, and the plan to get his job done come hell or high water. Speaking of "the plan," there is no one plan that fits all when dealing with a critic who is on attack. When dealing with cynics, you have to handle challenges on a case-by-case basis. This means that you will need to know something about your critics, before you can respond to them. Critical people love knowing much about others, but sharing very little about themselves. You might have family and friends who love listening to you and commenting about your life, but when you reverse the table, they "don't want to talk…I got to go." Ask your skeptics questions, "What are your views? How do you feel? What made you think of that? What am I doing that makes you feel the way you do? Why do you say that? What witnesses or evidence do you have that proves what you are saying is correct? How did you come by that opinion?" Seek God on how and when to respond to your critics.

Now maybe your critics might be lethal and mentally unstable. It would make sense to protect yourself and family. Don't sleep on crazy critics. Your door should never be left wide open for your enemy to take comfort. Teach your family not to be so open with everyone when you know you have enemies. Put escape plans in place, save money, choose friends wisely, and most of all stay prayerful. There may be those moments in your life that you may have to go underground, meaning you will need to stay out of public view for a time. Find information that will help you take cover from a lunatic enemy, but don't become so paranoid that you lose sight of God.

We read in the Scriptures, prophets in the Bible were used to give kings, individuals or crowds: a message from the Lord, a set of instructions, a warning, and other things that God wanted them to do. The Lord prepared each of his followers in advance. Now, if we choose to listen to God when it comes to some details, incorporate our own philosophies or others' opinions in matters, for some of us, doing these things might get us killed. We ought not to do some, but all of what God wants and consult God on who or what we should be including on his project, sermon, mission, and other things. What if God had been warning those pastors about pending danger in advance? Of course, this information is not in those articles. Besides, that wouldn't look good in the newspapers that a "pastor ignored God's voice before he died." Sometimes God is whispering to us, "Don't move on this yet…Wait. Don't live here, but live there. Avoid trouble by going this way…" But what do many of us do? Think about the inconveniencies and how God's directions might hinder us or disrupt our plans. Meanwhile, all God is trying to do is save you some time, money and even your life. Acting stubborn, impatient, or slow when God wants you to be still, move at a certain time or act quickly on something might cost you some blessings in the past and more in the future. Surrender your do-it-yourself mentality over to the Lord and permit him to help you get there from here.

You most likely don't smoke, drink, curse, or argue. So the unsaved critic or backslider decides he or she wants to make small talk, but the Bible instructs, "Go from the presence of a foolish man, when you perceive not in him the lips of knowledge" (Prov. 14:7, AKJV). The critical person may leave your presence before you leave him or her if you should talk often about Jesus. Some Christians may welcome a debate with the unrighteous, but it won't be long before one's temperature rises and words meant to uplift become harsh. The ungodly will begin to defend their lifestyle with lies; while the Christian will offend his or hers with biblical truth. You might be a church-goer, worshiper, bible study teacher, even a good friend of the pastor. There are those individuals who will assume that because of the titles you carry, you might be a trouble-maker. They might have had bad experiences with "those type." Therefore, they do their best to avoid you and people like you.

I think of a time when I first came to Christ overly excited about God's Word and carelessly talking about it to whoever whenever. I sincerely wanted to share my church experiences and biblical studies with others, because I wanted them to feel just as joyful. But oftentimes, I was given the cold treatment. The unbeliever, backslider, and even fellow believers didn't want to hear about God or the Bible. It was okay for some on Sunday, others on Saturday or when a Christian show was on TV to talk about God, but apart from these times, talking about spiritual things was often met with objection. However, years prior to my accepting Jesus into my life, I could share stories about my nightclub experiences almost any time with these same individuals and receive laughs, stories, and encouragement to "live your life...just have fun!" But once I became saved, I had a better outlook about what I wanted to do with my life. I had falsely assumed people would be happy for me and bless me with godly instructions, but I was wrong.

There will be those moments that a critic will leave you no choice, but to respond to his or her negativity depending on how the criticism is phrased. He or she will ask questions that most likely you never thought of or can't answer. The naysayer may add an insulting remark when speaking to you especially if you should share positive things about your current lifestyle. Wicked critics will mention sensitive information from your past in order to arouse angry feelings. Overall, the critical person who has already formulated a negative opinion about you and your God will not assist you in being the best you can be.

The critic enjoys making those he or she doesn't like, crack under pressure. If you are going to speak to a public audience, be prepared for that attention-grabber in the audience who is going to question your faith. When you don't know an answer to a question, just say. "I need to further my study on that subject." Some Christians when feeling under pressure will blurt out, "I don't know." That answer is fine when speaking to those closest to you. But when speaking before large audiences or representing a business, that answer is unacceptable. Answer questions as the Lord leads. Always ask someone for help when in doubt. Remember, God knows your enemy better than you. I think of how Jesus answered the Pharisees' objections. From time to time he answered a question with a question, used body language, told a parable, made convicting statements, or did other things that caused his naysayers to think critically. If we are believers in the one true God, we will not always be well-received by our critics; therefore, we must do the best we can to represent for team God!

Don't Deny the Pain of Criticism

Your critic expresses how she feels about "People like you…" She admits that she "can't stand Christians." Your adversary motivates your brother to "tell you about yourself." He fills the air with curse words, finger pointing and threats. If you have experienced similar things, then you know you didn't walk away without feeling hurt, confused and bitter. You tell yourself, "All I was trying to do was help. Why would she say such horrible things to me? Why was my brother yelling at me?" Later that day, when a relative or friend asks, "How are you?" You answer with a lie, "Fine." Knowing full well, you are deeply wounded emotionally. Being a Christ follower is no easy task and you will feel like at times the weight of the world is on your shoulders.

Critics cause pain. Some people don't mean to abuse, but many of those described in this book, intentionally hurt others because they have been repeatedly hurt as children and then again as adults. When bitter remarks come off the wicked tongue, some Christians allow them to resonate in their spirits. They take words and actions personal; rather than giving their emotional pain over to the one who can bare it all, Jesus! The hurt Christian may deny that he or she is affected by negative events, resist wise counsel, or oppose others who are only trying to assist. This man or woman of God may act in ways that are not typical of his or her personality. He or she may lash out at others, blame others for ill feelings (whether guilty or not), act aggressively, or do other things that look like the world. When this happens, a believer may act like an abused dog backed in a corner, assuming that everyone is out to get him or her. When approached about one's erratic behavior, the angry Christian might cover up true feelings with a smile and act polite. He or she will most likely come up with excuses. "I guess I'm feeling this way because of the weather…or maybe it's the stress I'm under at work…" Some may go so far as to say, "I don't know what you're talking about. All is well with me."

Offenders take their pain and dump it on the unsuspecting. They feel insulted when truthful statements are made about the things they say and do. When you speak truth, the offended shows his or her teeth while preparing for the opportunity to attack. We can make matters worse by denying that we too have been wounded by some truth said to us. But we must remember, God was there, he saw our pain. He knew what the critic was going to say before he or she said it. As we all know criticism hurts more when we didn't see it coming and when it comes from relatives and friends. We may ask God, why would he let that person act so foolishly and say such mean things? We have to bear in mind that God permits all men and women to move freely in their lives whether their actions or reactions are right or wrong. It is up to us, to guard our hearts from a potential avalanche of emotions. But what do some of us do? Avoid talking to God about the things that hurt us the most. Instead, we converse with people who can't heal us from painful feelings. Here's a thought, "Forget the former things; do not dwell on the past" (Isa. 43:18). We are to wait on God for his comfort rather than man, woman or child's.

For some believers, they think pretending to be emotionally stable will bring them healing. They say things like, "I just know I'm good…I don't need any help, I got God…I know I act strangely, but that's alright I got God…I know I have an addiction, but God will heal me!" They are unfortunately in denial. "They claim to know God, but by their actions they deny him. They are detestable, disobedient and unfit for doing anything good" (Titus 1:16). There are many believers who obsess with the following things like: entertainers, sex, food, sodas, gossip, getaways, Internet activities, jobs, shopping, church events, bad advisors, and more. Rather than turn over their troubles to God, they distract themselves with everything but God. Rarely does anyone warn people about these kinds of obsessions because usually they are guilty of the same behaviors, and besides these addictions don't affect others' lives like alcohol, drugs, pornography, and prostitution. Therefore, some individuals' fixations go unnoticed for years. Those who are emotionally and physically troubled will ask for prayer, but don't do much else to deal with painful past events. We have to realize that God gifted many doctors, counselors and others to assist us mentally and physically if we are unwilling to see how our actions negatively impact others and be willing to change then we will continue to suffer with addictive habits. Think about this, Jesus had to touch some people while others he just spoke to. Some he went to and others came to him. We need the Lord to anoint the hands of his chosen to heal. Just praying for someone verbally, is not enough sometimes. Seek out professional help when voices in your head don't go away, when the words of others hurt so badly that you want to hurt yourself or someone else, and when actions are causing unnecessary confusion for self and members in your household. Then trust that God will do the rest.

We all should know that too much of anything isn't good for us. Eat and drink too much and you will have health issues. Lying often about your spiritual condition or someone else's will only move God to one day expose you. Consulting with advisors that are participating in ungodly lifestyles will only tempt you to do things just to avoid addressing those hurtful moments in your life. Fighting critics on a daily basis both on and offline, will tire, depress, and disturb your faith. "Cast thy burden upon the Lord, and he shall sustain thee: he shall never suffer the righteous to be moved" (Ps. 55:22). Once you do this, allow the Lord to direct you to the right people, places and things and yes, sometimes he will use people we don't like to direct us toward some help.

Test the Critic

There will be those moments when we don't know why a critic is set on attacking us. But some of those critical people around us may still have some unfinished business with God's children. They may be our employers, teachers, parents or friends. Money could be at stake, mental health, and other things that if we prematurely run a critic out of our lives, we might stand to lose a lot. This is why we must seek God for wisdom on how to react to a critic.

In Exodus 20:20, during the journey to the promise land, Moses noticed the people were fearful when they saw the thunder and lightning, heard a trumpet and saw a mountain in smoke. "And Moses said unto the people, Fear not: for God is come to prove you, and that his fear may be before your faces, that ye sin not." God may be using various situations to test you too. Keep in mind his trials are not to lure you back into sin, but to teach you to stop sinning.

When we know for certain that we have critics who mean to do us harm, we don't challenge them to a fight. Maybe at one time in your life, you did that, but not now. "Therefore, if anyone is in Christ, he is a new creation; the old has gone, the new has come!" (2 Cor. 5:17, NIV).

Consider this, when David realized Saul was determined to kill him, he left. He didn't stick around to see if something bad would not happen to the king nor did he try to do something bad to his enemy. David didn't even know why Saul was angry with him. For a time, Saul had hidden his jealousy and angry feelings from David (I Sam. 19). Initially, all David knew was that the king could no longer be calmed down with his music and service. Saul didn't like the way the people reacted to David. He was also disappointed that every test he gave David, he passed. The king was especially angry that his daughter, Michal, loved David as much as she did. David was that nice guy that seemed to have everything going for him looks, skills, fame, and fortune and Saul was looking for any reason to kill David, because he knew that he could effortlessly replace him as king.

You don't want to remain in the presence of a critic who doesn't like or want you around especially if you know that this person is mentally unstable. Negative emotions can get the best of the most successful people in our world. They may look normal to outsiders, but those closest to them know differently. Jonathan, King Saul's son, was close enough to his father to know that something was terribly wrong. While David was fleeing from Saul, he used Jonathan to test his father. David wanted to know was it safe to return to Saul. But after Jonathan sat with his dad and others at a feast that lasted over a period of days, by day two, Jonathan found that his father was still very angry with David. When his son asked the king about his reaction to David, Saul gave him no explanation. We see the same animosity that Saul showed David when Solomon discovered that God chose Jeroboam, his servant, to be the next king. Solomon tried to kill him.

People with mental illnesses are all around us. Today, the medical profession would put a label on Saul and give him a prescription. But the Bible says that the Spirit of the Lord left Saul. So no matter what man or woman comes up with, it is obvious that Saul didn't have the presence of God living inside of him. Therefore, when one is dealing with a mental condition, he or she is going to experience those embarrassing times when he or she will be critical of others for what appears to be no apparent reason. It doesn't matter how much you counsel, pray, service an individual's needs, or give this person good gifts, someone with mental challenges might be determined to undermine you and discredit you to others because of reasons that are important to him or her, but seem petty to others. I went through a situation for years with a young person who had a mental handicap that was aggravated periodically simply by my presence. Because I didn't know what this troubled teen's problem was, I thought of her like you would a bully, and had prepared myself to fight her physically if needed. The opportunity never came and instead one day she simply apologized for acting so ugly toward me over the years and I in turn said I was sorry for the things I said and thought about her. We never spoke again after that.

For some of us, who try to quiet conflict, we might strive to rectify any matters with a difficult person that could have caused discourse in the past. Yet, with all of our hard work to remedy a situation, a person who is set on never liking you, is a problem for God to solve in the meantime all we can do is pray and keep on going with our own lives. If you are in a situation like this, know that God sees and hears all. He will avenge your enemies. Sooner or later that thorn in your side will be plucked out! Then there are those, who aren't our enemies at all, they are just godless, pray for their souls. You may remember the times that you turned down invites to talk with Christians, attend gatherings and might have been upset that religious people kept coming around telling you about the Word of God, so what did you do? You criticized them and when you did, you may have blasphemed the Holy Spirit—thank God for his mercy!

For further study to help you if you are being attacked by a critic, consider reading the following: Prov. 24:7; Prov. 17:24; and Eccles. 2:14. I pray that the Lord will provide you with the wisdom to witness effectively. Let not your heart be troubled by any criticism, because you serve an awesome God, in Jesus name!

7. Put on the Whole Armor of God

A soldier must prepare for battle. He trains, studies and trains some more. Then one day he has to make that journey into the enemy's camp. For days, weeks, months, even years, you may have studied the Bible, attended church, and participated in some activities to help you deal with Satan and his demons. You heard about those who didn't like you and watched the critics talk about you and your faith. You may have even internalized what the critics believed God wanted for your life. Maybe you have already confronted a critic or two. But the battle isn't over, one day the serpent is going to show up again like he did when Eve was in the garden. As mentioned in other chapters, he will present an offer you might not refuse. You will need to speak truth boldly and courageously and might even have to go so far as to physically fight like David with Goliath (1 Sam.). After you complete this book, get *Face Your Foe* by me because I will be explaining more in that book about battling with an enemy.

A child of God will have to do the following when dealing with his or her critics. Take a stand, and avoid the temptation to compromise truth. At times, turn the other cheek, but don't flip-flop on societal or personal issues and most of all, avoid being silent about what is evil and what is good. To walk with the Lord, means there is no sugar-coating the gospel or pretending! Every believer must have a moral compass, (based on biblical principles), that uplift and encourage others as well as self. Without it, the soldier enters battle without a prayer and a plan. He or she will easily fall into a trap strategically set before his or her feet. One must know that the battle for truth, in all its forms, can get quite ugly sometimes. There is a long history of men and women who suffered for telling the truth. John was murdered. Paul was put in jail. Jesus was tortured, hung and then left for dead. You might have been ostracized, beaten, manipulated, or wounded because you told the truth over the years. I have a history of being ridiculed, shunned, cursed, and physically assaulted for standing up to angry men and women, liars, players, control freaks, and narcissists and exposing them on their wrongs. Wayward believers don't always behave. Backsliders don't always listen. The unsaved don't always walk away. As for God's chosen, they aren't always right, wrong or quiet.

Let's review the armor God has provided for his soldiers, line by line as it relates to dealing with a critical person. Beginning with Ephesians 6:11 "Put on the whole armor of God, that ye may be able to stand against the wiles of the devil. For we wrestle not against flesh and blood, but against principalities, against powers, against the rulers of the darkness of this world, against spiritual wickedness in high places" (v. 12). God is telling us that we wrestle with unseen forces. This proves that there are powers that are not in our best interest and cannot be fought with human strength. These powers operate with ulterior motives, evil secrets, dark thoughts, and negative feelings. This is why you just get that "feeling something ain't right" sometimes when dealing with people.

"Wherefore take unto you the whole armor of God, that ye may be able to withstand in the evil day…" (v. 13). God is preparing us for what is ahead. If you thought walking with the Lord would be boring, think again. And if it is boring to you, then I have to question what are you doing or not doing to help the lost, unsaved, confused, miserable, or poor? When you take this Scripture and apply it to your life, you know the day is coming when the enemy is going to use someone to verbally or physically attack you—that evil day is coming. What will you do? Further, the Scripture instructs, "…and having done all, to stand. Stand therefore, having your loins girt about with truth" (v. 14). The belt of truth is what you will often refer to when the critic comes trying to get you to swap truth for lies.

The breastplate protects you from the enemy's fiery darts, because when he shoots his darts, he is aiming for your heart. "…and having on the breastplate of righteousness;" (v. 14). We are to stand for truth and conduct ourselves in ways that if anyone is witnessing us getting attacked by difficult individuals, they will just know that we are children of God. "And your feet shod with the preparation of the gospel of peace;" (v. 15). Your feet are prepared to take you wherever you need to go to deliver God's truth. Despite being in a spiritual battle, you know that your duties will eventually bring an end to the war.

In the same Scripture passage, "Above all, taking the shield of faith, wherewith ye shall be able to quench all the fiery darts of the wicked" (v. 16). Notice, the enemy will attack. What do fiery darts do? They burn you. Evil comments make your temperature rise.

"…And take the helmet of salvation" (v. 17). A helmet protects one's head from injury; your belief in Christ guards your heart from the enemy's schemes to keep you away from God. However, sometimes even when we wear a man-made helmet, we are still wounded. But when you wear your helmet of salvation, despite physical wounds, you still know that your inner being is protected no matter what happens on the outside.

When someone challenges you about your beliefs, know why you believe what you believe. Why are you saved? Who do you serve God or worldly gods such as: money, TV, family, sports, celebrities, etc.? The critic will come to knock off your helmet like a bully snatching off a small boy's baseball hat and then running with it. Once he has your helmet off your head, the whole body is open for destruction. You are going to try to get your assurance of your salvation back, but he is going to dangle it over your head while you jump for it. Then when you start pushing and punching him with no plan and no skill, he is going to wait for you to leave yourself wide open, then he is going to hit you with a right and then a left. After that, you and your hat will be down on the ground while he is standing over you laughing saying, "See, I told you, you aren't a Christian!"

Your sword of faith, when used correctly, will cut your critic before any of his fiery darts do any damage to you. "…and the sword of the Spirit, which is the word of God:" (v. 17). Notice, we aren't bringing guns, knives and the posse to the fight—for some of you, back in the day you did these things without hesitation, but now you are a new creature in Christ. If we sincerely trust in the Lord, like we say we do, then we will let the words of his Bible speak to us on what to do before we do it—trust in him for a plan. In addition, the sword of the spirit is used to cut up or cut out the following: a critic's ideology, argumentative spirit, foolish living, and any number of things to get this naysayer to re-think his or her position. The sword need not be used with loud voices and curse words attached to it while being swung at someone's head—those are nothing more than distractions that could be used to get the best of you when in battle. The mere presence of a child of light, with sword in hand, will intimidate or offend sinful men and women and draw attention to what God wants to do in and through them. It's not the tone of voice that does the cutting, but it's the Word of God both in print and through the voice of the Holy Spirit that does it all.

The last part of this Scripture sums it all up, "Praying always with all prayer and supplication in the Spirit, and watching thereunto with all perseverance and supplication for all saints…" (v. 18). We are asking and pleading with the Lord to make some things possible in our lives. We desire an answer. We need to be assured that God hears us and will do something about our dilemmas. For those who believe and trust in God, he listens and meets our needs not in our time, but in his.

We can be saved from the critic's harsh words and physical assaults by standing on the principles of God. "For the word of God is quick, and powerful, and sharper than any two edged sword, piercing even to the dividing asunder of soul and spirit, and of the joints and marrow, and is a discerner of the thoughts and intents of the heart" (Rom. 10-17). The Apostle Paul reminds us to pray and give praise to our Creator. This is how we stay strong in our beliefs. Otherwise, we will waver in our thoughts, begin to worry, act irrationally, and eventually return to ungodly lifestyles.

Think about this, the heart is the central part of the nervous system, if it is severely wounded, the whole body dies. "Always keep your heart guarded. Keep thy heart with all diligence; for out of it are the issues of life" (Prov. 4:23).

8. In the Name of Jesus

To say something be done in the name of Jesus is declaring this power. "And Jesus came and spake unto them, saying, All power is given unto me in heaven and in earth" (Matt. 28:18). The power of Jesus' name is beyond comprehension. Many men and women have attempted to explain the overwhelming influence that the name of Jesus gives to the worshiper. A forum poster (Nairaland.com) explained it like this, "Jesus Christ has given Christians the right and authority to use his name. This means that Christians have been given the power of attorney. Legally, power of attorney is the authority to act in another person's behalf, at their request. It is authorization given by one person (Jesus) permitting another (Christians) to take action on his (Jesus Christ's) behalf." The Bible says, "And whatever you ask in My name, that I will do, that the Father may be glorified in the Son. If you ask anything in My name, I will do it." (John 14:13,14)

The unspiritual critic doesn't understand nor know of the divine power manifested in the believer. In Acts 19:2, "He (Paul) said to them, Have you received the Holy Ghost since you believed? And they said to him, we have not so much as heard whether there be any Holy Ghost." Nowadays many believers are still responding to that question the same way, they believe in God, but they do not have the gift of the Holy Spirit. The Holy Spirit is the gift that Jesus left behind for every believer when he ascended to heaven.

When Paul spoke to the Thessalonian church about the Holy Spirit, he said, "For we know, brothers loved by God, that he has chosen you, because our gospel came to you not simply with words, but also with power, with the Holy Spirit and with deep conviction. You know how we lived among you for your sake. You became imitators of us and of the Lord; in spite of severe suffering, you welcomed the message with the joy given by the Holy Spirit" (1 Thess. 1:4-6, NIV). So how does one receive the Holy Spirit, he or she asks the Lord. "If you then, though you are evil, know how to give good gifts to your children, how much more will your Father in heaven give the Holy Spirit to those who ask him"(Luke 11:13, NIV)!

If a believer sincerely has the gift of the Holy Spirit, something about his or her lifestyle would exemplify that gift. He or she would be focused on what God wants and not so much on what he or she desires. This person would be concerned about helping others, appeasing the Lord, exhibiting self-control when tempted to sin, teaching others about Jesus, be humble, generous, and more. If you are a reader who questions whether or not you have the Holy Spirit, I encourage you to pray and ask God for his gift. Also, read Scriptures and study books about the gifts of the Holy Spirit. Bear in mind, critics, especially wicked ones, focus on people and what they can get from them. When you are powerless, you are unable to pray effectively, stand up against difficult people and you also lack the access to obtain the knowledge that God so much wants to share with you.

Wise men and women use the name of Jesus in conversation in ways that uplift, rebuke, correct, etc. but critics find fault with all things righteous. The critic will debate over things he or she may or may not be knowledgeable about as it relates to the things of God. Eventually, when he or she has been proven wrong, this person will begin to tire of debating especially when he or she feels the Spirit of God in the midst. Some critics will even go so far as to say, "You know what, forget what I said, it's unimportant." The devil has tried to conquer believers for generations by casting doubt within them about their faith. One of his many ways is by use of words. "Are you sure God is speaking to you? You really don't know enough about the Bible to talk to people about God. The Lord wouldn't use someone like you to do that. You don't have a license or a degree to teach people about Jesus. You know you have always been fearful of being in front of people, why don't you leave that up to someone else. God wouldn't want you to get up there and make a fool of yourself."

Satan moves a man or woman to rebel against God's will through fear. He desires to get one to emotionally feel guilty about his or her circumstances; therefore, a weak-minded Christian will allow the following to happen: tiredness or busyness to prevent one from sharing the gospel, fear to keep from doing God's will (think: Jonah), fleshly desires, childhood trauma, and other issues. The tired believer, with unresolved issues, just doesn't have any energy to do or say anything to a pessimistic critic, therefore, he or she just goes along with whatever program to avoid having to defend truth. "I will just collect a paycheck…it's not that bad I have experienced worse…I'll be okay," she reasons away the critic's ugliness and may even blame herself. She says, "Well if I would have just done what the man asked…I'm always doing so much, maybe that's why he reacted that way. I'll do better next time and maybe he will be nicer to me."

The busy, lukewarm believer doesn't want to have to cope with the issues that come with standing for truth. For instance, expressing his or her thoughts about one's ungodly ways, or witnessing to the backslider, unsaved, and others might cause him to lose friends and make enemies, so he tries to avoid rocking the boat by sharing what God has laid on his heart. Instead, this person will simply usher believers and unbelievers from one church event after the other without a care. The church worker does what he is told by leaders, blames others when souls aren't won for Christ, and so on. Rarely, does this overwhelmed believer make time to have a serious one-on-one conversation about his faith with anyone. Some believers, like this, spend years at jobs they don't like, never receive the pay that they deserve and can be difficult with those who they work closely with while being nice to strangers. They are often impatient and irritable with relatives and friends because they don't speak up when their leaders are being unfair or unreasonable. These passive aggressive types internalize much, and will take out their issues in little ways while hoping their sneaky behaviors go unnoticed. You got a glimpse of this kind of believer earlier in this book. Hopefully, this doesn't describe you.

On PsychologyToday.com, passive aggression is defined this way, "…a deliberate and masked way of expressing covert feelings of anger. The chronically passive aggressive person expresses anger through such indirect means as procrastination, sulking, 'forgetting' and intentional inefficiency across most situations, almost all of the time. Yet, even those who are normally honest and direct in their dealings, may choose to behave in passive aggressive ways at certain times." People act like this are described as sneaky and will bad-mouth others.

Then there are those believers that fear doing the things of God and don't act on the following Scripture, "For God did not give us a spirit of timidity, but a spirit of power, of love and of self-discipline" (2 Tim. 1:7, NIV). With people like this in the church, it isn't any wonder why so many are lukewarm. We have to ask ourselves, what kind of faith do we really have? Let us remember, "...we are more than conquerors through him that loved us" (Rom. 8:37). According to Merriam-Webster dictionary, a conqueror is "victorious," able "to gain mastery over or win by overcoming obstacles or opposition."

I have observed that all critical individuals go through a spiritual process in their lives (whether children of God or children of Satan) like that of a caterpillar who one day turns into a butterfly. He or she starts off crawling but eventually flies right into God's calling on his or her life. Some butterflies evolve into beautiful masterpieces; while others are moths, void of color and sickly looking. They fly here and there looking for something to feed off of whether a flower or a sweater. Some can be a nuisance while others can simply be something interesting to look at from a distance. If I am a child of light, someone should feel like there is something about me worth getting to know. But if I am a child of darkness, then observers might consider me a nuisance. Discerning Christians must know the difference between those who are sent by God to enlighten, reprove, correct, and encourage and those who are clearly marked to do nothing more than cause spiritual chaos in our lives. Hopefully, one day a beautiful butterfly will emerge from the critic who sincerely wants a relationship with Christ, but until then, watch as well as pray.

Your Savior is Jesus, not man, not a statue, a child, a celebrity, symbol, or anything else that becomes shabby, breaks or dies. No matter how many people have done great things in this life, when man and woman dies (along with his or her unbelief), Jesus is still the only one left standing. He is the one who you can call on when no one else cares or wants to be around you. You may have read the Book of Job and could relate to some of his personal struggles. Despite all of his trials, when all was said and done, God blessed Job and his family. He then used Job's story to be a blessing to others for centuries. This true man of God, like Jesus, was used in a glorious way at the end of all his suffering. Both men were like caterpillars that grew into extraordinary butterflies.

Jesus is moving men, women and children to assist you and I spiritually and physically while the enemy is using others to break us down. In the past, the Holy Spirit placed you in settings at the right place at the right time. You had to crawl before you could walk. The Spirit of God ministered to you while you slept and you received orders to do things for the Lord. You recall that Jesus opened doors that no man could open. As you know, he is the author and finisher of our faith. So who are you? A man or a woman who has the Word of the Lord in one hand and your testimony in the other, for some of you readers, go do something with both in Jesus name! You are God's divine plan!

The power in the name of Jesus is evident in the gospels. People, who heard that the Messiah was in town, knew that he had the power to do miraculous things in their lives. Jesus inhabits a power so rich, pure and true—a power that comes from the Father and shared with his Son! How many earthly fathers are really walking in the name of Jesus? How many are blessing their sons and daughters with the Holy Spirit power of Jesus? When I attempted to share the gospel, after dedicating my life to Christ, with those in my circle who were unsaved, they acted uninterested and really had no understanding of the Holy Spirit. Rather than being open to talking about spiritual things, they preferred to talk about themselves. Needless to say, I got to a place where I spiritually matured and learned to put the rebellious and hard-hearted in God's hands and stopped delivering "God said…" messages.

Centuries ago, before Jesus' arrival, there was nothing out there like him back then. People didn't have the kind of access we now have in Jesus name. In past centuries, men, women and children looked up to the sky and elsewhere for a sign from God. It wasn't until Jesus came and left believers with the Holy Spirit that we were able to tap into his power. There is an abundance of spiritual riches that we won't enjoy until we all get to heaven—I am excited about the future, and you should too, with an advocate like Jesus speaking to his Father for us, who are weak, lost and confused at times. We have no choice but to give honor and thanksgiving to a holy God who loves and cares about us so much that he gave us the option to choose eternal life! "But when the kindness and love of God our Savior appeared, he saved us, not because of righteous things we had done, but because of his mercy. He saved us through the washing of rebirth and renewal by the Holy Spirit, whom he poured out on us generously through Jesus Christ our Savior, so that, having been justified by his grace, we might become heirs having the hope of eternal life (Tit. 3:5, NIV).

You and I have come a long way since the time we accepted Jesus into our lives. But then again, maybe some readers have yet to take God seriously and become saved sanctified and Holy Ghost filled, there is still time. For he says, "In the time of my favor I heard you, and in the day of salvation I helped you" (2 Cor. 6:2, NIV). I tell you, now is the time of God's favor, now is the day of salvation. But if one "remains stiff-necked after many rebukes will suddenly be destroyed--without remedy" (Prov. 29:1, NIV). In John 6:4, Jesus said to his disciples, "No one can come to me unless the Father who sent me draws him, and I will raise him up at the last day" (John 6:44, NIV). We must pray to the Father daily, get around the like-minded, read his Word and allow it to convict us so that we can make those burdensome changes in our personal lives.

We have all seen things in people that may have disgusted and discouraged us, but this is no excuse not to draw near to the Lord. He says, his "Spirit will not strive with man forever" in Genesis 6:3. Some readers may have believed less in the one true Christ, because of people's negativity concerning his existence and believed more in the attitudes, appearances, actions and things of men and women. May I suggest you take your eyes off people and their opinions and lifestyles, and put them on Christ? "Let this mind be in you, which was also in Christ Jesus: Who, being in the form of God, thought it not robbery to be equal with God: But made himself of no reputation, and took on him the form of a servant, and was made in the likeness of men: And being found in fashion as a man, he humbled himself, and became obedient to death, even the death of the cross" (Phil. 2: 5-8, AKJ). Has anyone sacrificed their life for you in the way that Christ has? We are all flawed. No words or deeds of mere men and women can surpass the awesome power of that name, Jesus Christ. "Why God also has highly exalted him, and given him a name which is above every name. That at the name of Jesus every knee should bow, of things in heaven, and things in earth, and things under the earth; And that every tongue should confess that Jesus Christ is Lord, to the glory of God the Father." (Phil. 2.9-11, AKJ). So why not use his name in appropriate ways? Pray with the name. Use the name when in need and when you aren't. Trust in it since you can't trust anyone or anything else. Know that in Jesus name, he is holy, a healer, wonderful, magnificent and worthy to be praised! Why observe your bother or sister in Christ hallowing the name of Jesus? Join in on the praise! "Praise ye the Lord. Praise God in his sanctuary: praise him in the firmament of his power" (Psalm 150:1). You may have heard brothers and sisters in Christ say, "When the praise goes up the blessings come down?" How? When a believer exercises his or her faith in Jesus things happen. "Let us fix our eyes on Jesus, the author and perfecter of our faith, who for the joy set before him endured the cross, scorning its shame, and sat down at the right hand of the throne of God" (Hebrews 12:2, NIV). Here's what happened when we made the choice to believe in the one true God and answer his calling, "And you also were included in Christ when you heard the word of truth, the gospel of your salvation. Having believed, you were marked in him with a seal, the promised Holy Spirit…" (Eph. 1:13, NIV). So if you have yet to praise the Lord today or have welcomed his Spirit in your heart, then the following words does both for you today! Say the following out loud, "Jesus, Jesus, Jesus…I know that you loved me first! I know that you care for me! If it wasn't for you I would have no heart-beat! You put breath in my body! When no one liked or wanted me around, you were there! When people talked about me and said I was not qualified, couldn't do, wasn't this, and unable to do that, you gave me the wisdom, you blessed me, you saved me, you left your Holy Spirit for me! Man was no where around! Woman had no time! But God, but God! I believe that you will make me the head and not the tail in every challenge that I face! I receive you: the Father, Son and Holy Spirit this day! I want you in my life! Put the desire in my heart to want to learn more of you and your functions in the spiritual realm like you did for the disciples, prophets and others in your holy Word of days old! Order my steps! I'm giving my all to you, this day! I declare at the sound of your name—Jesus, Jesus, Jesus, my enemies will retreat—go back wherever they have come from! Keep away from me with all their negativity! I bind Satan in Jesus name and all his plans for my destiny! Thank you, Lord for peace, love and the wisdom to know who I am in Christ, in Jesus name!"

Try reading the text aloud. Listen to how it sounds. Think about all you have went through and why it is so important to trust in the Lord. He is all we have when the day is done! Do you feel uplifted, renewed, and ready to do something for God's kingdom? Then read the text again, slowly this time and trust that the Lord will speak to your spirit. Make this kind of praise a part of your daily routine and who knows what turn God will make in your journey with him! Oh yes, there is a power in the name of Jesus "…every knee shall bow, every tongue shall swear" (Isa. 45:23, AKJ).

How would you have reacted had you heard of a man named Jesus with the power to heal coming to your town? Today, the feeling of knowing that God loves you so much that he sent his only Son to save you and me from an eternal death is enormous! The devil knows this that is why he does everything to keep Jesus out of print, off the television screen, radio, music, various Internet websites, and definitely out of public education. Jesus is hated because he represents goodness! And if you are a sincere believer in Jesus, then you will be hated too by unbelievers, backsliders and apostates. "And ye shall be hated of all men for my name's sake: but he that shall endure unto the end, the same shall be saved" (Matt. 13:13).

Many worldly men and women of today are interested in everything, but Jesus (sports figures, musicians, partners, children, jobs, etc.) because they don't sincerely believe that they need Jesus. Some doubt there is power, freedom, and wisdom in the Christian faith. Why is this? The explanation is simple; far too many Christians have allowed people with secular views, traditions, unholy unions, and gods to come into their lives and in their church settings (whether at home through the TV screen, Internet or radio or in local buildings) to infiltrate God's plans for their lives. Believers and unbelievers make changes in the things of God so as to make teachings more palatable to the masses and of course obtain the most money they can. So like a bear caught in a trap, ministers, teachers, and others are howling, crying and wishing for God to come to their unholy structures and anoint unscriptural programs. Rather than coming to God and admitting they have made a mess of things and hearkening to the Lord, they decorate their mistakes with pagan traditions, false beliefs, and unwise, attractive looking counselors so as to draw more money to their organizations. If only the lost, confused, ignorant money-loving ministers would have just listened when God's Holy Spirit whispered to them, "Walk away, this is not of God. Don't sign your name on that contract. God is not in that program. This person is working for Satan…" Instead, they ignored the voice of God, continued to sleep, ate so much food until they couldn't function, became distracted by one's wealthy lifestyle, ideas and more, then went on and shook hands with wicked critical men and women. They entered into business with Satan and without Jesus. It is unfortunate, but leaders as well as followers are all suffering because of both past and present foolish decision-making. "For out of the heart come evil thoughts, murder, adultery, sexual immorality, theft, false testimony, slander. These are what make a man 'unclean'; but eating with unwashed hands does not make him 'unclean'" (Matt. 15:19, 20, NIV).

Too many centuries have gone by where Christians (or those pretending to be) removed the name of Jesus from certain circles, books and more to make their man-made gospels more pleasing to the masses. The name of Jesus doesn't go over too well when one is clearly more interested in serving self than an entity he believes he can't see, hear, taste, touch, or smell.

The Blood of Jesus

The blood covering of Jesus is profound. For when he died on the cross his blood was shed to wash away our sins. "This is the one who came by water and blood--Jesus Christ. He did not come by water only, but by water and blood. And it is the Spirit who testifies, because the Spirit is the truth" (1 John 5:6, NIV). If it wasn't for the blood, he wouldn't have been a sufficient enough sacrifice for the one true God. We know this to be true, because from the beginning of time, God's people gave sacrifices that had to be pleasing to the Lord. But when Jesus came, he was the perfect sacrifice! "…we have been made holy through the sacrifice of the body of Jesus Christ once for all" (Heb. 10:10).

It is with great adoration that we look to Jesus and humbly bow before his feet. What man has shed blood that washed away centuries of people's iniquities? There was an eternal covenant made between Christ and his followers when his blood was shed upon the cross. According to Heb. 13:20 (NIV), "May the God of peace, who through the blood of the eternal covenant brought back from the dead our Lord Jesus, that great Shepherd of the sheep..." One can't enter the Holy Place without Jesus. Believers of the faith demonstrated this in the Bible, "Therefore, brothers, since we have confidence to enter the Most Holy Place by the blood of Jesus..." (Heb. 10:19, NIV). They were certain of what would get them to God, belief in Jesus. Those that were far away from Christ "...have been brought near through the blood of Christ" (Eph. 2:13, NIV).

You must understand that without the shed blood of Christ there is no sacrifice, but gradually this teaching is being diluted and in some cases removed from bibles and sermons. Jesus paid the price for our sins. No other spiritual teacher did what Jesus did! "And from Jesus Christ, who is the faithful witness, and the first begotten of the dead, and the prince of the kings of the earth. To him that loved us, and washed us from our sins in his own blood" (Rev. 1:5). No man has to ever kill another man to be secure in his position with Christ or make a point he is a righteous man by cutting himself or someone else. Yet, many men take unnecessary blood oaths to prove loyalty, gain approval, obtain material wealth, and more from godless men and women. God says, "Jesus paid it all!" In Proverbs 14:12, "There is a way which seemeth right unto a man, but the end thereof *are* the ways of death." Nowadays all we have to do is go to the Father through his Son Jesus. Trust in HIM and know that we are covered by his blood.

There are those born-again believers who will say "by the blood of Jesus, Jesus cover my children with your blood, may your blood cover my home, job and family..." and other similar phrases. This is nothing more than one encouraging his or herself about one's belief in Christ and what he has done for man, woman and child. It is not a magical spell, it doesn't keep men from committing wrongful acts and it is not meant to keep people from speaking ugliness. People will continue to behave any way they see fit around the one who says, "Nothing but the blood of Jesus..." but what those simple declarations of one's faith does is call attention to the awesome power of that living Spirit who every Christian calls, Jesus.

The power of the blood of Jesus covers people's sins, if you want the same power to cover you when engaging in war with your critic, you must be mindful of the Holy Spirit's presence. In order to truly experience the Spirit of Jesus, you must silence your own voice long enough to listen. I ask you the following questions, "Prior to Jesus dying on the cross, how much talking did he do?" Did he address every concern, statement, and question his critics posed as he walked toward his death? When he was resurrected did he spend time defending his actions? Did he tell everyone about his Father's will? We mustn't forget that Jesus walked as a man on this planet at one time. He had many of the same experiences we encounter today with the wayward, unsaved and ignorant. Although he was the Messiah, he suffered too. He was tempted to sin. He cried, got angry, and needed to eat, drink and relieve himself just like us. Jesus had moments where he spent much time with people, but then there were times when he got away from people and prayed to his Father. At one point nearing his death we are shown just how great the burden was that he would carry because he said, "Father, if thou be willing, remove this cup from me: nevertheless not my will, but thine, be done" (Luke 22:42).

Sincere believers in Christ, who know they are bought with a price (1 Cor. 7:23) and know the power of the Son, need not explain God appointed deeds or defend God. It is the man or woman who acts apart from God who stands and argues why he or she said or did something wicked or acted in rebellious ways. We don't have to act like the unrighteous when we know who we are in Christ and are obedient to him. There are times that we have no choice, but to deal with the critic in order to get to the person or object that we really need. Many times I was put in a position where I knew I was covered with the blood of Jesus when I walked in my enemy's camp. The room was cold, eyes rolled, deep sighs, and whispers, while the offender pretended as if all was okay with us when I knew otherwise. Some of you reading this live in towns that you have to go through certain streets, you rather not, in order to get to where you need to go. When you go through those streets, are you going in Jesus name? Are you protected by the blood of Jesus?

We might question who exactly are we in Christ and what purpose does Jesus serve in our lives? We can get so distracted by routines that we don't bother to take that time to go to God for further revelation of our purposes. There will be moments in this walk when we need a fresh anointing, a new perspective on an old one, further knowledge of who we are, and what our purpose is for living. Young people look to us for wisdom to help them understand who they are and what they need to do to become better in God's sight. We should not hesitate to direct them toward Jesus Christ!

You know that Christ dying on the cross was to save us from eternal death. Long before we arrived on this planet, there were problems that only God could solve by sending his only begotten Son. We know that men and women experienced great evils of the past, like we still do today. In addition, we have noticed that many acknowledged a personal Savior which is often referenced in the Holy Bible as well as in countless other documents around the world. There is no question that Jesus is real!

To question whether you are a believer in Jesus is to question, who do you believe resides over your life? For many, money and sports are all-too-important gods in the lives of both believers and unbelievers. For others, they worship relatives and friends, and for plenty more believers, they worship self—one believes that he or she reigns over his or her own life despite acknowledging that there is a Creator. When a person approaches the one true God, he or she must come in his Son's name Jesus, he must believe in his Son. "And this is his commandment, That we should believe on the name of his Son Jesus Christ, and love one another, as he gave us commandment" (John 3:23). When one has made up in her mind, to believe in the Son of God, he or she will not have to worry about where the soul goes after death. "He that believes on him is not condemned: but he that believes not is condemned already, because he has not believed in the name of the only begotten Son of God" (John 3:18, AKJ).

9. Why Love an Enemy?

What does it mean to truly love an enemy—more specifically one's critic? Does it mean laying one's life down for the offender? Does loving our unrighteous critics indicate we are supposed to entrust them with personal information, entertain, buy gifts, or do some other nice things so as to appear like we have forgiven them? What does loving an enemy who may have robbed, stolen, lied, criticized, murdered, raped, or done other things that left us feeling like we could never trust him or her really signify?

While writing this, I heard the Holy Spirit say that we must realize the true aspect of what it means to love the wicked critic, who just might be our neighbor. You recall the passage of Scripture about loving one's neighbor as yourself? The Pharisees were telling people in the Old Testament to hate their enemies (Matthew 5:43), but when Jesus came he turned their twisted words around. "But I tell you: Love your enemies and pray for those who persecute you, that you may be sons of your Father in heaven" (Matt. 5:44:45). The Old Testament law, according to Leviticus 19:18 (NIV), said "Do not seek revenge or bear a grudge against one of your people, but love your neighbor as yourself. I am the Lord." When we treat someone how we want to be treated, we are giving them the best. When you shop, you look for items that are flawless. When you sit down to eat, you expect to be eating a meal that is tasty, healthy, and the best in quality. When you are in need of something a product or service, you get it, don't you? In Proverbs 25:21-22, "If your enemy is hungry, give him food to eat; if he is thirsty, give him water to drink. In doing this, you will heap burning coals on his head, and the Lord will reward you."

Society doesn't teach us how to love wicked people or those who have inadvertently or purposely hurt us. It was never God's intention to make an issue out of loving one's enemy, making it so technical to the point that we find ourselves analyzing every word, but because of critical people who doubt the word of God, men and women of faith do just that; rather than just take God at His Word.

Let's talk about what loving an enemy doesn't mean. It doesn't mean tell people that you forgive an enemy when you know you really haven't. God would consider such behavior as deceptive. Love an enemy also doesn't mean blindly share your world with him or her knowing that this person can potentially destroy you and your family. The Lord would call that, foolish. Further, it definitely doesn't mean participate in sinful acts to show an enemy that you love him. God would cast you out of his sight, because you would be rebelling against his commandments. But what love your enemy means is simply to love like Our Father who has shown love to us. We were once enemies of God and his children.

You might have no problem loving the wayward, unsaved, lost, and confused when these enemies are dear relatives and friends. You act respectful despite how they have acted toward you. When an enemy is close to you, you may or may not say anything to him or her about the offense, but if he or she were a stranger you might vow to get even. In Proverbs 24:28-29 (NIV), "Do not testify against your neighbor without cause, or use your lips to deceive. Do not say, 'I'll do to him as he has done to me; I'll pay that man back for what he did.'" God wants us to be fair, respectful, loving, kind, etc. with all people whether we know them or not. We are to leave it up to God to deal with our enemies. He is the one who hates the ways of the wicked.

Loving an enemy isn't connecting with someone on an emotional level like you would your mother, father, sister, or brother. You wouldn't drop your guard with someone who you know is jealous, angry or bitter toward you or with a stranger. You know that would be foolish and dangerous. A relationship with an enemy isn't bad or good it just is. God isn't interested in our labels, categories or personal opinion or feelings when it comes to dealing with our enemies, he just wants us to listen and obey as the Spirit leads. When we are so focused on what we want, how we feel, and what others think of us, that's when we end up falling into traps.

I have learned, after years of fighting with former enemies, you never want to make them feel like you are all-too-willing and able to do something like destroy their reputations or worse murder them—you never know when God is going to use them to service you. If you put your foe at ease, he or she might not feel the desire so much to want to attack again. However, your actions or lack thereof against an enemy doesn't guarantee anything. You will also want to avoid the temptation to psychologically or physically control an enemy in order to get the upper-hand. In addition, you don't want to use the godless critic's tactics described in this book to launch a counter-attack. If anything, pay close attention to how you react to situations and try hard to exercise self-control over your behavior when dealing with wicked people who love to launch verbal attacks, ignore or speak negatively about you to others.

So many believers have attempted to dissect the Lord's directive, "Love your enemy," to the point that they follow worldly men and women's definitions whose sole intention is to obtain selfish gain and build on their reputation with God's commandment. If you find yourself still struggling with what it sincerely means to love your enemy, ask yourself, "What does loving my enemy sincerely mean to me?" Then check to see that your definition aligns with Scripture.

Why Do You Love Your Enemy?

I didn't fully comprehend what it meant to love my evil critic until I saw the benefits. One day, I reasoned I could sincerely love an enemy, because he or she showed me a lot about myself through my own personal trials and tribulations. If I could love the new me, then surely I could at least appreciate what my enemy did for me through the process – no matter how bad! I have realized over the years to trust God for healing and to permit him to use me to love an enemy in ways that only he can.

I did come up with some reasons, as to why I have come to love a couple of my enemies over the years (with that Christ kind of love) and I have included a tad bit of humor about the subject in the following list.

- I love my enemy, because God used him to fill my pockets even when he didn't know that was what he was doing. *You can't help but love a person who helps pay the bills!*

- I love my enemy because he thought he had the upper-hand on me with his lying, covering up, and manipulations, but the Lord reminded me, "Vengeance is mine." I got to see my enemy take a God-ordained butt whipping which kept me from getting one! *So I thank my enemy for taking the butt whipping that could have been meant for me!*

- I love my enemy because when I was weak for him, God used him to make me strong. *Shattering those rose-colored glasses made me see the truth!*

- I love my enemy because I know that I could have paid him back in the worse way, but I didn't which made me a better person because I spared his life. My enemy taught me compassion when I thought I had none (*sometimes I can be colder than ice cubes!)*

- I love my enemy because his lack of appreciation when I assisted him (and her) encouraged me to help others. Those who received gifts and opportunities intended for him say just want to say, "Thank you!"

I know that some might not see the benefit of loving one's enemy and may have turned his or her nose up about my list. But this is how I remain peaceful with those who don't like me. Of course, loving an enemy is not the kind of love a mother has for her child or a love that someone has for a favorite meal or game. Love your enemy also doesn't mean to sacrifice who you are for a person either—no matter the title! In addition, God's command also doesn't mean to do things that grieve the Holy Spirit so that one can appease an enemy. To love is simply the opposite of hate. It encourages positivity and discourages negativity. Therefore, I will love my enemy because it brings out the best in me and who knows, it might make an optimistic impact on him or her. If I am doing what's right by my enemy, I feel less burdened and am not concerned about being judged by God and others. Remember: just because you love your enemy doesn't mean that our Creator expects you to do the following: be a fool for your enemy, compromise your beliefs, go along just to get along or any other weak-minded thing the devil would like to convince you is "the Christian thing to do."

When Your Critic Brings Up the Old You

Now let's say, you may sincerely love your enemy and no matter what negative thing this person has done or said to you, there are critics who always seem to remind you of how you once hated this person.

Consider doing the following when dealing with this cynical foe who loves to remind you about your past:

- ✓ Observe this person's ways. Watch how he or she hurts others. Note what you see and question his or her actions. So many people spend more time talking with a critic and less time watching one's actions that it isn't any wonder why the unsuspecting is blind-sided by wicked strategies.

- ✓ Pray about your observations. We falsely assume someone is an enemy, when in fact he or she just might be going through some challenging times.

- ✓ Find out what you can about the critical person's belief system, his or her past and other relevant information without talking negatively about the individual to others. Most often, mean-spirited criticism is coming from a wounded heart.

- ✓ Look at the contradictions in this person's views. Compare truths and lies. Check the Bible for further understanding.

- ✓ Be prepared to stand for what you believe when the chance comes.

- ✓ Keep quiet when you know a critical person is trying to use seduction, anger, frustration, manipulation and other tactics to tempt you to commit a sin. Remove yourself from his or her presence.

- ✓ Avoid the temptation to attack an adversary; rather discuss your thoughts and feelings with God and be still until you hear from him. In other words, wait on the Lord!

Think of the many tribes who were at war in the Bible. Some didn't fight without God and those that decided to go their own way lost their battles. Some biblical stories involved a tribe that may have been "minding their own business" per se, and then along comes another tribe that wants their land. Others may have had an enemy that ordered a surprise attack, but thanks to God, they were prepared to fight because they wore their spiritual armor. When we, believers, are just living our lives drama free (so we think), at some point, the enemy is going to come and disturb our peace. He will use those closest to us to hit us where it really hurts. For some believers, finances are constantly under attack, health is a close second, and some of our family members seem to always be on the front page news in our lives for one too many wrong reasons.

We worry and cry periodically, while hoping that God will answer our prayers, but there are those moments when he seems so far away. If we sincerely trust in Him, like the many saints in the Bible that had been faced with various trials and tribulations, we will be able to overcome Satan's devices.

We must remember that our critics, who are constantly at war with us, from those little irritating battles to those screaming matches, are outside of the presence of God. These people are usually no longer prayerful or reading their Bibles. They often play the blame game and wish evil on those who are trying to live righteously. These people believe if they try to do something different with their lives (at the prompting of others) then they are showing signs of weakness. Therefore, they usually do the opposite of what their advisors tell them to do especially if they don't like nor respect them. We have seen evidence of this sort of behavior in the Bible, where God's prophets would come to warn kings and rather than listen, the leaders would do what they wanted (Read the book of Jeremiah and Kings for starters).

Critical people are also selfish. You saw this repeated pattern of behavior throughout this book. Their needs are often put above wisdom and unfortunately those around them pay for selfish decision-making. It is when the godless sees they are in trouble that they will allow themselves to be open for prayer. God doesn't always answer prayers no matter who might be praying for the selfish critic. These ungodly offenders will accept wise counsel, but may not follow it until days or weeks later. Then when they do, they will usually take credit for something they didn't think about nor create. I think of times when I shared simple tips with people on and offline and rather than doing what they were advised, they tried to find faults. There were other moments when I attempted to share God's Word about one's actions or inactions on a matter and was quickly cut off or ignored. In Mark 6:4, "Jesus said to them, 'Only in his hometown, among his relatives and in his own house is a prophet without honor.'"

While studying our enemy, we should also learn a lot about ourselves. God warns us prior to an attack by using a variety of ways from messengers to visions, so that we can prevent something from happening or change a behavior that could be further aggravating a situation. However, there are times when a warning doesn't come. We can use those challenging events to do better in our lives. Some Christians refuse to listen to God and his prophets, despite losing battles. They rationalize their involvement, or lack thereof, in a situation even when God was never in the plan. Weak believers are defeated often by Satan, because they refuse to listen to wisdom. They rather focus on the actions of their enemies. Unfortunately, there is nothing God can do with a man or woman who fights against His will.

10. Know the Power of Faith

Believing in God is one thing but acting on your belief is quite another. Many talk about the Lord, but don't always believe what they say. If you are a soldier in the army of the Lord, then act like one. When dealing with a person critical of your belief in Christ, you must use your conversation to strike him or her in such a way that your blow doesn't kill this person, but it does send a message such as this, "I am a soldier in the army of the Lord and I am given my orders to share a Word with you from the Lord." Now some would take such a statement like this and say, "I need to tell people how God (and I) really feel about their tacky lifestyle." To that, God would obviously say, "No. Wait for your orders. It's not what you say, it's how you say it." But what the statement demonstrates is that one knows who he or she is in Christ. The Apostle Paul knew who he was in Christ. He was not ashamed of the gospel. He also showed he wasn't fearful.

A believer must first know why she is battling with someone. I would take much time to seek the Lord which means to pray and fast before dealing with a critical enemy. I personally spent 40 days seeking to learn more about God and how to live amongst both the saved and unsaved. He called me to a liquid fast during a time when I had no one around who did such a thing other than an aunt who family members said was deceased. It wasn't easy spending 40 days with little or no spiritual support. I had no church home at the time and even those who attended church had never participated in a fast like the one God had called me to, so I was alone. Of course, I couldn't seek the Lord without criticism. There was also enemy schemes used to get me to stop fasting, but I kept going in Jesus name, and found I had more energy than many who weren't fasting. My belief in God and the reading of his Word is what sustained me from August 18, 1997 to September 26, 1997. This was the spiritual fast that catapulted me in my faith. When he was tempted by the enemy during his 40 day fast Jesus said, "It is written, Man shall not live by bread alone, but by every word that proceedeth out of the mouth of God" (Matthew 4:4). You must know that God is with you before attempting such a feat. I had to mentally and physically prepare myself for at least two weeks prior to going without solid foods.

There are three points I would like to make when dealing with an enemy when one is putting his or her faith into practice.

First, if you don't know who or what the cause you stand for is, then how do you know what to say to the opposition or how to defeat your foe spiritually? Spend time with the Lord and ask him to reveal a plan to help you solve your dilemma. Next, when face-to-face with an enemy, be sure your enemy knows who you represent and on what authority you come to speak especially if the Lord has used you to give a prophetic word or word of knowledge to someone. Your mere introduction will most likely offend the one who chooses to start a verbal battle with you. "Oh, you are one of them Christ followers? You think you know God, huh? Well what did he tell you to tell me?" Lastly, a soldier in Christ must know when to end the battle. You can identify yourself as a soldier without attacking and killing your enemy spiritually. You can even sit down with an enemy and still have your hand on your sword without using it. You must realize God's truth doesn't kill a person's spirit, but it can penetrate one's being and cause backsliders, the unsaved and others to think about what just transpired between you and them. The seed has been planted now permit God to do the rest!

Sometimes we tend to get so caught up in battles with enemies that we can't see clearly what really matters to our Creator. Consider what King Hezekiah said about his enemy, the king of Assyria, in 2 Chronicles 32:8, "With him is an arm of flesh; but with us is the Lord our God to help us, and to fight our battles. And the people rested themselves upon the words..." God is our source of strength, the power of our faith, and the one who when we seek him, outlines our next battle. When we listen to the Holy Ghost, he conveys what God wants from us. God blesses us with insight regarding our enemies, it is then that we can look at our critics and see the blessings they give us without them even knowing it!

Know that You Can Defeat Your Enemy

All of my critics inspired me to write books, articles, art work, jobs, and more. Because of their comments about what I shouldn't do, what I better not do and why I lack this or that while eye-rolling and deep sighing, the Lord used them to give me the motivation to keep on listening to his instructions. These naysayers' protests, back-handed remarks, name-calling and talking behind my back, helped me grow closer to the Lord. I thought of the prophet Jeremiah who said, "Alas, my mother, that you gave me birth, a man with whom the whole land strives and contends! I have neither lent nor borrowed, yet everyone curses me" (Jer. 15:10, NIV). These pessimistic individuals must have forgotten God was listening to my pleas and their insults. I heard some critics' anger, frustration, irritation, jealousy, and bitterness in their voices (after our conversations) and I asked the Lord, "You know this person has made me so angry, what can I do with this?" God would then instruct me to record my feelings and then apply what I have learned to my own life. He would then move me to share my journeys with others by putting a burden in my spirit. Like a mother expecting a child, with each project, I labor for a period of time and then give birth to what the Lord has put inside of me. Thanks to the power of faith!

You may have a raging inferno, passion, or burden on the inside of you to do something for yourself, others, and for the Lord. Why not ask God to help you gain some insight on how you can release what's inside of you in the most productive way? Taking what the enemy meant to curse you with and turning it into something positive would be a win for Team God and a loss for Team Satan!

Overlook Distractions

We don't realize the power that comes from Jesus, because we allow the world's distractions to get the best of us. We choose to focus on the frivolous things that provide us with temporal happiness. After the item we bought no longer satisfies us and the event is over, we are on to the next person or thing that will hopefully give us a little more happiness then the next and the next and so on. The essence of our joy should come from above. "And on that day they (God's people) offered great sacrifices, rejoicing because God had given them great joy" (Neh. 12:43, NIV). Many church services are modeled after what took place in Nehemiah 12: 27-47. Creating an atmosphere of praise and thanksgiving will cause one to be joyful. We should ask our Lord, "How might I be joyful today about living? Bless me with wisdom concerning joy I can have in you. Direct me to something or someone who can teach me how to be grateful for what I already have." How many readers would honestly set aside time to watch and wait for those gold nuggets of God's wisdom that teach us how to be content? How many would stop accepting people and things that give us a less than satisfactory lifestyle?

Let Your Faith Shine

The power of our faith should not only come out in our conversations, but also in the way we look, feel, and help others. Fellow brothers and sisters should feel comfortable in our presence knowing that we are all on one accord (at least for the moment). Notice I didn't say unrighteous critics since most anything we say, as it relates to the Lord, will make them feel uncomfortable. People who don't like the things of God won't feel at ease with believers. This is why sinners hide behind political correctness hoping that Christians will keep their opinions of right and wrong to themselves. However, Christ followers should feel like they are at home when they are with one another. Since we all are supposed to be new creatures. "Therefore if any man be in Christ, he is a new creature: old things are passed away; behold, all things are become new" 2 Cor. 5:17. But of course, we don't live in a perfect world, and we will feel at times, even with fellow believers, to do the following: moved to do something in order to get something, burdened to respond to an offense, or suspicious as to what a brother or sister's motives might be. I pray that God will deliver us from any feelings concerning others that might be hindering our walk with him. Unnecessary stress, only makes some Christians look elsewhere for peace of mind.

A young or old believer shouldn't have to wrestle with feelings of whether or not they should ever again fellowship with you. But deep inside of all of us, there are secrets that others may never know and they may sound like this, "I really don't want a certain brother and sister in my life anymore. I really feel like this person is draining my spirit. I really wish that I had never met this person. God, please help me deal with this individual." Why would someone feel like this about a fellow believer? Because chances are there was something said or done that caused the relationship to be challenged. While any one of us could be thinking like this about other believers, someone might be feeling like this about you or I. When you know who it is, it hurts particularly if you don't know why they don't like you. David didn't know why Saul didn't like him during a time when he was running away from him. The future king didn't know that God's Spirit had left Saul. This could be the case with our Christian critic or it might be cause for concern with some readers. Talk with the Lord about your present spiritual condition, consult with wise counsel and read the passages of Scripture that relate to your issues.

When we are dealing with mental, physical and "other people" challenges that upset our heads and stomachs, our faith must be able to sustain us. Jesus encouraged his disciples by saying, "Let not your heart be troubled: ye believe in God, believe also in me" (John 14:1, NIV). Our belief in Christ and personal convictions brought on by the Holy Spirit should make us want to be better parents, teachers, leaders, employees, artists, singers, dancers, and more for the Lord.

One day we will have to give God an account of the things we did and said in this life. "For the Lord your God is God of gods, and Lord of lords, a great God, a mighty, and a terrible, which regardeth not persons, nor taketh reward…" (Deuteronomy 10:17). Take the time to apologize now to God, yourself and those you may have offended. "I think I may have said something wrong…I hope I didn't hurt you. I apologize, my brother and sister for mentioning something to you that may have offended you." Keep in mind you can't apologize for things God hasn't revealed to you, so don't beat yourself up about an apology like Satan does with his children of darkness. Some become depressed, bitter, angry, and spend years obsessing over past offenses. What you know about, apologize for and if you can't articulate the words, bless someone with a gift of love, peace, prosperity, or something else. "Take heed to yourselves: If thy brother trespass against thee, rebuke him; and if he repent, forgive him" (Luke 17:3). I have learned such things by being a failure at many. Thank God for the power of faith! "So then faith cometh by hearing, and hearing by the word of God" (Rom. 10:17).

I couldn't keep my faith in God without choosing to hear his messages in a variety of forms (ie. church, radio, TV, Internet, etc.) while shutting out the worldly ones. This meant doing the following: cutting off ungodly TV programs, turning off secular music, limiting my phone conversations, avoiding busybody relatives, coworkers and neighbors, and above all else refraining from activities that were distracting me from God.

Trust God

When tempted to fight an enemy, the new Christian often makes the mistake of calling on everyone, but God himself. He doesn't listen to the Holy Spirit either. Does he really utilize the prayers that he or she is given from instructors to pray for an enemy? Does this person search for ways to bring peace of mind to one's self or others? Does he often spend time worrying over the "what ifs" of his or her life? Does one contemplate suicide, murder or revenge? Whatever the battle, the believer must have a great faith in knowing that God will indeed deal with both his seen and unseen enemies in HIS TIME. It doesn't pay to rush God or think that somehow if you think long enough about a situation something bad will happen to your critic. Sometimes believing for strange occurrences to happen to your offenders have a way of backfiring, after a while, you are wondering why you are in trouble while your critical relative or friend enjoys the wonderful perks of just living. Before you jump to conclusions, consider this, every battle between men and women will always have those tempting prideful moments before they fall. "Pride goeth before destruction, and a haughty spirit before a fall" (Prov. 16:18). Your enemy may praise you and your faith today only to set you up to fail tomorrow. Then if you should fall on your face, witnesses will talk. We can both surrender to the Lord and permit him to teach us or fight him and others every step of the way. In the end, who do you think will win?

There is always something good that happens during a spiritual battle that gives your foe false hope and security. Think of how many movies you watched where an enemy is sitting at home or in a restaurant, peaceful, and minding his own business. Despite causing so much strife in other's lives, he appears to have a good life. Then suddenly he is murdered. The story ends with justice being served. The enemy seduces the godless into having faith in things like one's own power, wealth and connections. But when an individual's back is up against the wall, what do the wicked really have? In reality, more specifically God's reality, he instructs us all to wait on him, to trust in him, to seek him, and to do other things that take our minds off the enemy and on our Creator. When you know you have a friend, like Jesus, watching your back, you can't help but shout, scream, speak in tongues, grow faint from his overwhelming presence, and whatever else moves your spirit. There are those readers who realize the power of the Holy Spirit and who understand the significance of praise and worship. It is because of all that you have done in honoring the Lord that when times get rough, you keep right on going. You praise God when it's sunny and when it's stormy. Know that God has your back and Satan can't do or say anything to you without God's permission.

11. Casting Out the Enemy

When Jesus casted demons out of various people in the Bible, what he did back then, looked nothing like what many ministers, teachers, evangelists and others are doing today. Did he use his gift to entertain the masses? Did he go around and tell everyone about his gift? Did he make his love for his Father a great mystery? Did he make his disciples jump through hoops to attain the gifts of the Spirit? No. So why does a supposedly godly man or woman take the gifts that God has given and make them out to be so mystifying that God's children must do the following: pay money, give time, boast, act emotional, travel, starve, give up their lives and other things? God has already given his Holy Spirit filled believers spiritual gifts for free! One doesn't need to do anything spectacular, difficult or harmful for God to use you in his own special way. If God is going to move you to cast a demon out of the mouth of an evil person, he is going to do it whether you have had a class on using his gift or not. There are those who put a price tag on God's gifts then make Christians go through lengthy programs to achieve them. By doing this, they are putting God's people in a box, while glorifying their selves, meanwhile God is calling brothers and sisters in Christ to perform his will.

When God is ready to use you to cast out demons, you will know it because he will give you instructions that may seem peculiar to you and others. You will feel his presence in such a way that you may not have ever felt him before. It will feel as if you are in a waiting room within your mind while God is manifesting his power through you. That critical person, who is standing watch ready to offer his or her opinion of what God does and doesn't do, will know something is different about you too. God may have the critic choke on his or her words, become silent, or avoid you altogether while he uses you to perform his will. Don't allow the enemy's words of doubt, envy or upset permeate your spirit and definitely don't grieve the Holy One because you are fearful or worried about what others think. When God is using you, man and woman need only to step aside. I have personally observed some strange things related to casting out demons and talk more about them in this chapter.

Crazy critics are riddled with demons. They may look and act ordinary, but once they open their mouths, you know almost immediately that Satan has filled their hearts. We see evidence of this with those who were demon-possessed in the Bible.

Casting out the enemy from a person or his or her lifestyle, is nothing new under the sun. For centuries, when men and women detected an evil entity amongst them, they practiced all sorts of chants, rituals, spells, and more. When they wanted an evil spirit to do something for them, they also participated in similar activities. "They sacrificed their sons and daughters in the fire. They practiced divination and sorcery and sold themselves to do evil in the eyes of the Lord, provoking him to anger" (2 Kings 17:17, NIV).

In a book entitled, *Demons: The Answer Book*, author Lester Sumrall writes, "Church leaders in every age have recognized the evil presence of man's great foe, the devil, and have exerted dominion over him." He mentions Augustine, Thomas Aquinas, John Calvin and Martin Luther as examples. Do we have the power to resist the devil? Yes. "Dominion is for you if you are seeking to be a disciple of Jesus. After a person is converted, the devil attempts in every way to continue deceiving him. He promotes the idea that Satan is not real," Sumrall pens. "Failing that he tries to keep the new Christian from knowing there is dominion over the devil, Satan knows that when the believer is aware of his privileges and power, he (Satan) will be completely defeated and his works destroyed."

To date, if you visit certain homes or buildings you will see occult symbols and statues supposedly to keep evil away and similar things to evoke spiritual entities. I say supposedly because darkness can't cast darkness out. The devil can't reside where he isn't welcome. However, those believers and unbelievers practicing things that contradict God's instructions will possibly see, hear or experience supernatural things that might cause more harm than good mentally, physically or both.

You recall reading in the Bible when the Israelites put blood upon their doorways to prevent their firstborn children from being killed by the death angel? God showed us in this example how he can use what was intended for evil and turn it around into something for our good. "And it shall come to pass, when your children shall say unto you, What mean ye by this service? That ye shall say, It is the sacrifice of the Lord's Passover, who passed over the houses of the children of Israel in Egypt, when he smote the Egyptians, and delivered our houses. And the people bowed the head and worshipped" (Exod. 12:26-27). To this day, many Jews and Gentiles still recognize the Passover with a feast.

Believers know the significance of bloodshed throughout history, but rather than place animal or human blood on one's doorway, nowadays many Christ followers will place anointed oil, water, and other things and consecrate them to the Lord both in and out of their homes, workplaces and other environments they spend time. But do such things cast the enemy out of one's presence? No. They are nothing more than symbols, and "feel good" items. It is the presence of God that keeps demons away. "Ye shall receive power, after that the Holy Ghost is come upon you" (Acts 1:8). The casting of a demon comes from the power of Christ not from things or from humans. Once the evil entity is gone, it moves on to his or her next assignment.

Christians who cast out demons don't typically interview with the media, call up relatives on the phone boasting about what they have done, or stand before men and women in the church talking about one's experience casting demons out of people, animals and things—unless he or she is in a setting to teach. Backsliding men and women, who were once used by God to cast out demons, eventually find out, they no longer have this kind of power especially when they choose to brag about it to others and give the appearance as if they are a god. "But let him that glorieth glory in this, that he understandeth and knoweth me, that I am the Lord which exercise loving-kindness, judgment, and righteousness, in the earth: for in these things I delight, saith the Lord" (Jer. 9:24).

What God gives, he also takes away (Job1:21). A brother or sister in Christ may falsely assume that the leader or teacher who once was chosen by God still has the gift of casting out demons, when in fact; God has long rejected the braggart because of his or her prideful heart. Unfortunately, some will then look to witchcraft to restore what God has taken away, meanwhile giving a false impression that God is still with them when he is not. Earlier in this book I mentioned Saul who knew he couldn't hear from the Lord any more so he sought a witch at Endor for information (I Sam. 28:3-25). There are believers who do similar things and wonder why God rejects them. Read about the psychological manipulations used in so-called revival meetings. You will find that there are Christian leaders who will use various tactics to give an appearance like God is with them when he really is not. There are many writers who have exposed the trickery used in many religious as well as secular groups to arise the emotions of the masses. Visitors wonder why they still battle with afflictions after leaving a church service. The answer is quite simple, God operates in his time. He may not be with some who are self-appointed demon-busters, ministers or healers. Look at one's track record. Can anyone say recently that because of a certain man or woman's prayers, that a demon or affliction had left his or her body? If yes, you have yourself a person in your midst that God is indeed using but if not, you will want to seek out someone believers that can pray with you. One who once followed Christ, who is now more concerned about selfish gain, will talk a lot about what he or she can do for God's people. God is not with men and women who are consistently disobedient to His word.

I have had the experience of casting demons out in the name of Jesus and it was no pretty site! There was foam coming out the corner of mouths, tears, demonic laughing, and finally sighs of relief when the Holy Ghost showed up and took over. I have also witnessed people (of various faiths) attend church who needed a few demonic entities removed from in and around them, but unfortunately, they weren't troubled enough to ask anyone for prayer nor was it God's will to do anything with those who were reprobates. Even worse, some church leaders were too busy singing and teaching, to allow for a move of the Holy Spirit to cast demons out in Jesus name. I must admit I didn't interrupt service to tell leaders about a need to cast out demons, although sometimes I wish I had; rather I prayed quietly and hoped that someone would be moved enough in the audience to shout those demons out of their body and out of the church. At times, God would answer prayers and people would experience a Holy Ghost take-over.

Casting out demons may not be what everyone in God's kingdom will do (although all have the authority in Jesus name to take on such a feat). "And these signs shall follow them that believe; In my name shall they cast out devils; they shall speak with new tongues..." (Mark 16:17). But what God requires is obedience. Unfortunately far too many believers avoid doing anything that makes them feel uncomfortable. When you are called upon to cast a demon out, listen to the Lord and do what he says in Jesus name. Otherwise, you might be like Jonah, running away from God's calling. God doesn't want us to fear his commands, he just wants us to do them. "For God hath not given us the spirit of fear; but of power, and of love, and of a sound mind" (2 Tim. 1:7). God will ensure that you get all the information you need before he assigns you a task. There are those who are called to teach about certain gifts and exercise them. However, be mindful of those who practice witchcraft to cast out demons. "Regard not them that have familiar spirits, neither seek after wizards, to be defiled by them: I am the Lord your God" (Lev. 19:31). Know that the witch and warlock will at times disguise themselves behind harmless sounding names like: spiritualist, healer, psychic, prophet, and others. Know the difference between light and darkness because sometimes God's people are also called similar names.

Those of demonic influence will criticize hypocrites of the Christian faith. They know who is of God and who isn't. Those who are evil workers name-call, spit, hit, cry, scream, curse and use various tools to help them conjure up assistants. Some create images, visions, cold chills, sickness, weird smells, and the like to either cast revenge on lukewarm Christ followers, drive them mad, cause them to run in fear, die, or even murder. They will also use all sorts of tactics to keep believers away from their territories among other things. Repeatedly, I have warned in this book about relatives and friends, who are susceptible to enemy schemes, because they are not following the Lord, know that a demonic spirit can use people, places and things to prevent you from casting him or her out of your life or keep you at a distance depending on the individual's spiritual condition.

A former witch from the 1960s now a Christian pastor wrote an article entitled, *Former Witch Exposes Harry Potter* (Jesus-is-Savior.com). The Harry Potter series that appears to be harmless has been read by millions of young people. Pastor David J. Meyer writes, "In order to succeed in bringing witchcraft to the world and thus complete satanic control, an entire generation would have to be induced and taught to think like witches, talk like witches, dress like witches, and act like witches." He continues, "The occult songs of the 1960s launched the Luciferian project of capturing the minds of an entire generation. In the song *Sound Of Silence* by Paul Simon and Art Garfunkel, we were told of seeds that were left while an entire generation was sleeping, and that the 'vision that was planted in my brain still remains.'" Meyer cautions, "How serious is this? By reading these materials, many millions of young people are learning how to work with demon spirits. They are getting to know them by name. Vast numbers of children professing to be Christians are also filling their hearts and minds, while willingly ignorant parents look the other way." The Harry Potter series isn't the only books that are filled with various forms of witchcraft references, but many of the popular C.S. Lewis books are as well. So how do you combat this kind of evil? Don't welcome it into environments that you have control over and for those areas that you don't, you pray about your concerns in Jesus name. We learn in the Scriptures, "Many of those who believed now came and openly confessed their evil deeds. A number who had practiced sorcery brought their scrolls together and burned them publicly. When they calculated the value of the scrolls, the total came to fifty thousand drachmas. In this way the word of the Lord spread widely and grew in power (Acts 19:18-20, NIV).

The Apostle Paul repeatedly dealt with satanic attacks. One of his challenges was quite personal and the Scripture never reveals what that could have been. However, Paul gives an explanation for his trouble. "To keep me from becoming conceited because of these surpassingly great revelations, there was given me a thorn in my flesh, a messenger of Satan, to torment me" (2 Cor. 12:7).

Understand that when one is called upon for a specific task by God, he or she must be prepared for anything! This is why it is very important to have witnesses when praying outwardly for others. Be sure to protect yourself. As I mentioned in other places in this book, even a child can be used by the devil to attack an unsuspecting Christian! Don't try things like casting out demons without a support system. In one situation, I could have been badly hurt, because I chose to undertake this task one day without a witness. Spirits can jump off of the victim and on to you if you aren't careful. This happened in Acts 19:16, "And there were seven sons of one Sceva, a Jew, and chief of the priests, which did so. And the evil spirit answered and said, Jesus I know, and Paul I know; but who are ye? And the man in whom the evil spirit was leaped on them, and overcame them, and prevailed against them, so that they fled out of that house naked and wounded." Scriptures to further your study on demon possession see: Luke 4:33; Luke 8:29; Luke 9:42; Mark 9:25; Mark 5:2, 5:8; Mark 1:26; Mark 7:25; and Matt. 12:43.

In a way that is less mysterious and supernatural, like casting out demons, a Christian can cast his critic from his presence simply by speaking truth. He can allow God to use him or her to minister great truths about the critical person. The kind that would leave him or her speechless when in the presence of the wicked, the Christian could remain quiet, ignore the critic or enlist some help. There are many ways to shut the mouth of a opinionated person. I have found, for me, what works best is silence. Evil critics love a good argument, when you don't feed into them they have nothing to say, at least to your face. Notice what the critics said about Jesus after all of the good he had been doing, "Then they brought him a demon-possessed man who was blind and mute, and Jesus healed him, so that he could both talk and see. All the people were astonished and said, "Could this be the Son of David?" But when the Pharisees heard this, they said, "It is only by Beelzebub, the prince of demons, that this fellow drives out demons" (Matt. 12:22-28, NIV). If the critics can say this about the Son of God, what do you think they will say about you? Jesus didn't allow people's criticism to stop his progress.

After all your study, you may have concluded that the one who continues to debate, bad-mouth, lie, confuse, abuse, and do other things that keep you praying to your heavenly Father, is nothing more than a human being with a demon or demons. He or she is challenged by something within his or her spirit that cannot be removed simply by telling it to, "Be quiet" or "Come out," for man doesn't have that kind of power without Jesus. A demonic spirit must be removed by the authority of Christ, in Jesus name, by the Spirit of God, by the blood of Jesus or other similar statements of faith. No matter what you choose to say, notice you cannot leave

God or his Son out! There is power in the name of Jesus! Demons tremble over his name, says the Lord.

You can bind up the strong man. When men and women claim that God is not with you or God doesn't do that, think about the following Scripture, "…how can anyone enter a strong man's house and carry off his possessions unless he first ties up the strong man? Then he can rob his house. He who is not with me is against me, and he who does not gather with me scatters. And so I tell you, every sin and blasphemy will be forgiven men, but the blasphemy against the Spirit will not be forgiven" (Matt. 12:29-31, NIV).

Think of those people who tried to help you in the past without acknowledging God or the Son of God. Maybe their efforts worked for a time or maybe not at all. Do you recall witnessing a moment when someone tried to pray for a person plagued with demonic spirits and the only thing those spirits did was jump off the sick, and onto the one doing the praying? Maybe you were that person. Not everyone is called to pray for certain individuals no matter what their title. They may say, "Jesus, Jesus" but the Son in heaven may not be listening.

When there is someone around you with a demonic spirit, where are the people who you entrust to pray with you or are you doing all the casting by yourself? Is God sincerely in the plan when you pray? What have been the results of your prayers? How might you gather up enough courage to combat a demonic spirit? Demonic spirits aren't reasonable. They don't sit nicely for long. They have temper tantrums. Some even use magic and other tricks to either earn a Christians respect or scare him or her away. You must get your spiritual nourishment each and every day just like you eat and drink each day. Stop fearing the darkness—walk boldly in Christ!

Learn about the various demonic spirits, but don't allow your mind to follow their teachings—you must be stronger than that! Find out how other believers have casted out demons from human bodies, households and other places. However, don't be surprised if you don't find many around you, because as I have said before, some churches and their leaders are not permitting a move of the Holy Spirit to fall on them so that they can do Christ's works.

Some believers will pray in Jesus name and go out into the most unlikely places as God leads. Others use not only biblical text, but carry along various anointed things to symbolically take back a territory. There are Christians who use music, art, written and spoken words of God to drive out demons as God wills. What talents or tools has God led you to use to communicate his righteousness and expose the works of darkness? At some point in your spiritual walk, your critic is going to come ready to do war with you and he will have a legion of demons within him. How will you handle his insults, her spitting, or even a possible physical altercation?

During Jesus' ministry, he casted out demons in human beings, there were eyewitness accounts of what transpired during his ministry and some of those stories you may have recalled reading in your Bible surfing the Internet and watching on television. Re-read those biblical stories, this time seeking new information you may not have thought of in the past. Ask God for wisdom.

The people who were plagued with demons never left Jesus' presence the same way they approached him. You must be like Jesus, don't argue or accept a challenge to physically fight with a demon. Use prayer and silence. If there is no time to pray, just call out his name, "Jesus!" Also, don't tell a demonic spirit to "shut up" or insult him or her with statements like, "I will stomp on your head devil, I hate you!" Consider this, in Jude 1:9, the archangel Michael didn't insult the devil despite their disputing. The Bible says, "Yet Michael the archangel, when contending with the devil he disputed about the body of Moses, durst not bring against him a railing accusation, but said, The Lord rebuke thee."

If you don't know what to do or say when in the presence of a demonic spirit, just be still and wait for the Lord to give you wisdom. The demon will be taken aback by your silence. He or she won't know what to do except fill up the quiet atmosphere with more rants, snide remarks and the like. Let the Holy Spirit that Jesus left us with, after he ascended up into heaven speak into your spirit (Acts 1).

Practice in your mind, a scenario between you and a demon-possessed human being. He or she is angry that you just offended him or her again with your God talk, now what? Do you apologize? That's weak. Do you hold her hand and comfort her? Be careful she might be a witch. Do you ignore the demon and walk away? If you do, who has your back? Don't drop your head to the floor, Soldier! You face your enemy. You look at him or her like Jesus did as depicted in many movies. Jesus wasn't smiling or joking with someone carrying a demonic spirit. If you are too fearful of the eyes or feel you may be tempted to sin, look pass him or her while still keeping this person in view. Keep in mind, the following Scriptures when dealing with those who use their eyes to curse, fight or weaken you spiritually. "Wisdom is before him that hath understanding; but the eyes of a fool are in the ends of the earth" (Prov. 17:24). "My son, give me thine heart, and let thine eyes observe my ways" (Prov. 23:26).

Are you quiet while the devil is spitting, red-eyed, and fuming? Maybe you picture the devil gentleman-like or very beautiful like a model in a magazine, but at some point those nice eyes and staged mannerisms will be threatening. Remember, Jesus angered some people in those gatherings by what he said. He didn't sugar-coat truth. If you are sincerely speaking the Word of God, at some point, the devil is going to show up and show out! Be prepared to do something or nothing at all as God leads.
Remember the Scripture, "Resist the devil and he will flee?" (Jas. 4:7). Truth will cause the devil to leave your presence during the battle or afterward. You shouldn't always be the one storming away when the smoke clears. God will call us to stand and then the enemy will have no choice but to move! However, if you are tempted to sin, you should always be prepared to walk or run out.

Maybe one day you will be put in a situation where you can't scream out, "Come out devil in Jesus name!" especially when dealing with family members and close friends. However, what's wrong with the power of your mind? You might be too nervous in the enemy's presence to hear from the Lord at the time. You could fold your hands, place your right hand or both hands up and begin to pray. You can't be concerned with eyewitnesses. Was Jesus concerned about what others thought or said? Did he wait for someone to bring him special tools to heal people? Don't allow the critics to tell you what is of God, what isn't and whether something is in the Bible when you are hearing from the Holy Spirit. Not everything God commands is in the Bible.

You may have something like anointed oil or a Bible in your hand when the enemy launches his or her attack, don't use either of these like they do in the movies and just throw it on an enemy even though this might have worked for some people you know. I did this once, it didn't help matters. A careless action such as this will only make your enemy want to attack you. Wait for the demon-possessed to surrender. He or she may show up at your church function, sob at your dinner table or become ill at your workplace. Use your spiritual tools in a peaceful way, like a minister marking a new believer's head with anointed oil. Consecrate your environment and personal belongings to the Lord. Privately anoint your hands lightly with oil before meeting and greeting people. There is a good possibility, an enemy won't raise his or her white flag in a spiritual war and that's okay. Pray for your enemy and do what God calls you to do for him or her.

Many Christians think they are failures when they can't get an enemy to submit to God. Remember don't take any spiritual battle personally. Spiritual warfare is in the hands of God—it's HIS battle we are just the instruments used to get HIS job done! Keep praying anyway. If you have the gift of tongues, use it to edify yourself. If you have a word of knowledge or a prophetic word to share, use them to help not hurt your enemy. God will convict his or her spirit, not you!

Any of your spiritual gifts will come in handy when in battle. But always be sure you are wearing your spiritual armor because you never know when the enemy will come to disturb your peace. Sometimes simply reciting the word of God will keep your enemies distant or even better cause them to drop to their knees sobbing. And there was in their synagogue a man with an unclean spirit; and he cried out, Saying, Let us alone; what have we to do with thee, thou Jesus of Nazareth? art thou come to destroy us? I know thee who thou art, the Holy One of God. And Jesus rebuked him, saying, Hold thy peace, and come out of him. And when the unclean spirit had torn him, and cried with a loud voice, he came out of him" (Mark 1:23-26).

In an article that appeared on the Good Morning America website, a victim of a robbery had prayed with a thief. "…Montez, 43, started to talk to the alleged robber about God, Smith began to tell her about his hardships and asked her to pray with him," the report said. "The incident took an even more surprising turn when Smith removed the bullet from his gun and gave it to Montez, police said."

This was a moving story, fortunately for this woman everything worked out for her good, but the robber's as well. He may not have his physical freedom, but he has a mental freedom with Christ. Fortunately, this situation didn't result in death. We must be wise. Sometimes our critics pretend to have the Spirit of God when they know we are on to them. They may cast out demons and know the kinds of things to say like, "Be released of that demonic spirit…bind the enemy…go back to hell evil spirit…" and other similar statements. The false believer may pretend to speak in tongues, laugh as if happy, or act as if slain in the Spirit, and do other spiritual things that may look like he or she is filled with the Holy Spirit. *Don't be fooled!* The devil is a liar and the truth is not in him! A wicked critic may purposely act like Christians to make a negative point.

Keep praying and fasting for that one you are burdened to see set free! While everyone else in the church, family, workplace or somewhere else is convinced that the enemy has let go of that lost soul, be the one in the crowd who isn't so sure. Test the spirits. God is righteous and our judge, he will reveal the truth! Our Lord provides us with the courage to stand against the enemy—we can't win a war all by ourselves, we will always need God's help! Keep in mind, God works in mysterious ways. Don't be surprised if he uses the most unlikely sources to fight your battles!

You may know of someone right now who is talking crazy, acting crazy and doing other things that medical professionals have labeled. Go to God in prayer and ask him whether what a person is battling with is an illness, a demon, or something else—know the difference. You don't want to be embarrassed one day calling something a demon when the issue may be nothing more than a temporary setback caused by something they have been eating or drinking. Understand that just because someone has prayed for a person's demons to leave that they all will go away immediately. It is up to God when he will remove them and how many he will eliminate. Casting out demons might be an ongoing process that might last hours, days, weeks, or years for some victims. We also need to be humble when a man or woman is freed from their affliction and showering us with praise. Remind this person, "To God be the glory!"

Your heavenly Father has his reasons for miraculously healing some and not healing others, so who are we to question him about that? Rather, keep doing what God has led you to do in the kingdom and give him all the praise, even if you don't see the following: the blind able to see, the crippled able to walk, the deathly ill come back to life, and so on in your time. Use what the world calls, a "fail," you call it a blessing! God has his reasons for doing what he does. It is through one's suffering that we learn to be more compassionate toward one another. In the Bible, we are reminded to appreciate the blessings we already have. We are encouraged to keep fighting the good fight. We are moved to be simply grateful for being a child of God!

You and I must learn to accept responsibility for the things that are within our power to change, but for things that we have no power over, we must learn to let them go. Otherwise, we give place to the devil. He will riddle us with guilt feelings, depression, suicidal thoughts, and other negative emotions from the past to keep us from performing God's will today.

Ask yourself the following the next time you see one who is demon-possessed, "If that were me, would I want help?" How you answer that question says a lot about how much you love yourself. Conduct an even deeper study on yourself, and you will discover how much or how little compassion you have for the lost. Some would say, "I would probably just want to be left alone." Others would say, "No, free me!" Still others would answer, "I don't know if I would be sane enough to know I needed any help." This last statement is key. Those that have demons don't know that they have them. Just like a person who unknowingly walks around with cancer until strange symptoms show up and his or her doctor confirms it. Some Christians prefer not to say anything at all about one's spiritual condition even though they know that the person who stands before them is battling with a demon. But in their minds, they feel they are sparing the person hurt feelings by not calling it what it is, "a demon." These days that isn't considered the politically correct thing to say to anyone. Many churches have avoided any study about casting out demonic spirits for fear they might offend someone. Its unfortunate, but these churches play right into the hands of the enemy. We are to "Study to shew thyself approved unto God, a workman that needeth not to be ashamed, rightly dividing the word of truth (2 Tim. 2:15).

So when the Holy Spirit moves you to cast a demon out of a person or environment, do it in Jesus name! When it comes to dealing with demonic spirits, try on your spiritual armor, see if it fits, walk around in it, then start using your equipment. Walk as Jesus walked. Don't half-step, don't beat around the bush, don't skip down the path, don't run like a track star, and most of all don't hide.

I think of Ecclesiastes 9:11 (NIV) which says, "I have seen something else under the sun: The race is not to the swift or the battle to the strong, nor does food come to the wise or wealth to the brilliant or favor to the learned; but time and chance happen to them all."

12. The Worst Enemy of Them All

By nightfall when your head is lying on your pillow and eyes are prepared to rest, the images of the day might pass through your mind. Besides thinking of those memorable exchanges between you and those you care about, you may recall those disturbing moments when you were at fault.

For some, they will blink away the truth revealed during their waking hours while rolling over and going to sleep. Others will momentarily ponder wisdom and possibly make a right wrong. But then there are those, who unfortunately keep drama going hoping to experience their own sort of peace. Yet, for the God-fearing, they will arise out of bed, confess their sins and repent of their ways while asking the Lord what would you have me to do to fix my situation? The Christian is a work in progress, never perfect, forever flawed until Jesus comes back again! I think of Paul struggling with sin according to Romans 7:18-20. "I know that nothing good lives in me, that is, in my sinful nature. For I have the desire to do what is good, but I cannot carry it out. For what I do is not the good I want to do; no, the evil I do not want to do—this I keep on doing. Now if I do what I do not want to do, it is no longer I who do it, but it is sin living in me that does it."

While we are thinking about what others have said about us, sometimes we have to stop and think about what we say about us to ourselves and others. Sometimes it isn't what someone has criticized us about during our waking hours that tend to upset us most by nightfall, but it is our response (or lack thereof) to the criticism that makes us angry, depressed, confused, etc. It is what we personally feel about ourselves that bind us spiritually, mentally and physically. We have a choice: learn from our actions or ignore life lessons while placing blame on others. You may have been guilty of calling yourself a name or two when you've made an error. Other times you might have falsely assumed someone had ill feelings toward you. So you took this person's opinion of you and read too deeply into it. Unfortunately, we overreact and don't like ourselves or others just because we simply misunderstood.

According to an article entitled, *Christianity is its Own Worst Enemy* by Wesley Ellis (Whateverisgood.blogspot.com), he writes, "I've long felt alienated from the mainstream of my own faith and I've always found that Christians are the ones who make Christianity so difficult." He adds, "My most profound crises of faith have come not from the challenges of people outside the Church but from the people inside it who look nothing like Jesus... not just in the fact that they struggle but that their "worldview," for lack of a better term, and their political, economic, and philosophical orientations are so diametrically opposed to those of Jesus (of course I'm speaking from my own perception of Jesus, not to claim any more certainty than what is possible from my own perspective)." So the following question popped into my mind, why would a man feel this way if many of our sisters and brothers are supposedly "alright with God and self?" What are believers doing to one another that make it so difficult to walk this walk? The truth of the matter is whatever we are dealing with behind closed doors within ourselves, we may or may not want to deal with it head-on. Therefore, in some strange way, it surfaces out into the public and if not dealt with, it begins to spread like a contagious virus. By then, we have the choice to do the following with our personal struggles: deal with them, hide them or run from them. A few brave believers might pray that a brother or sister's visible sickness will be gone in Jesus name. However, when a Believer is ill with a not-so easily recognized illness such as: hate, greed, maliciousness and more, it becomes a challenge for the Christian community to take care of their own, because they may be struggling with the same issues as well. But if we are walking as children as light, what do we have to fear? Jesus didn't concern himself over catching a case of leprosy, blindness, death, a demonic-spirit, or other issues; rather he set the captives free without taking their problems so personally to the point that he might fall away from the Lord. As believers sometimes we internalize other people's personal struggles so much in fact that we debilitate ourselves spiritually.

Some believers consume their time with much feel-good Christian activity so that they don't have to face personal dilemmas. When sincere believers come along with the power to cast out devils, weak Christians will do the following: attack (before they are found out), ignore, cover up or lie about an issue, discredit a fellow brother or sister in Christ, or do other things to keep from their weaknesses being exposed. Others will often drink, eat, entertain, or drug themselves to a state of peace, sleep or temporal happiness. Some believers and unbelievers will feed their flesh with everything but God just to get by each day. With issues like these, it isn't any wonder why some sisters and brothers argue, physically fight, sue, and even murder one another. Their faith is based on what makes them happy and not on what God wills for them to do with their lives.

We are all battling with something on the inside of us including Ellis who wrote his opinion piece about Christianity being its own worst enemy. Something on the inside of every one of us becomes easily frustrated when the right button is pushed. Outsiders can't push our buttons like those we care about. This is why many believers can remain cool with those outside the family home, but act like fools around those who know them. People, who are closest to us, know what sets us off. Maybe your prayers have gone unanswered, people have disappointed you, or worse you failed at not sticking to your personal goals, plans, or what the Lord told you, these things happen. However, don't let your personal issues affect those who God has assigned to you to teach, uplift, advice, and correct. Ask God to reveal the things within you that might make you potentially your own worst enemy and eventually an enemy to someone else.

As believers, instead of using the knowledge we have received from the Holy Spirit in positive ways, sometimes we are venting and beating ourselves and others up mentally until there is no soul left within willing to receive godly things. We tell ourselves we are not going to do XYZ again, yet we do it. Then we temporarily get upset about what we have done only to later look for someone to blame about our actions. Sounds crazy doesn't it? We shouldn't permit the enemy to move us to say or do something that hurts us or others, but we do it anyway.

CNN Contributor and Christian, LZ Granderson, wrote on CNN.com, "For all of the rhetoric about Christianity being under attack in this country, oftentimes it feels no one does a better job of hurting Christianity than the people who call themselves Christians. Especially after a national tragedy." He then lists Christians in the mainstream media who got caught saying some insensitive things after the September 11 terror attacks, Hurricane Katrina, the 2010 earthquake in Haiti and the theater shootings in Aurora, Colorado. Maybe these Christians felt bad about what they said, maybe not. But something on the inside of them moved them to say what they did, without thinking about the timing or anything else. Insensitive actions like this made by Christians is fodder for the wicked critics. They use believers wrong-doing as recruiting tools to get those in the middle of the road, when it comes to walking with the one true God, to come join their secular groups. "See, I told you Christianity isn't right…look at what this one did!" The ignorant doesn't consider the fact that Jesus wasn't calling men to men, but to his Heavenly Father. As much as we all would like to be perfect like Christ, we could never be, so if one's faith revolves around what people say and do to them, then he or she is in a sorry state of mind. To believe and trust in the Lord is to follow his example not mom's, dad's, the man on TV spouting off the mouth, your Christian neighbors or the woman at the local church.

When you find yourself wallowing in self-pity, doubt about your faith, and concerned about what others are saying and doing, pray. Ask the Lord to bless you with peace of mind, turn your burdens over to him, and most of all be honest with yourself. We are not perfect and wonderful, we are all flawed! We think that because we don't commit this sin or that one and we do this deed but not that one that somehow our actions and in-actions makes us better than the poor, the rich, the uneducated, the backslider, the untrained, the ghetto, the blind or the crippled, be sure to check your heart. Maybe you are physically rich, but spiritually poor. Maybe your "blessings" is what is keeping some of you from being obedient to the Lord?

Our voice should be softer than God's. Our walk should exemplify a need to follow Jesus. Our children should reflect a desire to do what's right. Our hearts should be filled with love and compassion. However for many of us, this is not the case especially without Christ. Our lack is not an excuse to sin. God blesses us with messengers, miracles, signs, wonders, and more. At times we become enemies of ourselves, because we simply refuse wisdom. We do what we think is right void of God and his teachings.

13. Creating Distance from the Critic

No matter what you say or do, there will be those relatives, friends and co-workers who will have their "opinion" on an issue and it isn't always going to be a wise one, a right one, a wrong one, or a sincere one. For some of you, you may have argued far too many times with a select few individuals always ending with, "All I was trying to say was...But you misunderstood me." The critical person will keep sharing his or her personal feelings despite a trail of broken hearts, angry relatives, lost jobs, opportunities, friendships, and blessings. She cries out when confronted, "I don't care! I had to tell him the truth! So what, God knows how I am!" There is always a consequence to pay when we don't let the teachings of Christ show up in our daily activities with others.

We already know the tempter will come looking to start some trouble, when Jesus was approached by Satan he used God's word to stand up against the enemy. "Resist the devil, and he will flee from you" (Jas. 4:7). For 40 days, Jesus fasted and he was faced with opposition according to the Holy Bible. Fasting requires great dedication and discipline, but when you trust in the Lord, he will lighten your burdens. Many people make the mistake of telling others about their spiritual fasts. Knowing that Satan and his demons are on the loose, it isn't wise to share your information with others unless absolutely necessary. The Bible instructs, "When you fast, do not look somber as the hypocrites do, for they disfigure their faces to show men they are fasting. I tell you the truth, they have received their reward in full (Matt. 6:16).

When you have decided to fast from certain people, places and things that is when the temptation to do what use to do seems to be even stronger. If you should mouth to others what you're intentions are, such as wanting to stop participating in a certain activity so that you might draw closer to the Lord, the critical voiccs will risc up against your fast saying things like: "You don' really want to stop talking to...you all were the best of friends. Surely, you don't want to stop going to our favorite hangout. You know the group has done a lot for you. Why would you want to break away now?"

The adversary will send others to criticize your actions during times of fasting. He will use people to tell you that bad things might happen if you cut certain people off. But when you know that God is moving you to distance yourself from hurtful individuals, follow his lead! "I urge you, brothers, to watch out for those who cause divisions and put obstacles in your way that are contrary to the teaching you have learned. Keep away from them." (Rom. 16:17).

The enemy will attempt to make you feel guilty about your actions by attacking you mentally, physically and spiritually using things like: lies, false accusations, name-calling, and false humility. You may lose finances, favor and more before, during and after your spiritual fast, but consider what God will do for you, if you continue to seek Him.

The enemy will pretend to come in peace, when in fact, he or she desires to argue or debate with you. Separate from him or her when you detect in this person's voice tension or see a negative disposition come upon his or her face.

Avoid the temptation to defend your actions such as why you don't come around the critical person like you use to and why you don't feel like it is necessary to share your personal feelings about another person or situation. Keep right on doing what God has called you to do.

Don't destroy what God has not instructed you to tear apart, get rid of, or break up (ie. a job, friendship, business partnership, intimate relationship, etc.) Sometimes people walk away from everything when God is only trying to draw their attention to one or two things that might be causing problems in their personal lives. When we can't hear from God on the specifics of what he is asking, besides not eating, we should also fast from other distractions including: television, phone, sex, shopping, and other personal pleasures we typically do daily. God will provide you with details at the appointed time of what exactly you need to do to create some distance from your trouble-making critic.

Lastly, be prepared for the difficult person to bring you food, drink and anything else to cause you to break your spiritual fast. For some backsliders, they know the power of fasting so they might actually be used by the enemy to hurt you. However, others may not know anything about fasting and may simply be concerned about your safety. Remind those who are aware to continue to pray for you. When they object to your fasting, tell them that what you are doing is consecrated to the Lord and that you trust in him.

14. Satan is Under Your Feet

Do you really know who Satan is? By now you should. You learned about some of his wicked tactics and how he uses people, especially some relatives and friends, to get us to turn away from our faith. You might recall reading or hearing someone talk about Satan or demonic spirits like they are friends and guide him or her in life. I must remind my readers that no matter how nicely one describes Satan, he is not your friend! Yet, I see an increase of adoration for the devil in things like music, magazines, videos and movies. Followers (or those who have empathy for the fallen angel) refer to him as Lucifer, the name given to him before his fall. They talk about him as if he is wise and helpful. Satan knows his job description and he also knows that one day his job is going to come to an end, so being helpful to human beings is not on the agenda. In the meantime, he is going to do his best at his job of destructing mankind until his job is complete.

I have noticed we are too proud at times of our own accomplishments that God has to remind us to humble ourselves; therefore, he temporarily appoints "a devil" for a boss to test us. The evil one then uses his demonic spirits to act as supervisors. The supervisors then enlist the help of their assistants to act as our critics. The assistants' jobs are not to encourage, uplift, edify, correct or rebuke; rather they are told to break us down until we have no choice but to cry out, "Jesus!" When you come back to the Lord with a humble heart, he will then place Satan under your feet. You may have witnessed people dance, shout, and speak to the devil like this, "You thought you had me Satan...you assumed that I was going to stop trusting in the Lord...you said that I was this and that, but by God's mercy and grace, I am able to say Halleluiah, praise the Lord!" You can say this as well as many other phrases to usher in the sweet feelings of victory! God knows the heart of his children, evil critics don't.

Unbelievers, backsliders, and others observe believers' actions, come up with conclusions, and then speak about their observations in such a way that they sound like curses. When you are not knowledgeable of the enemies' deeds, you will succumb to his schemes. The devil prides himself on being everything to everyone in deceitful ways. He pretends to be that wise teacher, that best friend, a great parent, and other things, but after closer inspection, you realize everything you thought a person to be is incorrect. While he deceives you and those who think they are "great, wonderful, clean, nice...," he gets you to fight with those who are in fact chosen by God to help you see through the smokescreen. But what do many believers do? Defend satanic people and their lifestyles while accusing children of light of being insensitive, ignorant, rude, envious, or argumentative for not embracing a variety of viewpoints and things that go against the teachings of God. I think of many individuals over the years in my own family that looked the other way when myself and others were open to all sorts of satanic influence and actually enabled us to keep on doing what we were doing. However, when God came into our lives, they questioned our motives, became critical of us because we spoke of God, and looked for faults within us so that they could go back and negatively talk about us to others. When they were confronted about wrongdoing, they vehemently denied saying or doing one thing or another and pretended to be supportive of all things Christian. As mentioned in another chapter, the devil is a liar and deceives even those who think because they pray and attend church periodically that they are alright with the Lord. Without experiencing spiritual regeneration inside and out, Satan will be everywhere but under your feet! Ask the Lord to deliver you from your own personal demons. Seek counseling and get amongst like-minded believers. Read the Bible and pray daily. Shut out, shut off, and shut up anything that keeps you from experiencing the presence of the Holy Spirit. When you confess your sin, invite Jesus to come into your heart to renew you spiritually and begin to listen and obey Him, then you will begin to experience victory in your life.

Who Do You Trust Yourself or the Lord?

We all want more money, time, power, and other things that will make our lives easier. There is nothing bad about wanting these things. But what is wrong, is doing the devil's work in order to obtain them. How is Satan ever going to truly be under a believer's feet when he or she is focusing on worldly things? Many Christians sit in church for decades and never experience that wonderful joy in knowing that God has won and the devil has lost, because they can't let go of the devil's false promises created to look like they are their own ideas. Many believers are still holding on to expired dreams, unequally yoked partners, bad jobs, and more. Satan has even gone so far as to move on the spirits of vulnerable men and women to tell others, "I don't love you, I hate you. I didn't want to tell you the truth, so I lied! I never wanted you. I wish I never met you! I didn't think you were ever going to amount to much of anything, so that's why I don't help you! I was going to give you something, but I changed my mind. Besides, you don't need anything!" Imagine sitting in church with burdens like these placed squarely on your shoulders from people who don't believe that what they say or do is wrong, deceitful, ignorant, or downright rude! What's worse, many Christians never release such hurtful comments to the Lord and ask him to deal with those who have upset them. Rather, they orchestrate plans inside their minds to pay someone back only to feel further angered, bitter and even guilty for having answered a wrong with a wrong.

You can't dance for the Lord when you have a headache, heartache, and chains around your feet. You have to be willing to give it ALL to the Lord, not some of it, or part of it. If you can't remember what keeps you bound, list it on a piece of paper. Then take your note to the church and set it down at the altar symbolically giving it the Lord. Then rip the list up because you are letting go and letting God deal with your issues.

"Get that Jesus joy," as one person once told me by accepting that some stuff you can't change without God, and those things that you can change, ask God for strength. Satan has worked hard to get you to a place in your walk with the Lord filled with indecision, depression, upset, and confusion. Now it's time for you to shake all that off in Jesus name, place Satan under his feet and keep on walking, my friend! When you perform these actions, the evil one will take his cue and go away for a time. When he comes back (he always does and brings some friends with him) to tempt you, hopefully you will be like Jesus in the desert and stand on the word of God!

Knowing that there is an enemy who is determined to destroy all of God's creation, we must remember not to aid him in his destruction. Be mindful when speaking to men, women and children. Ask God to put the right words in your mouth when speaking to those who are faced with doubts, fears, and other negative emotions. Say things that will not only rebuke and correct, but also comfort and uplift—some of us are far too good about telling people what they should do, but not so good about encouraging them live righteously using kind words.

At times, God will move us to say and do things that might not initially look like we are being very helpful to others. However, we must trust that if God is using us, he is also directing those around us toward peace whether in the short or long term, and sometimes that doesn't come without a battle.

Also, consider asking yourself the following, "What kind of life am I living for Christ?" Are you consistent in the way you behave both at work and home? Occasionally we think that acting honest and respectful is reserved for certain dates, places and events. However, we are to act righteously wherever we go (including at home) even if the end result is that we are least favored, disliked, unpopular, or labeled a trouble-maker. We are not to behave and reason like godless individuals. "Do not conform any longer to the pattern of this world, but be transformed by the renewing of your mind. Then you will be able to test and approve what God's will is—his good, pleasing and perfect will" (Rom. 12:2).

I close this book speaking the following blessings over your life:

May the words of (your) mouth and the meditation of (your) heart be pleasing in God's sight… (Ps. 19:1, NIV).

May God bless you with unspeakable joy and love in Him!

May he provide a compassionate heart in you for those who may not like or love you!

May you come up higher in your daily walk and live victoriously!

May God give you favor, healing restoration, and prosperity!

May God keep you grateful and humbled as your blessings come in!

Bind the enemy of fear and worry this day! Walk in peace in Jesus name!

About the Author

Nicholl McGuire is a lay teacher with an apostolic anointing. She is not formally trained in religious studies but has been marked as a representative of God by the Holy Spirit. Her gifts have been verified by God appointed leaders and witnessed by many. Her responsibility is to deliver messages to those whom the one true God has chosen in both religious and secular settings. Nicholl is a believer in the Father, Son and Holy Ghost and attends church in her local neighborhood. She has been writing and speaking online via videos, blogs and articles about subjects such as: relationships, spirituality, family and business since 2007.

30952663R00155

Printed in Great Britain
by Amazon